AFRO-
AMERICAN
LITERATURE

AFRO-AMERICAN LITERATURE

The Reconstruction of Instruction

Edited by

Dexter Fisher and Robert B. Stepto

for the Commission on the Literatures

and Languages of America

The Modern Language Association of America

New York   1979

Published by The Modern Language Association of America
62 Fifth Avenue, New York, New York 10011

Preparation of some of the essays in this volume was aided in part
by a grant from the National Endowment for the Humanities.

"The Blues Roots of Contemporary Afro-American Poetry" by Sherley
Anne Williams is reprinted, as revised by the author, from *The
Massachusetts Review*, © 1977, The Massachusetts Review, Inc.

Contents

Preface   *vii*

Introduction   *1*

AFRO-AMERICAN LITERARY HISTORY   7

1. *Teaching Afro-American Literature: Survey or Tradition*
   The Reconstruction of Instruction   8
   Robert B. Stepto, *Yale University*

2. *Rivers Remembering Their Source*
   Comparative Studies in Black Literary History—Langston Hughes, Jacques Roumain, and Négritude   25
   Melvin Dixon, *Williams College*

3. *Preface to Blackness: Text and Pretext*   44
   Henry-Louis Gates, Jr., *Yale University*

BLACK FIGURATIVE LANGUAGE   71

1. *The Blues Roots of Contemporary Afro-American Poetry*   72
   Sherley Anne Williams, *University of California at San Diego*

2. *Dis and Dat: Dialect and the Descent*   88
   Henry-Louis Gates, Jr., *Yale University*

AFRO-AMERICAN LITERATURE AND FOLKLORE   121

1. *Are You a Flying Lark or a Setting Dove?*   122
   Robert Hemenway, *University of Kentucky*

2. *Riffs and Rituals: Folklore in the Work of Ralph Ellison*   153
   Robert G. O'Meally, *Wesleyan University*

Contents

THEORY IN PRACTICE   *171*

I. *Introduction*   *172*

II. *Three Studies of Frederick Douglass'*
    Narrative (1845)   *177*

1. *Narration, Authentication, and Authorial Control*
    in Frederick Douglass' Narrative *of 1845*   *178*
        Robert B. Stepto, *Yale University*

2. *Frederick Douglass' 1845* Narrative
    The Text Was Meant to Be Preached   *192*
        Robert G. O'Meally, Wesleyan University

3. *Binary Oppositions in Chapter One of* Narrative of the
    Life of Frederick Douglass an American Slave Written
    by Himself   *212*
        Henry-Louis Gates, Jr., *Yale University*

AFRO-AMERICAN LITERATURE COURSE DESIGNS   *233*

1. *Rethinking the Afro-American Literature Survey*
    Course   *234*

2. *Rethinking the Afro-American Genre Course*   *244*

3. *Rethinking the Interdisciplinary Course Embracing Afro-*
    American Literature   *250*

Appendix   *256*

Preface

Sponsored by the Modern Language Association's Commission on Minority Groups and the Study of Language and Literature and funded by the National Endowment for the Humanities, a two-week seminar on "Afro-American Literature: From Critical Approach to Course Design" was held at Yale University under the direction of Robert B. Stepto in June of 1977. Unlike most books that are the end products of seminars, this volume is not so much a document of the seminar, assembling everything that was spoken or written, as a carefully orchestrated presentation of the central ideas and even the key metaphors that sparked the meetings and, in retrospect, seemed to be those features defining the session's significance.

Five scholars in the field composed the seminar staff: Dexter Fisher of the Modern Language Association, formerly of Hostos Community College, CUNY; Henry-Louis Gates, Jr., of Yale University; Robert O'Meally of Wesleyan University; Robert Stepto of Yale University; and Sherley Williams of the University of California at San Diego. Twenty-four participants were selected from colleges and universities throughout the Northeastern and Atlantic states to come together with the seminar staff to "reconstruct the instruction" of Afro-American literature—in this case, to design courses in, and to refine critical approaches to, Afro-American literature yielding a "literary" understanding of the literature. Since the seminar was one of the first efforts of its kind in the Afro-American field to pursue aggressively such issues as folklore as process, intertextuality, black speech as poetic diction, and the distinction between literary history and literary chronology, it soon became apparent that a volume presenting our collective ideas on these matters as they relate to the study and teaching of Afro-

American literature would be useful and, quite possibly, essential to teachers and scholars within and without the field.

Part I of this volume offers essays on various critical approaches to the literature, and we must thank the aforementioned seminar leaders as well as Melvin Dixon, Williams College, and Robert Hemenway, University of Kentucky, for their significant contributions to the seminar and to this book. The course designs appearing in Part II represent the collective effort of the seminar participants, whom we gratefully acknowledge for their skills, patience, and commitment to improving the study and teaching of Afro-American literature. They are Abu Abarry, State University of New York at Buffalo; Owen E. Brady, Clarkson College; Diane Dippold, Strayer College; Melvin Dixon, Williams College; Brian Gallagher, LaGuardia Community College; Leroy E. Giles, Catonsville Community College; Shelley Halpern, Empire State College; Robert Hemenway, University of Kentucky; Gloria Hull, University of Delaware; Chidi Ikonné, Harvard University; Jennifer Jordan, Howard University; Marcia Keizs, Queensborough Community College; Charles Lynch, Empire State College; Eugene McCarthy, College of the Holy Cross; Candace Oglesby, Onondaga Community College; Margaret Perry, University of Rochester Library; Stewart Rodnon, Rider College; Lance Schachterle, Worcester Polytechnic Institute; Fahamisha Shariat, University of Massachusetts at Boston; Joseph T. Skerrett, Jr., University of Massachusetts at Amherst; Eleanor Traylor, Montgomery College; Jill Weyant, Eastern Connecticut State College; Barbara Whitehead, Hampton Institute; and Wilburn Williams, Jr., MIT. We wish also to express our appreciation to Yale's Afro-American Studies Program for hosting the seminar, and, for making possible the opportunity of the seminar and this publication, we are grateful to the Modern Language Association and the National Endowment for the Humanities.

Dexter Fisher
Robert B. Stepto

Introduction

Of the many anthologies of Afro-American literature and criticism published during the last two decades, few are devoted exclusively to critical discussions of the literature, and none focuses specifically on critical issues that are especially pertinent to designing courses in Afro-American Literature. Even a cursory look at college-level literature curricula (and even graduate school offerings) reveals this deficiency. Many schools still do not teach Afro-American literature, while other institutions offering courses in the field seem to be caught in a lockstep of stale critical and pedagogical ideas, many of which are tattered hand-me-downs from disciplines other than literature. Clearly, what we do *not* need is yet another elementary volume replete with historical overviews and book lists that, in effect, "proves" the "existence" of Afro-American literature. The literature fills bookstore shelves and, increasingly, the stacks of libraries; symposia and seminars on the literature are regularly held; prominent contemporary black writers give scores of readings; and so the question of the literature's existence, at this juncture in literary studies, is not at issue. The need is rather for an intermediate or advanced volume on Afro-American literature that presupposes an awareness of the literature and, from that posture, not only demonstrates the links between various critical approaches and course designs but also pursues this activity with considerable emphasis on what is literary (as opposed to sociological, ideological, etc.) in Afro-American written art.

This book, *Afro-American Literature: The Reconstruction of Instruction*, which grew out of the lectures and course design workshops of the 1977 Modern Language Association/National Endowment for the Humanities Summer Seminar on Afro-American Literature, attempts to meet this need. It begins with three essays that discuss views or interpretations of Afro-American literary history. As a unit, the essays advance a pedagogical commitment to literary history that transcends a pedagogical submission to literary chronology. Furthermore, they suggest that instructors may begin to move beyond the lockstep of the chronological literary survey by examining the "historical consciousness" of art forms and pursuing the dialectic between the various black literatures of the New World as well as that between the literature and its criticism (including, especially, the commentary that is so often appended to texts). Drawing on ideas about literary myth, tradition, and transition suggested by Northrop Frye, Geoffrey Hartman, and Octavio Paz, Robert Stepto argues in the first essay that an Afro-American literary history may be charted—and hence a survey course may be organized—by studying the "pregeneric myth" in motion through historical and linguistic time. While the essay concentrates in this way on describing the course of Afro-American literary history, Stepto's remarks on the extraliterary values, ideas, and pedagogical constructions that have plagued the teaching of the literature are central to his essay and, indeed, to this volume as a whole. In the second essay, Melvin Dixon suggests that histories and surveys of Afro-American literature that confine themselves to North American authors and texts mistakenly overlook the "international vision" of prominent authors such as Langston Hughes. Dixon's study of Hughes, Jacques Roumain, and the international Négritude movement reexamines the issues of translation, multilingual intertextuality, and definitions of literary periods and canons when the literature examined crosses national boundaries. In this way, it is a functional model for further comparativist scholarship and teaching. The third essay of the group surveys the prefaces to Afro-American texts of several centuries and is thereby a valuable examination of the place of critical writings, past and present, in Afro-American literary history. Written by Henry-Louis Gates, Jr., the essay argues that heretofore most criticism of Afro-American literature has been entrapped in a hermeneutical web of "race and superstructure," which compels many modern and contemporary critics to redress the "superstructures" fashioned by Thomas Jefferson, William Dean Howells, and other notable litterateurs far more than to study the literature itself. At the heart of the essay lies a call for the breaking of this web and for the investigation of the history of criticism in Afro-American literature courses.

While the first unit of essays discusses what is literary about Afro-American literature by studying literary history, the second unit pursues this goal by concentrating on aspects of black figurative language. Here, in its study of relatively small, distinctly Afro-American linguistic units, the second group of essays offers models for the teaching of discrete literary texts that are inherently interdisciplinary (e.g., blues) and often multigeneric (dialect voicings in all written art forms). As a unit, the essays suggest various ways in which an instructor—especially one who is committed to interdisciplinary activities such as Afro-American Studies or American Studies—can present a collection of art forms and still respond to the literary qualities of many of those forms in the course of the presentation. In the first essay, Sherley Williams' discussion of the blues roots of contemporary Afro-American poetry offers several fresh approaches to the study of the poetry and addresses the rather complicated issue of how one charts the transmissions and interminglings of oral and written forms. Her remarks on the blues poems of Lucille Clifton are especially noteworthy because they transcend the elementary stage of merely identifying blues features to demonstrate how a distinctly Afro-American poetry is formed by "a synthesis of black oral traditions and Western literate forms." The second essay, by Henry-Louis Gates, reminds us that dialect is a kind of figurative language and that a study of Afro-American dialect—of "linguistic masks"—informs our understanding and teaching of the dialectic between language and authorial control. While most discussions of dialect veer inevitably in the direction of extraliterary and "race and superstructure" concerns, Gates's remarks culminate in a careful examination of dialect language itself. Indeed, this essay is one of the few by a literary scholar that scrutinize the literal and figurative complexities of Afro-American dialect expression.

The third group of essays examines Afro-American folklore *and* Afro-American literature as well as Afro-American folklore *in* Afro-American literature, and does so for at least two reasons. On the one hand, the distinction drawn here between the two types of studies bears directly on the issue of the primacy of the literary text in critical and pedagogical thinking. On the other, the acquisition of a methodology for an integrated study of Afro-American folklore and literature equips the scholar-teacher with tools for examining alike discrete texts and large units of literature. Overall, the crisis before the Afro-Americanist planning to study and teach folklore and literature is much the same as that confronting those pursuing history and literature or music and literature, in that the frequent result of such enterprises is that folklore, history, and music are taught (or at least, "artifacts" of the three are unearthed and held up to the light), while literature is not. At the same time, however, the rewards for creating an effective criticism and pedagogy of folklore and literature are high since all such strategies represent one of the few ways to achieve an interdisciplinary study of oral and written expressions.

In the first essay, Robert Hemenway examines folklore and literary art in Zora Neale Hurston's first novel, *Jonah's Gourd Vine*. To be sure, Hurston helps him along the way since it may be said that she rarely distinguishes between *presenting* folklore and *writing* fiction. But this in no way diminishes Hemenway's accomplishment of a critical and pedagogical model correctly and agreeably bound to an artistic construction. In the second essay, Robert O'Meally discusses the use of folklore materials in Ralph Ellison's fiction. The essay is most helpful in that it explores its subject in Ellison's shorter, uncollected works as well as in *Invisible Man*; but its greatest merit may very well lie in its demonstration of how, in his book reviews and essays, Ellison has forged a critical posture (if not precisely a full-blown methodology) sensitive to efforts to transform folklore materials into written art. In short, Hemenway and O'Meally examine different types of counterpoint between folklore and literature (on the one hand, Hurston's inextricable commingling of folklore and fiction; on the other, Ellison's intentional subsuming of folklore within literary artistic impulses), and in turn issue calls for different types of critical and pedagogical approaches to the study of folk-lore and literature (Hemenway urges an approach he calls "folklitics" while O'Meally champions Ellison's model).

"Theory in Practice" offers three critical studies of Frederick Douglass' *Narrative of the Life of Frederick Douglass an American Slave Written by Himself* (1845) that function collectively as a kind of coda for the volume's discussion of critical approaches to Afro-American literature. Robert Stepto's opening essay demonstrates how the Afro-American pregeneric myth of the quest for freedom and literacy described in his previous statement ("Teaching Afro-American Literature . . .") is revealed in both the events of Douglass' *Narrative* and Douglass' pursuit of authorial control over his personal history, once it assumes written form. The second essay, by Robert O'Meally, examines Douglass' "preacherly" voice and, in this way, draws on certain ideas presented earlier in the volume regarding the oral and folk roots of Afro-American writing. In marked contrast to the O'Meally essay, Henry-Louis Gates's discussion studies the *Narrative's* literary roots in prose forms such as the picaresque tale and sentimental fiction. Furthermore, Gates focuses far more than O'Meally does on Douglass' "written voice"—especially as it is manifested in the binary oppositions that introduce the seen and unseen world of the slave. All in all, while the Stepto essay suggests how Douglass both found and won his voice, the O'Meally and Gates discussions explore that voice's various dimensions and resonances. The thrust or goal of the unit is, then, to demonstrate how a literary scholar may explore questions of intertextuality, rhetoric, oral to written transferences, and structural linguistics in an Afro-American text —which is, in all its complexities, the "property" of many disciplines.

"Afro-American Literature Course Designs" are grouped under the broad rubrics of Survey, Genre, and Interdisciplinary Courses. The course designs draw on the critical and pedagogical strategies implicit and explicit in the preceding essays and reflect ideas generated in the seminar's course design workshops as well. Thus, the designs help to synthesize the ideas presented in this volume much as the essays on Douglass' *Narrative* do: All of them, irrespective of their assigned rubric, pursue the study of oral and written forms, make a distinction between literary history and literary chronology, examine intertextuality in both a broad and a particular way, and sanction the primacy of the literary text within the critical and pedagogical activities of the scholar. They are not offered as prescriptions or "lesson plans," however, any more than the seminar's reading list in the appendix is meant to be a definitive bibliography. Indeed, as suggested before, this volume, like the seminar that prompted it, is designed not for the purposes of merely disseminating information or of enabling what are called in the first essay "bibliographical repairs" but for the higher goal of sparking an instructor's critical and pedagogical imagination. In sum, the progression from criticism to pedagogy forwarded in these pages is completed in the most practical sense of the term only when the instructors reading this book begin to focus their own imaginative energies on the considerable and yet rewarding task of discovering and teaching what is literary and artful in Afro-American literature.

Afro-American Literature: The Reconstruction of Instruction presents a fresh and long overdue approach to the literature that was collectively discussed and shaped by almost thirty instructors of literature from twenty-five colleges and universities. Several instructors have remarked that the critical and pedagogical ideas collected here will have a great effect on their teaching of *all* literature. If this is indeed the case, then the time is certainly near when the committed Afro-Americanist can paraphrase Ellison's Invisible Man and say with great truth to colleagues in other literatures, "Who knows but that I speak for you?" If this volume plays even a small part in the realization of that exchange, then it will have succeeded.

                                                    Robert B. Stepto

Afro-American
Literary
History

Teaching Afro-American Literature: Survey or Tradition
The Reconstruction of Instruction

Robert B. Stepto

1: Survey or Tradition?

Tradition is extradition; art must become transitive
vis-à-vis its original site in history.
—Geoffrey Hartman

Our mode is our jam session
of tradition,
past in this present moment
articulated, blown through
with endurance
an unreaching extended
improvised love of past masters
instruments technically down
—Michael S. Harper

Survey is the bane of all literary studies, but it has had an especially cursed effect on the study of Afro-American literature. At a time in the academy when most language instruction is being curtailed, Afro-American literature, primarily because it is currently the most visible "minority" literature, has a larger responsibility than ever before in the great enterprise of nurturing young men and women who are literate; who are, regardless of their major discipline, articulate about the myriad cultural metaphors (textual and otherwise) in their world. By and large, however, Afro-American literature is not meeting this educational need and opportunity, primarily because of the antiquated ways in which it is taught and discussed in critical writing. On most campuses, Afro-American literature is still an agreeable entrée to black history, sociology, and politics. Of course, there is both a good side and a bad side to this: Historians and social scientists seem to employ Afro-American literature to illuminate their disciplines; for them, literature is part of a pedagogical strategy. Teachers of literature, however, more often than not attempt to become amateur historians and social scientists in their pursuit of the literature long before they actually get down to the business of teaching literary art. The most infamous proof of this is the rise of what I call the all-purpose Black Studies essay. For some understandable yet lamentable reasons, there are students in the land who have been led to feel that an essay containing an occult potpourri of references to Frederick Douglass, Frantz Fanon, and Richard Wright is acceptable in any Afro-American Studies course taught by any teacher regardless of the discipline in which the course is situated. Insofar as the literature teacher is responsible for this travesty, I would judge that the purveyance of survey approaches to both the taught and written critical discussion of the literature has done the greatest damage. And, really, it is the literature teacher who must make the most dramatic and complete reversal: Above and beyond the issue of extraordinary developments in literary analysis since the nineteenth century (which is where, in terms of sophistication, most criticism of Afro-American literature tends to reside) lies the simple, haunting fact that Afro-American history and social science are being taught while Afro-American language, literature, and literacy are not.

A definition is in order: A survey of literature is a presentation of discrete literary texts for the purposes of (1) explicating and distilling poetic rhetoric *in isolatio*, or (2) illuminating (however dimly) coded structures (Harlem Renaissance, Black Aesthetic), or (3) reviewing literary chronology (as opposed to literary history), or (4) miracu-

lously, accomplishing all of the above. Lest someone think
I am building straw men or tilting at windmills, let me illustrate my definition by constructing a hypothetical but no
doubt familiar survey presentation of a popular and often
taught black poet, Langston Hughes.

Let us assume that the presentation—to be completed in
at most three or four classes—begins with a kind of informal explication de texte of several early Hughes poems,
taken most likely from *The Weary Blues* or *Fine Clothes to
the Jew* or both but certainly not studied within the context
of these volumes because the critical and pedagogical tool
in hand studies discrete texts; the students are reading the
poems in an anthology or perhaps in a sheaf of photocopy
material and have not been encouraged to seek out the
Hughes volumes in the library; and the instructor, trained
as a survey teacher by other survey teachers, has not read
the poems—that is, for *pedagogical* purposes—in their
original setting. The explication is informal primarily because of a curious conspiracy between the instructor and
Hughes himself. Consciously or not, and for reasons both
textual and atextual, the instructor desires to sustain certain
theories (clichés, really) about the "clarity" of Afro-
American letters as opposed to the "convolutedness" of
"Angry-Saxon" art. In this, the instructor is abetted by
Hughes who, as perhaps *the* paradigmatic anti-intellectual
among modern Afro-American writers, created poetic surfaces offering collectively what might be termed a quasi-
aesthetic of the literal. One result of this conspiracy is what
the poet Michael Harper jocularly terms the "explain" approach to literature—the reading of maps as opposed to the
reading of landscapes—and the most recent edition of *The
Norton Anthology of Poetry* bears him out. There, in the
Hughes selections, one can find glosses for "Lenox Avenue"
("A main thoroughfare in the heart of Harlem"), for "W.
E. B. Du Bois," for "Sugar Hill" ("a section of Harlem
where the more prosperous Negroes once lived"), and for
"Virginia Dare" ("A brand of wine"). The classroom
equivalent of this sorry map-reading business may take up
one class of the three, but usually the count is two. Let us
say one class, however, assuming that the survey teacher is
"organized."

In phase two of the survey presentation, the instructor employs what Northrop Frye describes as documentary approaches to literature: approaches that attempt to return a text to its place in cultural and literary history without accounting for either the literary form or the poetic and metaphorical language of the literary work. As Frye notes, the most pervasive of the documentary approaches are the biographical, the historical, and the psychological (with some sort of inevitable Freudian base). Most documentary criticism of Afro-American letters concentrates on biographical and historical data and is in this way embarrassingly antiquated. Psychological studies of the literature, at least when pursued by literary scholars, have been viewed traditionally as being suspect, partly because they are rarely done well but mostly because of the somewhat xenophobic and certainly emotional premise that the theories of a fin-de-siècle Austrian Jew cannot possibly illuminate black American art and culture. Despite these disclaimers, one suspects that psychological approaches to Afro-American literature will continue to advance and prosper as younger scholars are exposed to the ideas of established critics (witness the recent "psychobiographical" discussions of black writers such as Ellison, which are clearly indebted to the writings of the anxiety school of romanticists) and are informed also by the more thoughtful critiques of Freudianism and its corollary arguments. Our survey instructor, however, is not about to mystify or convolute the study of Hughes's poetry with psychological speculation (few of the texts can bear that weight anyway); "pure" biographical reference will shade the map outlined before, and not incidentally get instructor and student alike through class number two.

Langston Hughes wrote two autobiographies, *The Big Sea* and *I Wonder as I Wander*, and so our instructor can draw on a veritable wealth of authentic—and authenticating—material while making his or her presentation. Because the course is a survey and there is "no time" for the students themselves to read the autobiographies, the draft is often literally an extraction of pertinent passages from such chapters as "Harlem Literati" in *The Big Sea*, orchestrated agreeably with additional anecdotes, allusions, and cartographical glosses by the instructor. If the instructor is reasonably artful in the creation of documentary mosaics, the students will be entertained (if not exactly enlightened about Hughes's verse) and the class will go down as a good one. Curiously, old but persisting doubts about the efficacy of committing the intentional fallacy will not surface, either because student and teacher alike have tacitly agreed that such ideas do not apply to the study of "minority" literatures or because the business of that particular class never really was the discussion of poetry.

At this point in the presentation—consciously or not, subtly or not—an intellectual and pedagogical crisis occurs, and how the instructor responds to that crisis determines nothing less than whether Hughes's poems will be taught at all. Class one, with its informal (possibly, aformal) explication of texts, timidly began that enterprise, while class two took matters in a far different direction. The crisis is, quite simply, whither does one go? Does one go to the poems, which at this point seems to be a disagreeable form of backtracking, or does one continue with documentation —with the essentially nonliterary activity of embellishing the Hughesian map? In most cases, the survey instructor chooses the latter activity, and this choice has both lamentable and alluring dimensions.

What is lamentable of course, is the abandonment of Hughes's texts and, worse, the innocent prostitution of those texts for the sake of potential intimacy with extraliterary concerns. The alluring dimension involves principally the joy of fashioning, albeit with the tools and rules of a false cartography, a reasoned if not envisioned whole. This whole may not be an interpretation of Hughes's verse, and certainly it is not a *reading* of it, but it does have weight and shape; it has presence and is therefore presentable, and this presentability in turn creates the illusion of an accompanying pedagogy. In our hypothetical survey classes one and two, a map—as opposed to both what Octavio Paz, among others, calls a landscape and what Geoffrey Hartman has termed a *genius loci*—has been outlined and, through reference to biographical information, carefully shaded. Although the biographical materials suggest boundaries and even topographies—of the autobiographies if not the poems—further embellishment and, more important, contextualization of the map are required. This, as suggested before, is the seductive, Luciferian quality of the survey enterprise: The map will not direct one to the grail, which is the various dimensions of literacy achieved within the deeper recesses of the art form, but mapmaking in and of itself is an engaging, self-contained activity. One assumes, in short, that these satisfactions at least begin to explain why the pursuit of nonreading is sufficiently resilient to remain au courant.

Contextualizing the map is most frequently the responsibility of historical documentation. In our hypothetical survey presentation of Langston Hughes, which is now entering its third and final day, the informal textual explications, glosses, and mosaic of biographical reference will be conjoined with coded historical reference and structure: The instructor, in short, will contextualize the map by grounding it in a somewhat amorphous but nevertheless celebrated historical and cultural watershed we have come to call the Harlem Renaissance. References to this Renaissance have no doubt reverberated in parts one and two of the presentation, but here in class three the subject becomes a veritable rumble. And with good reason: The presentation began with the microcosmic—the gloss, the parenthetical reference, the allusion, and aside—and now it is achieving macrocosmic proportions—Langston Hughes and the Black Map of Modern Western Civilization. With this level assumed, the last thirty minutes of the last class on Hughes can be devoted to a breathless sprint through the Big Questions: Langston Hughes and Black Nationalism; Langston Hughes and Protest; Langston Hughes, Architect of the Black Aesthetic; and Langston Hughes, Critic of the Bourgeoisie, which is, of course, a fresh sport of Langston Hughes, Poet of the People. A first-rate survey instructor might instead devote those final minutes to an equally breathless discourse on how Hughes's greatness transcends temporal boundaries, how he is representative not merely of the Harlem Renaissance but also of the entire Modern era. This instructor might even attempt to link Hughes's transtemporal qualities with his efforts and abilities in several literary genres, the immediate effect being that the macrocosmic element in the presentation achieves a truly grand scale. But the final effect of either closure is regrettably the same: The students will feel that they have "done" Langston Hughes, and, taking off from any of the topics in either hypothetical closure, they will write—or warm over —yet another all-purpose Black Studies essay addressed almost parenthetically to the art of dear Langston.

Sadly enough, after three organized and possibly charged classes on Langston Hughes, the students who have received this survey presentation cannot begin to answer any of the substantial questions concerning Hughes's art. For example, the students ought to be able to discuss intelligently whether Hughes, in writing his "jazz" and "blues" poems, merely duplicates folk forms or achieves what George Kent suggests when he describes the "real opportunity" before the "self-conscious," as opposed to "group-conscious" or "folk," artist: the rendering of new art not by revision but fittingly, as in jazz, by modal improvisation. A good answer to this question will include discussion of both the verbal *and* tonal poetic rhetoric (fulfilled and unfulfilled) in a very few carefully selected Hughes poems, but, of course, the students subjected to the hypothetical presentation just described are totally ill-equipped to pursue this issue. In their first class on Hughes, verbal poetic rhetoric was at best partially explored and tonal poetic rhetoric simply "unheard." What they know of the music in Hughes's verse is most likely anchored in coded cultural/historical referents: cabaret, rent party, Charleston, black bottom, flapper (black, tan, and white), Cotton Club, Jazz Age. And they might not know all of that. The instructor might have been of the multimedia persuasion and played "Take the A Train" and "Creole Love Song" in hopes that a history and culture might be gleaned by a kind of osmosis.

Most certainly, especially if the authors preceding and following Hughes are presented in more or less the same fashion, the students are incapable of placing Hughes in the continuum of Afro-American artists who have wrestled with these very same questions of form, verbal and tonal metaphor, authorial posture, textual control, and shared tradition. They have no basis whatsoever on which to compare Hughes with such early articulators of the musical dimensions to literacy as Frederick Douglass and W. E. B. Du Bois. They are equally incapable of making any comparisons between Hughes and Ralph Ellison or Hughes and Leroi Jones. The students ought to be able to bring into their discussion of Hughes's persona other personae, including James Weldon Johnson's Ex-Coloured Man and Sterling Brown's Big Boy Davis. But these are leaps that the implicit rhetoric of survey presentations discourages. On the whole, nonreading inaugurates a surprisingly rigid praxis; it encourages ingenious manipulation of nonliterary structures instead of immersion in the multiple images and landscapes of metaphor. In brief, the primacy of the text is obliterated.

Instead of achieving some facility at contextualizing the Hughesian map in nonliterary or, more generally, non-artistic structures, the students should be able to begin to place Hughes in the Afro-American artistic continuum of which literature is but a part, and in doing so, illuminate the text or texts by referring to the artistic whole. Those students who, as Ralph Ellison reports, persist in the illusion that they possess a "genetic" knowledge of black culture, may very well compose yet another all-purpose "black" essay. Others will take the harder but more rewarding path delineated—and in fact demanded—by the multiple forms of literacy, not "feeling," and draw from *all* their resources the requisite vision and energy to see author, text, and tradition alike.

Of course, the instructor, much more than the students, requires reconstruction. Ironically, the pedagogy he or she has employed is bankrupt because it is self-contained, and self-contained because of some of the procedures used to escape "confinement" in the art form itself. As we observed in the hypothetical classes on Hughes, what passes for pedagogy is an inevitable movement from the text to familiar nonliterary constructs such as the Harlem Renaissance. These constructs in turn become the grand, controlling themes of a survey course; and, when nonliterary structures are both the linchpins and goals of a teaching strategy, the "text" of a course, like a bad poem, yields documentary data stripped of metaphor. For this reason, the students, if asked, might very well explain that in the

course they studied slavery times, Reconstruction, the Ac-
commodationist Era, and the Harlem Renaissance, much as
they would describe too many Black Studies courses
couched in too many disciplines.

The intellectual and pedagogical problems before the
survey instructor become manifest when one speculates on
what will follow the sessions on Langston Hughes. Moving
chronologically, the next good poet is obviously Sterling
Brown, whose best volume of verse, *Southern Road*, saw
print in 1932. But beyond the all too apparent activities of
comparing, say, a Hughes "blues" with a Brown "blues"
and glossing "Casey Jones," "Ma Rainey," and "Four and a
half and M," our instructor has very little to say about
Brown. In contrast to Hughes, Brown has not yet published
his autobiography and, for reasons personal as well as historical, is not readily identified with the Harlem Renaissance era. These matters, we have good reason to fear, have
far more to do with why Brown is undertaught or considered "difficult" than the more substantial issue of what
his poems demand of their readers. In short, our instructor's
pedagogy is bankrupt because it neither allows proximity,
let alone intimacy, with writers and texts outside the normal
boundaries of nonliterary structures nor fosters the literacy
required to examine literature without respect to extraliterary concerns. If our instructor were free, in these senses
of the term, he or she might be able not only to read and
teach both Hughes and Brown but also to judge who is the
better poet, even if only along the lines of the aforementioned question of the "real opportunity" before the modern Afro-American writer. But obviously, our instructor and,
by extension, our students are not yet free—nor, sadly
enough, is the literature that they glimpse but cannot see.

II: Temenos/*Notes on a Course*

Once a mythology is formed, a *temenos* or magic circle is drawn around a culture, and literature develops historically within a limited orbit of language, reference, allusion, beliefs, transmitted and shared tradition.

—Northrop Frye

The path to freedom and literacy has many pitfalls, and among the most considerable of these is the trap of bibliography. Let us suppose that our survey instructor senses, despite reassurances to the contrary from questionnaire scores and enrollment figures, that something is mightily wrong with the map-reading system of teaching Afro-American literature. (This in itself is an act of courage; no one relishes altering habits of intellectual discourse that outwardly seem to work.) An initial response might well be to read new texts and to insert them here and there in the old course. No matter how sanctioned this revision might be by the various reading lists compiled by colleagues, committees, or "institutes," the instructor has done little more than perform what one might call a "bibliographical repair": the shuffling of texts like that of cards in hopes of a better "deal." This will not do. What the course needs is not simply new authorial names and textual faces but an aesthetic and rhetorical principle that summons the texts that properly shape a course. A course, as I have suggested before, is a kind of grand text; in its way, a good course assumes a place alongside the great works of a literary tradition because the interdependence of its integral parts (texts) reflects the artistic continuum both celebrated and subsumed in the great works themselves. In order to pursue this ideal of the good course, our instructor must be able to distinguish a literary tradition from a literary survey and an artistic continuum from a bibliography and to see the dialectical relationship between these two distinguishing processes. But before any of this activity is launched, our instructor must discover the Afro-American canonical story or pregeneric myth, the particular historicity of the Afro-American literary tradition, and the Afro-American landscape or *genius loci*.

The Afro-American pregeneric myth is the quest for freedom *and* literacy. Once this is absorbed, our instructor will be able to abandon freely most nonliterary structures because those structures, evolving as they do almost exclusively from freedom myths devoid of linguistic properties, speak rarely to questions of freedom *and* literacy. Because this is so, they are now, if not obsolete, only partially useful to our instructor.

The quest for freedom and literacy is found in every major Afro-American text but is perhaps most accessible in Frederick Douglass' *Narrative of the Life of Frederick Douglass an American Slave Written by Himself* (the last part of the title, as many have remarked, suggests the goal of literacy) and W. E. B. Du Bois' *The Souls of Black Folk*. I mention these works not only because they are familiar and central but also because each yields a remarkable expression of the multiple dimensions to literacy subsumed within a primary Afro-American archetype, the articulate hero. In both works, the hero (that is, a heroic voice created as much by its author's vision as by his condition) discovers the inextricable bonds among study, language, and "the pathway from slavery to freedom" and, in turn, especially with Du Bois, suggests that comprehension of his culture's tongues has led in part to the discovery of his own voice. Thus, the articulate hero achieves the posture of the custodian of the culture—an idea reinforced in other works by less articulate figures such as James Weldon Johnson's Ex-Coloured Man, who seems all too aware that his false mobility (false when compared to that of Douglass' self-become-metaphor and that of Du Bois' truly self-conscious hero-narrator) is a kind of illiteracy. What our instructor learns here is that the pregeneric myth creates both literate and illiterate, free and enclosed, heroes and landscapes, and that both types must be offered in teaching in such a way that what Du Bois termed a "total race consciousness" —as envisioned in art—is presented.

Aware of the quest for freedom and literacy, our instructor may now study how that pregeneric myth and its archetypes generate Afro-American literary forms. As in all literatures, these are bound to specific texts, so that the study of form invariably arrives at some inspection of discrete works. But I am speaking here of another activity as well: What must also be observed is the pregeneric myth *set in motion* in search of its form and, since it is bound to form, its voice. Here, the instructor discovers what is most likely the central intellectual and pedagogical enterprise in the study of Afro-American literary forms: the effort to define and discuss how the pregeneric myth both assumes and does not assume the properties of genre—notably, history, autobiography, fiction, and certain modes of verse. If an Afro-American literary tradition exists, it does so not because there is a sizeable chronology of authors and texts but because those authors and texts seek collectively their own literary forms—their own admixtures of genre—bound historically and linguistically to a shared pregeneric myth.

The historicity of the Afro-American literary tradition is, then, not the chronology of authors and texts but the history of the pregeneric myth in motion through both chronological and linguistic time in search of its form and voice. Thus, the history of tradition differs massively from that of survey in that surveys destroy linguistic time and the continuity of literary history by moving systematically from texts to nonliterary structures and passively allowing those structures to become collectively the "history" of a literature. Once this is absorbed, most of the remaining nonliterary structures impeding the *reading* of the literature will fall away, and, probably for the first time, our instructor will be set in motion, free to learn the rhythm of the history, free to *see* finally what binds, say, *Native Son* to the slave narratives, or a Robert Hayden ballad to a ballad by Sterling Brown or to the "Sorrow Songs," as Du Bois termed them. All this will have pedagogical ramifications. Our instructor's course will still unfold chronologically but will do so for reasons literary, not extraliterary: Literary conventions, archetypes, genres, and pregeneric forms will generate what Northrop Frye describes as "a sense of history within literature to complement the historical criticism that relates literature to a historical background." Obviously, nonliterary structures will still have a place in teaching, but they will no longer define the goals of the pedagogical strategy or control the reading of art. Instead of depicting history, our instructor's course will now illuminate the historical consciousness of an art form.

Once the pregeneric myth has been set in motion, we must concern ourselves not only with the chronicle of that movement, literary history, but also with that movement's direction and shape. In Afro-American letters, the shape of literary history is a circle, a continuum of artistic endeavor; and, like Northrop Frye's *temenos*, it is a magic circle —magical because it is full of resonance generated by artistic acts of modal improvisation upon the pregeneric myth of freedom and literacy. The interior of the Afro-American *temenos* is the culture's landscape or *genius loci* (spirit of place, but also spiritual center), the deeper recesses both attained and realized, as Du Bois instructs us, by penetration of the Veil. Afro-American literature abounds with metaphors for its culture's *genius loci*; the creation of them is indeed one of its major occupations. One of the more apparent is "the black belt," of which Booker T. Washington and Du Bois both write, and it is a good one for our instructor to begin with since it is essentially a geographical metaphor and comprehension of it will yield not only the *temenos* but also the distinction between the reading of maps and that of landscapes.

Put succinctly, Washington, in his public pronouncements if not so much in private exchange, was a mapmaker —a direct result of his great literary offense, the adoption of "the speech and language of triumphant commercialism" (to which, I think, the tongue of nonreading is linked ancestrally). When called upon to define the black belt, Washington wrote in *Up from Slavery*:

> So far as I can learn, the term was first used to designate a part of the country which was distinguished by the colour of the soil. The part of the country possessing this thick, dark, and naturally rich soil was, of course, the part of the

south where the slaves were most profitable, and conse-
quently they were taken there in the largest numbers.
Later, and especially since the war, the term seems to be
used wholly in a political sense—that is, to designate the
counties where the black people out number the white.

Obviously, Washington carefully avoids any suggestion that
the black belt possesses deeper recesses, let alone that it
might be the interior of the Afro-American *temenos*. His
gloss is that of a mapmaker or gazettist. He ventures into
politics not as a philosopher but rather as a demographer
and creates a linguistic surface that is thin except perhaps in
the rather wry phrase, "the part of the south where the
slaves were most *profitable*" (italics added). But, of course,
Washington had a very specific goal in mind (raising funds
for Tuskegee) in thus shaping the rhetoric of his gloss—
which parenthetically raises the question of what comparable goals, literary or extraliterary, our instructor had in
composing equally thin glosses for the poetry of Langston
Hughes.

The wicked subtlety and charm of Washington's description of the black belt are lost unless it is returned to the
canon of metaphors for the Afro-American *genius loci*.
There, Washington's language enters into dialectical play
with Du Bois' portrait of the black belt in *The Souls*: The
rhetorical map becomes engaged dynamically with the
rhetorical journey into the soul of a race. Our *reading* of
this dialectic is what allows us not only to interpret Washington's and Du Bois' language but also to see the black belt
whole. This act of reading within tradition affords a
pedagogical approximation of artmaking within tradition,
and it is reading of this sort that our instructor's new
pedagogy should both emulate and promote.

Just as we must learn to pass from metaphor to metaphor
and from image to image of the same metaphor in order to
locate the Afro-American *genius loci*, we must learn also to
move freely throughout the full compass of the Afro-
American *temenos*, from the *genius loci* at the center to the
outermost reaches of the *temenos* circumference. Geoffrey
Hartman speaks of the tension between Genius and *genius
loci* and how it takes the form of and also mediates "the

conflict between the universal and nationalistic aspirations of art." I would suggest a comparable tension exists in Afro-American letters not only between Genius and *genius loci* but also between the *temenos* (the magical cultural circle that is the most immediate interior region of the Veil) and the *genius loci* (the heart of the interior landscape). In the best Afro-American texts, the nationalistic tendency is not so much a baldly political compulsion as it is a drive to perpetuate the motion of the pregeneric myth of freedom and literacy. Artmaking—craftsmanship—demands a mediation between this nationalistic tendency and Genius. Of course, this produces what is extraordinary about Afro-American art forms: Mediation between the drive to perpetuate the motion of the pregeneric myth and the compulsion to follow Genius is an exquisite definition of modal improvisation; art that does not come from this mediation does not advance, in Octavio Paz's language, the Afro-American's "mode of association" within "the universality of history," and thus does not enter Afro-American literary history even though it does, in some sense, exist.

The reconstruction of an instruction is no simple task: The revised course must attain textual (that is, metaphorical) properties, and the complementing pedagogy must approximate the artistic act itself. This is not as difficult as it sounds once literacy is achieved, because the act of reading is not unlike that of writing. Both require a mediation between Genius and *genius loci* and between *genius loci* and *temenos*, and both require of their practitioners a sense of the counterpoint between texts (or courses) and the rhythm of the artistic continuum subsumed within *temenos*. Our instructor set out in search of a new map but discovered, fortunately, the eternal landscape instead. The new course will, like literary history itself, encompass the landscape, and, more important, the new pedagogy will, like artmaking, mediate between individual talent and the continuity of tradition. But perhaps most important of all will be our instructor's new, reconstructed self: Free to read, free to see, and free to attain that state John Coltrane termed wakefulness.

Wakefulness is not, however, an altogether blissful circumstance. Once sufficiently awake to reconstruct the old

Afro-American literature course, the instructor is cognizant also of the other, larger systems and constructs (curricula, departments, schools), which are, like the old course, infested with a kind of intellectual misery. The new course, generated by the artful act of reading, may now enable Afro-American literature to nurture literacy in the academy, but our instructor may ask quite rightfully why does this responsibility exist in the first place, and why must more and more of the burden be assumed by Afro-American letters? The first question will be wrestled with almost endlessly, primarily because it addresses intellectual and pedagogical failures at all levels of instruction; but the answer to the second will, I think, become ringingly clear. The great gift of the best Afro-American literature to its readers is its historical and linguistic portrait of a culture —once imprisoned by an enforced illiteracy—questing for, finding, and relishing the written word. If students can absorb this, they not only will know something important about Afro-American literature but also, quite possibly, will drink of the spirit of the tradition and achieve the discipline required to force a revision of their own verbal inadequacies. It is horrifically ironic that some of our students cannot write as well as Henry Bibb—a fugitive slave with three weeks of schooling—but then, when were they ever imbued with even an ounce of Bibb's motivation? Our mission as teachers is clear: Afro-American literature must be taught, and taught as a literature. Only then will our students learn of a culture's quest for literacy and in turn gain the literacy with which to sustain the tradition.

References

Bibb, Henry. *Narrative of the Life and Adventures of Henry Bibb an American Slave Written by Himself*. 1849; rpt. in *Puttin' on Ole Massa*. Ed. Gilbert Osofsky. New York: Harper, 1969.

Brown, Sterling A. *Southern Road*. 1932; rpt. Boston: Beacon, 1974.

Chapman, Abraham. "An Interview with Michael S. Harper." *Arts in Society*, 2 (1974), 463–71.

Douglass, Frederick. *Narrative of the Life of Frederick Douglass an American Slave Written by Himself*. 1845; rpt. New York: Signet, 1968.

Du Bois, W. E. B. *The Souls of Black Folk*. Chicago: McClurg, 1903.
————. "The Storm and Stress in the Black World." *Dial*, 16 April 1901, pp. 262–64.
Frye, Northrop. "The Critical Path: An Essay on the Social Context of Literary Criticism." *Daedalus*, 99 (1970), 268–342.
Harper, Michael S. *Nightmare Begins Responsibility*. Urbana-Champaign: Univ. of Illinois Press, 1975.
————, and Robert B. Stepto. "Study in Experience: A Conversation with Ralph Ellison." *Massachusetts Review*, 18 (1977), 417–35.
Hartman, Geoffrey. "Toward Literary History." In *Beyond Formalism: Literary Essays 1958–1970*. New Haven: Yale Univ. Press, 1970.
Johnson, James Weldon. *The Autobiography of an Ex-Coloured Man*. 1912; rpt. New York: Hill and Wang, 1960.
Kent, George E. *Blackness and the Adventure of Western Culture*. Chicago: Third World Press, 1972.
Paz, Octavio. *The Other Mexico: Critique of the Pyramid*. Trans. Lysander Kemp. New York: Grove, 1972.
Washington, Booker T. *Up from Slavery*. 1901; rpt. in Vol. I of *The Booker T. Washington Papers*. Ed. Louis R. Harlan. Urbana-Champaign: Univ. of Illinois Press, 1972, pp. 211–385.

Rivers Remembering Their Source

Comparative Studies in Black Literary History — Langston Hughes, Jacques Roumain, and Négritude

Melvin Dixon

I

Your heart trembles in the shadows, like a face
    reflected in troubled water.
The old mirage rises from the pit of the night
You sense the sweet sorcery of the past:
A river carries you far away from the banks,
Carries you toward the ancestral landscape.
    —Jacques Roumain, "When the Tom Tom Beats"

It is not culture which binds the peoples of partially
African origin now scattered throughout the world,
but an identity of passions.
    —Ralph Ellison, *Shadow and Act*

The single most resounding literary achievement of international scale in the twentieth century has been the development of Négritude, the celebration of a black consciousness through literature. Through Négritude, in its
broadest meaning first coined by Aimé Césaire,[1] an entire
continent renamed itself, and by this act of language,
whether indigenous or acquired through acculturation,
generations of blacks dispersed throughout the world re-
claimed a part of their identity as members of the African

Diaspora. Writers from the Harlem Renaissance in the United States, the *Revue Indigène* in Haiti, and *La Revue du Monde Noir* in Paris gave birth to literatures that, although established along lines of national language and culture, created an arena wherein blacks throughout the world could articulate their presence and condition. Each was a separate river remembering its source; each created a significant flow of theme and political passion ever circling the ancestral landscape, moving outward for independence and transformation of traditional oral forms of expression, and returning for renewal, regeneration, reunion with the past made present through language. Haitian poet Jacques Roumain has written:

> Listen to those voices singing the sadness of love
> And in the mountain, hear that tom-tom
>   panting like the breast of a young black girl.

Hearing the tom-tom cannot be wholly explained or dismissed as a passion. Nor would emphasis on this oral-aural contact establish for writers of African origin simply "an identity of passions" as Ralph Ellison has argued. In his effort to delineate an American literary landscape for himself and an American identity for black Americans, Ellison mistakenly separates feeling and form from their essential interaction in culture or art. He admits a shared feeling among Africans against racism and colonial oppression, but he too eagerly dismisses the question of form or culture that also might be shared among black writers who create, as Ellison does, a written literature from the continuous presence of the oral tradition.

James Baldwin, in a similar public statement in *Nobody Knows My Name*,[2] echoes Ellison's caution concerning the possibility of shared cultural forms among black writers. Baldwin, reporting on the First Congress of Negro Writers and Artists held at the Sorbonne in 1956, identifies his own ambivalence toward the cultural importance of an African presence in the world. From the assumed stance of an outsider, he discusses what might unite black writers in terms of feeling rather than form. He describes the delegates to the conference:

What they held in common was their precarious, their un-
utterably painful relation to the white world. What they
held in common was the necessity to remake the world in
their own image, to impose this image on the world, and
no longer be controlled by the vision of the world, and of
themselves, held by other people. And this ache united
people who might otherwise have been divided as to what
a man should be. (p. 29)

Baldwin may have been encouraged to take such a position
by none other than the Martinican poet Aimé Césaire.
When questioned at the same conference about the definition of Negro-African culture, Césaire responded, as Baldwin reports, that "no one is suggesting that there is such a
thing as a pure race, or that culture is a racial product. We
are not Negroes by our own desire, but, in effect, because
of Europe. What unites all Negroes is the injustices they
have suffered at European hands" (p. 54).

Césaire, Baldwin, and Ellison establish a context for a
public discussion of culture that is not reflected in the text
of their works. On the public level all three confirm "an
identity of passions," or a racial feeling, but shy away from
acknowledging a racial form. More openly sensitive to the
interrelation between feeling and form, between culture
and "passion," and between the African and the European
traditions was Richard Wright, who stated at that same conference: "I see both worlds from another, and third, point
of view" (p. 44). For Wright, that third point of view
meant identifying himself as a black man of the Western
world. And despite his misleading and exaggerated comment that the Negro is America's metaphor, Wright reveals
the challenge that modern black writers have faced—the
creation of a language that is faithful to the experience of
blacks in the New World, a language that expresses the
acculturation of traditional African and European forms
and the dynamic transformation and reinvention of self that
results. This cultural adaptation may, in fact, be the very
essence of the American experience, for it permeates every
multiethnic, multiracial society of the Western Hemisphere.
Its people, to extend Baldwin's and Wright's metaphors, are
those persons of color "who can speak of the West with real

authority, whose experience, painful as it is, also proves the
vitality of transgressed Western ideals." I would not go so
far as to say "Western ideals"; rather, what proves vital is
the ability of a dispossessed, captive people to re-create
themselves out of culture contact and fusion, resilience and
improvisation. These "American" persons of color, Baldwin continues, "could be considered the connecting link
between Africa and the West, the most real and certainly
the most shocking of all African contributions to Western
cultural life. The articulation of this reality, however, was
another matter. But it was clear that our relation to the
mysterious continent of Africa would not be clarified until
we had found some means of saying, to ourselves and to
the world, more about the mysterious American continent
than had ever been said before" (p. 21).

Fulfilling this challenge to say, or to speak, requires that
we use a language that expresses the American experience
of blending and borrowing from the old worlds of Africa
and Europe, that creates literature from the historical experience of the language and the peculiar cultural syncretism from which it was born. This mission for the black
writer is expressed poetically by Césaire in his moving epic
Return to My Native Land:

> I should discover once again the secret of great communi-
> cations and of great combustions. I should say storm. I
> should say river. I should say tornado. I should say leaf. I
> should say tree. I should be wet by all rains, made damp
> with all dews. I should roll like frenzied blood on the slow
> current of the eye of words like mad horses, clots of fresh
> children, curfews, vestiges of temples, precious stones far
> enough away to discourage miners. Whoever would not
> comprehend me would not comprehend the roaring of the
> tiger. . . . From looking at trees I have become a tree and
> my long tree-feet have dug in the ground long serpent
> holes presaging the pillage to come to high cities of bone
>> From thinking of the Congo
>> I have become a Congo buzzing with forests and
>> rivers where the whip cracks like a great flag
>> the flag of the prophet

The issue here entails a redefinition of black American
civilizations, or, one might even say, neo-African civiliza-

tions, for the literature that develops in modern Africa, the Caribbean, and the United States reflects a continuing confrontation between oral traditions and literary models; we discover, according to Edward Brathwaite, a culture that is "not pure African, but an adaptation carried out mainly in terms of African tradition," and, further, "a literature of negritude, and with it, a literature of local authenticity."[3] The writer merges with the singer, the dancer, the taleteller. And, as Wilson Harris has argued, "the community the writer shares with the primordial dancer is, as it were, the complementary halves of a broken stage."[4] The syncretistic locus for a comparative black experience emerges as the theme of the last stanza from Jacques Roumain:

> Your soul is this image in the whispering water where
>   your fathers bent their dark faces.
> Its hidden movements blend you with the waves
> And the white that made you a mulatto is this bit
>   of foam cast up, like spit, upon the shore.
>   ("When the Tom Tom Beats")

II

> I've known rivers ancient as the world
> And older than the flow of human blood
>   in human veins.
>   —Langston Hughes, "The Negro Speaks of Rivers"

Black America is a metaphor for the reinvention of the African self through a language that is the danced speech of its people. The quest for this language has both historical and textual significance. Both trends reveal how black literature, according to Wilfred Cartey's important study *Black Images*, is "an essential element in the process of self-discovery," a process through which the poet seeks to "remake the Negro image from within."[5] Cartey, echoing James Weldon Johnson's earlier plea for a racial idiom,[6] continues:

> Surely the most important task engaging the black man in
> Africa or America has been the remaking of his own image

> out of his own identity. Black poetry . . . as a mode of
> modern poetry, has been evolving in direct relationship to
> the evolution of the black man himself. (p. 183)

Historically speaking, the first decades of the twentieth
century witnessed the progress of the black man into as full
a participation in American and European society as the
racist and neo-colonial structures would allow. At least
he was no longer a slave. Capitalism, modernization, and
world war brought a global consciousness to all people.
Blacks in modern society, however, found the constrictions
of class replaced by the confines of race. The black man,
because of his race, was stereotyped as an exotic primitive.
But as a result of this pervasive racial identification and the
efforts of the United States government to protect the
Monroe Doctrine by occupying areas in the Caribbean,
blacks reversed the stigma of race and made it a banner for
national identity and a racial joie de vivre. Like their
cousins in North America, African and Caribbean students
in Europe found their adoptive France unreceptive to their
"racial" presence. And they soon discovered the roots of an
African contribution to world civilization within their own
ethnic identity.

The Harlem Renaissance occurred simultaneously with
movements throughout the Caribbean. The occupation by
American marines of several countries such as Haiti from
1915 to 1934 and Cuba in 1907 and 1917 inspired local
intellectuals to explore indigenous culture, particularly folklore, as the basis of a national and racial identity in the face
of an imposing foreign power that practiced racial discrim-
ination. Haitian and Cuban populations, previously divided
by an intraracial conflict between mulattos and blacks,
found a common black identity to be a good defense
against a foreign white authority. This shift in national consciousness meant that the Haitian identity was grounded in
racial as well as national sources. In 1927, Jacques Roumain
returned to Haiti from Europe, where he was educated, and
joined with Normil Sylvain, Dominique Hippolyte, and
Carl Brouard to establish *La Revue Indigène*, and from it
the indigenist movement became a precursor to Négritude.
Jean Price-Mars published his monumental *Ainsi parla*

l'oncle (1928), a collection of essays in Haitian ethnology that established a critical index of Haitian folk life from which these writers could derive the form and content, the feeling and language, of a native literature. The literature used folk beliefs of voodoo for symbolism and the figurative language of Creole for black speech patterns. Roumain went on to write the first Haitian peasant novel, La Montagne ensorcelée (1931), and culminated the genre with Gouverneurs de la rosée (1944).

Among Spanish writers in Cuba and Puerto Rico, Fernando Ortiz published Glosario de afronegrismos (1924), a compilation of African words in Cuban speech and words of Spanish origin with new Cuban meanings. In so doing, Ortiz called the attention of Cuban intellectuals to the rich source of black folklore in Cuba and may have countered the ideological effects of American occupation of Cuba in 1907 and 1917, the date of Ortiz's later work, Hampa afrocubana. By focusing on black speech patterns in Spanish, which used terms filled with African sonority, such as cumbancha, simbombo, chevere, sandunga, and mondongo, Ortiz paralleled Jean Price-Mars's pioneering study of the Creole language, where terms such as vaudou, yamvalou, petro, ibo, loa, and merengue identified dances of African origin and rhythm.[7] Ortiz' glossary paved the way for the magazine La Revista de Avance, the works of Puerto Rican poet Luis Pales-Matos (Tuntun de pasa y griferia, 1937), Ramon Guirao (Poesia afro-cubana, 1938), and the poetic achievements of Cuban Nicolás Guillén, whose volume Motivios de son in 1930 contained a glossary by Ortiz himself, which was no longer needed when his Songoro Cosongo, poemas mulatos was issued in 1931.

Ortiz and writers of La Revista de Avance ushered in a new generation of Hispanic writers who, like the Haitians of Revue Indigène, "demanded that poetry [indeed, all literature] bring into its cadence the rhythm of the spoken language"[8] and acknowledge its shared ancestry in African, Spanish, and French languages. Ortiz and Price-Mars may have served the same purpose as James Weldon Johnson in urging writers to abandon the imitative dialect of the popular plantation tradition and to create a racial idiom from within a more native poetic diction that allowed for the honest presentation of black character and theme. Following Johnson's lead, Langston Hughes created in his work what Jacques Roumain and Nicolás Guillén did in theirs—"a living transformation of a past into new artistic forms" (Cartey, p. 24). The rhythm and structure of the blues, like the danced speech of the Hispanic rumba and the Haitian Ra-Ra, became rubrics for a pregeneric New World literature. As Price-Mars has written:

> music and dance are for the black man an organic necessity. Together they give an undefinable, yet essential source of strength to a nervous system burdened by the weight of very deep emotionalism. They color all the manners of the black man's life.[9]

III

> Zumba mamá, la rumba y tambó
> Mabimba, mabomba, bomba y bombo
>
> Zumba mamá, la rumba y tambó
> Mabimba, babomba, bomba y bombó
> —José Zacarias Tallet, "La rumba"

The use of onomatopoeic words in the above refrain by José Zacarias Tallet gives an authentic structure, voice, and rhythm to a poem that describes the chase and eventual seduction—through the dance—of the woman Tomasa by José Encarnación. Here the poem transforms music by making it both a structural and a thematic element in the poem. It continues:

> Como baila la rumba la negra Tomasa,
> como baila la rumba José Encarnación
> Ella mueve una nalga, ella mueve la otra,
> él se estira, se encoge, dispara la grupa,
> el vientre dispara, se agacha, camina,
> sobre el uno y el otro talón.

> How she dances the rhumba, that black girl Tomasa,
> how he dances the rhumba, José Encarnación.
> She moves one buttock, she moves the other,

he stretches out, shrinks up, sticks out his rump,
the stomach thrusts out, he bends down, walks
on the one and then the other heel bone.

(Cartey, p. 80)

Note how the text transforms the raw material of music and folklore. Unobtrusively, the very rhythm and language provide theme and form. The reader becomes engrossed in the music as Tomasa becomes, literally, seduced by Encarnación. The reader participates in the dramatic action of the poem, which illustrates an important textual element of our critical vision: The text itself remakes the image of the black man or woman in the specific context of an African-American syncretism. Through the text, then, we come to agree with Wilfred Cartey that

> Although history, the political and economic sciences, ethnology and sociology, have done much . . . to begin to place the Negro before us, these disciplines do not match what literature has told us about the black man. This fact suggests that the task of making him known has required imagination in both cognition and perception. (p. 182)

In this specifically literary realm, Edward Brathwaite has distinguished four kinds of New World literature that evoke the African presence: (1) a rhetorical literature, which uses Africa as a mask and only says the word "Africa" or invokes a dream of the Congo, Senegal, Niger, and other place names; (2) the literature of African survival, which "deals quite consciously with African survivals in Caribbean society" but does not reconnect them with the great tradition of Africa; (3) the literature of African expression, "which has its root in the folk, and which attempts to adapt or transform folk material into literary experiment"; and (4) the literature of reconnection by writers who have lived in Africa and the New World and who "are consciously reaching out to rebridge the gap with the spiritual heartland."[10]

Most important of these developments, and the one most applicable to our study, is the "literature of African expression," for here the writer attempts to remake himself as he transforms folk material into literary experiment. Illustrating this process of self-discovery is Haitian Jacques Roumain, who took as models for his own literary expression the blues references of Langston Hughes, the sermons of James Weldon Johnson ("Nouveau Sermon nègre"), and his native Creole culture. Within this pattern of shared influence across linguistic lines one can speak of a cross-fertilization, an intertextuality among works of New World black literature. Not only was Roumain to learn from Hughes about the transformation of musical forms and folk material, but Hughes learned from Roumain, by translating his poetry, how to convey the peculiar Haitian assonance and sonority in English. In this respect, the poems "The Negro Speaks of Rivers" and "Guinea" present opportunities for interesting structural and thematic comparisons.

Both poems invest language with the power of transforming external folk material, atavistic reference, and the speaking voice itself. The speaker in Hughes's poem discovers a personal identity through his participation by means of language in an African past and a New World present. His racial knowledge is not abstract or romantic but grounded in personal and group behavior to create and re-create history. "I've known rivers," the poem begins, *because*

> I bathed in the Euphrates when dawns were young
> I built my hut near the Congo and it lulled me to sleep
> I looked upon the Nile and raised the pyramids above it.

Action within the past gives the poem an authentic voice for the present and rescues the work from an inappropriately romantic perspective. Man actively participates in human history. He earns his identity through the creation of civilization. The history outside him—rivers "older than the flow of human veins"—becomes his through the poem's near incremental repetition of the phrase "my soul has grown deep like the rivers."

Roumain, in a similar lyrical language, charts a journey into the future based on what the speaker in "Guinea" has inherited from the past. The word "Guinea" resonates for a Haitian audience not only because it signifies Africa but also because it identifies the popular belief in Haitian folk-

lore that upon death one will journey to Guinea and join
the ancestors. The lyrical tone of the poem differs from the
more religious language of James Weldon Johnson's "Go
Down Death," or Sterling Brown's more colloquial "Sister
Lou," but, nevertheless, it initiates Roumain's search for a
figurative language to express the form and feeling of his
people. The poem is descriptive of one speaker's journey
and prescriptive and instructive in the imperative mood for
his audience:

C'est le lent chemin de Guinée
La mort t'y conduira
Voici les branchages, les arbres, la forêt
Écoute le bruit du vent dans ses longs cheveux
    d'éternelle nuit.

C'est le lent chemin de Guinée
Tes pères t'attendent sans impatience
Sur la route, ils palabrent
Ils attendent
Voici l'heure où les ruisseaux grelottent comme
    des chapelets d'os

C'est le lent chemin de Guinée
Il ne te sera pas fait de lumineux accueil
Au noir pays des hommes noirs:
Sous un ciel fumeux percé de cris d'oiseaux
Autour de l'oeil du marigot
    les cils des arbres s'écartent sur la clarté pourrissante.
Là, t'attend au bord de l'eau un paisible village,
Et la case de tes pères, et la dure pierre familiale
    où reposer enfin ton front.

It's the long road to Guinea
Death takes you down
Here are the boughs, the trees, the forest
Listen to the sound of the wind in its long hair
    of eternal night

It's the long road to Guinea
Where your fathers await you without impatience
Along the way, they talk

They wait
This is the hour when the streams rattle
    like beads of bone

It's the long road to Guinea
No bright welcome will be made for you
In the dark land of dark men:
Under a smoky sky pierced by the cry of birds
Around the eye of the river
    the eyelashes of the trees open on decaying light
There, there awaits you beside the water a quiet village,
And the hut of your fathers, and the hard ancestral stone
    where your head will rest at last.

In the repetition of the droning phrase "C'est le lent chemin de Guinée," Roumain establishes a link to Haitian folk culture. And in his use of the "o" sound for near rhyme and rhythm, he approximates the open vowel sounds of the Creole language, as in "La mort t'y conduira."

When Langston Hughes translated the poem, he was particularly sensitive to this use of language and approximated the texture of the open, sonorous speech. Instead of the literal translation of the line to read "death will lead you there," he chose the sonorous, alliterative line "death takes you down" to maintain thematic clarity and to preserve the tonal quality of the language. The speaker in Roumain's original text, as in the translation, discovers a language through which he can experience death on the literal level and passage from the New World to Africa on the symbolic level. His experience is visual and aural: "Here are the boughs, the trees, the forest / Listen to the sound of the wind in its long hair / of eternal night." The speaker comes to know how the wind is animated, personified. And having established a primary contact with nature, he then discerns the voices of his fathers that accompany his passage through a decaying light that signifies no bright welcome. But rather than feeling an existential gloom, the speaker discovers "a quiet village" beside the water and the ancestral stone upon which he will rest. The repeated "long road to Guinea" suggests a passage that will test the speaker and, as in Hughes's "Negro Speaks of Rivers," make his presence one of active and earned behavior until he endures the darkness of his own fears and earns the rewarding, soft darkness of eternal rest.

Roumain's voice in the poem is that of a learned observer, instructing the uninitiated, who may still need to find—in the folk belief of spiritual and cultural redemption —comfort from the psychic dislocation and abandonment of his past in the New World. By its reference to Africa, Hughes's subjective voice affirms, indirectly, the historical, the folkloric, and, directly, the spiritual journey. Roumain is still groping for language that connects more fully to this rite of passage.

Roumain and Hughes were familiar with each other's work, but when Roumain began to write he composed melancholic, meditative verse that described his feelings of alienation upon his return to Haiti from his education abroad. Roumain's early poetry shows his search for a language to illuminate Haitian reality as the poet's own national identity. Other writers of the *Revue Indigène* were helpful to him, but so were writers of the Harlem Renaissance like Hughes and Countee Cullen. When interviewed by the review, Roumain suggested that Haitian writers become more aware of the flourishing North American black poetry. Years later, Roumain described indirectly how he learned from Hughes to depict the black figurative language of the blues. Note Roumain's direct borrowing of black American speech patterns in his tribute to Hughes:

> At Lagos you knew sad faced girls
> Silver circled their ankles.
> They offered themselves to you naked as the night
> Gold-circled by the moon.
>
> You saw France without uttering a worn, shop-made phrase;
> > *Here we are, Lafayette!*
> The Seine seemed less lovely than the Congo.
>
> Venice. You sought the shade of Desdemona.
> Her name was Paola.
> You said: *Sweet, sweet Love!*
>
> And sometimes
> *Babe! Baby!*
> Then she wept and asked for twenty *lire.*

Like a Baedeker your nomad heart wandered
From Harlem to Dakar.
The Sea sounded on in your songs—sweet, rhythmic,
    wild. . . .
And its bitter tears
Of white foam blossom-born.

Now here in this cabaret as the dawn draws near you
    murmur . . .
Play the blues again for me!
O! for me again play the blues!

Are you dreaming tonight, perhaps, of the palm trees, of
    Black Men there who paddled you down the dusks?
                                        ("Langston Hughes")

Roumain's sensitivity to colloquial speech, music, and folklore as a basis for indigenous figurative language is evident in his long, major poem, *Bois d'ébène* and surfaces again as a rhythmic device in his more political piece, "Sales Nègres" ("Dirty Negroes"):

Well then
here we are
we negroes
we niggers
we dirty niggers
we won't accept it any more
· · · · ·
that surprises you
after our: yes, sir
polishing your shoes
yes, father
to the missionary whites
yes, master
harvesting for you
the coffee
cotton
peanuts
in Africa
America
like the good negroes
poor negroes
dirty negroes

that we were
that we won't be any longer

But the creation of the peasant novel was Roumain's greatest achievement in Haitian letters. *Gouverneurs de la rosée* (1944), translated by Langston Hughes and Mercer Cook as *Masters of the Dew* (1947),[11] shows Roumain's masterful transformation of Creole language, music, and folklore into literary experiment.

In *Masters of the Dew* we encounter the peasant greeting of "Honor," which is answered by "Respect" when one peasant visits another. Roumain transforms that dialogue in the text to indicate an exchange of greeting between Manuel, the protagonist, and his homeland of Fonds Rouge. The hero, after fifteen years of working in the cane fields of Cuba, returns to his drought-stricken village and finds water to irrigate the land. The community, however, is divided by a family feud that prevents the peasants from working cooperatively to build an aqueduct now that water is found. Roumain's use of the oral exchange "Honor-Respect" establishes an internal dialogue between Manuel and himself, and an external one with Nature, with whose life forces he renews his primal covenant and from whom he eventually gains redemption in his martyrdom and sustenance for his community:

> [Manuel] was dull of happiness despite the stubborn thoughts that haunted him. He wanted to sing a greeting to the trees: "Growing things, my growing things! To you I say 'Honor!' You must answer 'Respect,' so that I may enter. You're my house, you're my country. Growing things, I say, vines of my woods, I am planted in this soil. I am rooted in this earth. To all that grows, I say, 'Honor.' Answer, 'Respect,' so that I may enter."
>
> He proceeded at that long, almost nonchalant but graceful gait of a Negro of the plain, sometimes cutting a path with a swift stroke of his machete. He was still humming when he reached a clearing. (p. 35)

Note furthermore how Manuel's exchange with nature necessitates dialogue with his fellow villagers:

Manuel began to talk to the peasants, one after the other. For years hate had become with them a habit. It had given an object and a target to their impotent anger against the elements. But Manuel had translated into good Creole the exacting language of the thirsty plain, the plaint of growing things, the promises and all the mirages of the water. (p. 115)

By thus focusing on Roumain, we can see how the black writer re-creates language from within the specific boundaries of his native culture and speech. Moreover, Roumain's achievement—transforming specific oral, musical, and folk forms into literature—links him to Hughes in the United States, Guillén in Cuba, and Léopold Sédar-Senghor in Senegal. Oral traditions, transformed, are the cultural elements shared by these black writers. They accomplish the very dictum articulated earlier by Jean Price-Mars that "nothing will be able to prevent tales, legends, songs come from afar or created, transformed by us, from being a part of us, revealed to us as an exteriorization of our collective self."[12] And these writers of New World literature have responded in their way to Derek Walcott's contemporary caution:

> How choose
> Between this Africa and the English tongue I love?
> Betray them both, or give back what they give?
> How can I face such slaughter and be cool?
> How can I turn from Africa and live?
> ("A Far Cry from Africa," *In a Green Night*)

IV

Black writers of the Caribbean, North America, and Africa confront European civilization on the cultural level, not merely on the level of feeling or passion. The form of their response to acculturation has been to combine the best of traditional African oral heritage with the most useful European vocabulary. African languages in motion and in contact with Spanish, French, and English have created something different, something new—not a pidgin or dialect version, but a language that seeks within its national oral foundation a synthesis based on racial characteristics and allegiance.We must argue against Ralph Ellison's assertion that "since most of the so-called 'Negro cultures' outside Africa are necessarily amalgams, it would seem more profitable to stress the term 'culture' and leave the term 'Negro' out of the discussion." In the same spirit Ellison continues to disregard culture as an aspect of race and to mislead his readers:

> It is not culture which binds the peoples who are of partially African origin now scattered throughout the world, but an identity of passions. We share a hatred for the alienation forced upon us by Europeans during the process of colonization and empire and we are bound by our common suffering more than by our pigmentation. But even this identification is shared by most non-white peoples, and while it has political value of great potency, its cultural value is almost nil.[13]

Fortunately, the literature of the African Diaspora, whether on the continent itself or in the West Indies, tells a different story. We find that through the shared history of oppression racial identity and folk life have created the means by which men acquired language: a national language built upon the resonance of folk forms and rhythmic syntax of speech that approximated the African gift of music and appropriated a vocabulary of convenience from Europe.

By acquiring language and imbuing it with terms directly related to New World experience through music and folklore (indigenous creations), black writers created a bond among themselves through literature. Ellison and Baldwin fail, at least publicly, to make this re-creation and reconnection vital to their work. They fail to learn from the literary experimentation of writers like Hughes, who was the most important cultural ambassador throughout the Diaspora during and after the Renaissance years.

As critics, writers, and teachers of Afro-American literature we need to return to what Hughes discovered through his translations, personal travels, associations, and creative work, so that we too might identify the shared cultural forms used by black writers to reconnect to a common, ancestral resonance. This kind of cross-cultural comparative criticism can illuminate the dimensions of a black sensibility in literature and effectively shape our understanding of literary history. Furthermore, our willingness to approach black writing by going beyond specific geographic or historical boundaries can add to the different ways in which survey courses are organized. By identifying uses of language in terms of shared cultural forms among black writers in French, English, and Spanish we free Afro-American literature from the confines of the North American cultural prison that automatically relegates it to minority, secondary, and thus inferior status. We also discover modes of universality within the individual text and a resonant intertextuality with literatures that share a common historical background and linguistic synthesis. In response, then, to Walcott's searing probe, "how can I turn from Africa and live?," we must answer that each New World literature is a river that remembers its source while continuing its individual direction, shape, and depth where language swims and *all* our nets pull.

Notes

[1] *Return to My Native Land*, trans. Emile Snyder (Paris: Présence Africaine, 1971). Critics have taken from Césaire a broader definition, which includes "the awareness of being black, the simple acknowledgment of a fact that implies the acceptance of it, a taking charge of one's destiny as a black man, of one's history and culture." See the translator's introd. to Lilyan Kesteloot's *Black Writers in French: A Literary History of Negritude* (Philadelphia: Temple Univ. Press, 1974), p. xviii.

[2] *Nobody Knows My Name* (New York: Dial, 1961). All further references to this work appear in the text.

[3] "The African Presence in Caribbean Literature," *Daedalus*, 103 (1974), 78.

[4] *Tradition, the Writer and Society* (London: New Beacon, 1973), p. 52.

[5] *Black Images* (New York: Teachers Coll. Press, 1970), pp. 24–25.

[6] See Johnson, pref., *American Negro Poetry*, rev. ed. (New York: Harcourt, 1931).

[7] G. R. Coulthard, quoted in Cartey, p. 25.

[8] Cartey, p. 28.

[9] Jean Price-Mars, quoted in Cartey, p. 78.

[10] Brathwaite, pp. 80–81.

[11] *Masters of the Dew*, (New York: Reynal, 1947). All further references to this work appear in the text.

[12] Jean Price-Mars, quoted in Cartey, p. 24.

[13] *Shadow and Act* (New York: Signet, 1964), p. 255.

Spanish	English	French
Negrissmo (Cuba, Puerto Rico)	*Harlem Renaissance (U.S.A.)* (Harlem, Washington D. C., etc.)	*Négritude* (Paris, Haiti, Martinique, Senegal)
1907 American Occupation of Havana	1903 *Souls of Black Folk*, Du Bois	1921 *Batouala*, René Maran; Prix Goncourt
1917 *Hampa afrocubana*, Ortiz Second American Occupation of Cuba	1910 *Crisis Magazine*	1927 *La Revue Indigène*, Roumain et al. (Haiti)
1924 *Glossary of Afro-Cubanisms*, Ortiz	1922 *American Negro Poetry*, ed. J. W. Johnson	1915–34 American Occupation of Haiti
	Batouala reviewed in *Crisis* Cullen writes "Dance of Love"	1928 *Ainsi parla l'oncle*, Price-Mars (Haiti)
1928 *La Revista de Avance* (Cuba)	1923 *Cane*, J. Toomer *Opportunity Magazine* est.	1930–34 *La Revue du Monde Noir*, Nardal/Sarjous (Paris)
La Revista de las Antilles (Puerto Rico)	1925 *Color*, Countee Cullen *The New Negro*, ed. Locke	1931–32 (?) *Légitime défense*, Radical students (Paris)
1930 *Motivios de son*, Guillén (w/glossary by Ortiz)	1926 *The Weary Blues*, Hughes	1934 *L'Étudiant noir*, Damas, Césaire, Senghor (Paris)
1931 *Songoro Cosongo, poemas mulatos*, Guillén	1929 *Banjo*, Claude McKay	1937 *Pigments*, L. Damas
1937 *Tuntun de pasa y grifería*, Luis Pales Matos (Puerto Rico)	1932 *Southern Road*, S. Brown	1939 *Cahier d'un retour au pays natal*, Césaire
1938 *Poesía afro-cubana*, Ramon Guirao	1935 *Mules and Men* Z. N. Hurston	1941 *Tropiques*, Césaire (Martinique)
	1940 *Native Son*, R. Wright	1944 *Gouverneurs de la rosée*, J. Roumain (Haiti)
	1947 *Masters of the Dew*, trans. Hughes and Cook	1947 *Chants d'ombre*, Senghor *Présence Africaine* founded
	1952 *Invisible Man*, Ellison	1948 *Anthologie de . . . poésie nègre*, ed. Senghor (Paris)
		1952 *Peau noire, masques blancs*, Fanon (Paris)
		1956 First Congress of Negro Artists and Writers (Paris)

Preface to Blackness:
Text and Pretext

Henry-Louis Gates, Jr.

For Soule is forme, and doth the bodie make.
—Edmund Spenser, 1596

Music is a world within itself, with a language we all understand.
—Stevie Wonder, 1976

I

The idea of a determining formal relation between literature and social institutions does not in itself explain the
sense of urgency that has, at least since the publication in
1760 of *A Narrative of the Uncommon Sufferings and Surprising Deliverance of Briton Hammon, a Negro Man,*[1]
characterized nearly the whole of Afro-American writing.
This idea has often encouraged a posture that belabors the
social and documentary status of black art, and indeed the
earliest discrete examples of written discourse by slave and
ex-slave came under a scrutiny not primarily literary. Formal writing, beginning with the four autobiographical slave
narratives published in English between 1760 and 1798,
was taken to be collective as well as functional. Because
narratives documented the potential for "culture," that is,
for manners and morals, the command of written English
virtually separated the African from the Afro-American,

the slave from the ex-slave, titled property from fledgling human being. Well-meaning abolitionists cited these texts as proof of the common humanity of bondsman and lord; yet these same texts also demonstrated the contrary for proponents of the antebellum world view—that the African imagination was merely derivative. The command of a written language, then, could be no mean thing in the life of the slave: Learning to read, the slave narratives repeat again and again, was a decisive political act; learning to write, as measured by an eighteenth-century scale of culture and society, was an irreversible step away from the cotton field toward a freedom even larger than physical manumission. What the use of language entailed for personal social mobility and what it implied about the public Negro mind made for the onerous burden of literacy, a burden having very little to do with the use of language as such, a burden so pervasive that the nineteenth-century quest for literacy and the twentieth-century quest for form became the central, indeed controlling, metaphors (if not mythical matrices) in Afro-American narrative. Once the private dream fused with a public, and therefore political, imperative, the Negro arts were committed; the pervasive sense of fundamental urgency and unity in the black arts became a millenial, if not precisely apocalyptic, force.

I do not mean to suggest that these ideas were peculiar to eighteenth-century American criticism. For example, we learn from Herder's Prize Essay of 1773 on the *Causes of the Decline of Taste in Different Nations* that in Germany "the appreciation of various folk and Gothic literatures and the comparative study of ancient, eastern, and modern foreign literatures (the criticism of literature by age and race) were strongly established, and these interests profoundly affected theories about the nature of literature as the expression of, or the power that shaped, human cultures or human nature in general." William K. Wimsatt also remarks that Friedrick Schlegel "only accented an already pervasive view when he called poetry the most specifically human energy, the central document of any culture."[2] It should not surprise us, then, that *Poems on Various Subjects, Religious and Moral, by Phillis Wheatley, Negro Servant to Mr. Wheatley of Boston*, the first book of poems published by an African in English,[3] became, almost immediately after its publication in London in 1773, the international antislavery movement's most salient argument for the African's innate mental equality. That the book went to five printings before 1800 testified far more to its acceptance as a "legitimate" product of "the African muse," writes Henri Grégoire[4] in 1808, than to the merit of its sometimes vapid elegiac verse. The no fewer than eighteen "certificates of authenticity" that preface the book, including one by John Hancock and another by the Governor of Massachusetts, Thomas Hutchinson, meant to "leave no doubt, that she is its author."[5] Literally scores of public figures—from Voltaire to George Washington, from Benjamin Rush to Benjamin Franklin—reviewed Wheatley's book, yet virtually no one discussed the book as poetry. It was an unequal contest: The documentary status of black art assumed priority over mere literary judgment; criticism rehearsed content to justify one notion of origins or another. Of these discussions, it was Thomas Jefferson's that proved most seminal to the shaping of the Afro-American critical activity.

Asserted primarily to debunk the exaggerated claims of the abolitionists, Thomas Jefferson's remarks on Phillis Wheatley's poetry, as well as on Ignatius Sancho's *Letters*,[6] exerted a prescriptive influence over the criticism of the writing of blacks for the next 150 years. "Never yet," Jefferson prefaces his discussion of Wheatley, "could I find a Black that had uttered a thought above the level of plain narration; never seen even an elementary trait of painting or sculpture." As a specimen of the human mind, Jefferson continued, Wheatley's poems as poetry did not merit discussion. "Religion," he writes, "indeed has produced a Phillis Whately [sic] but it could not produce a poet." "The compositions published under her name," Jefferson concludes, "are below the dignity of criticism. The heroes of the *Dunciad* are to her, as Hercules to the author of the poem." As to Sancho's *Letters*, Jefferson says:

> his imagination is wild and extravagant, escapes incessantly
> from every restraint of reason and taste, and, in the course
> of its vagaries, leaves a tract of thought as incoherent and

eccentric, as is the course of a meteor through the sky. His subjects should have led him to a process of sober reasoning: yet we find him always substituting sentiment for demonstration.[7]

Jefferson's stature demanded response: from black writers, refutations of his doubts about their very capacity to imagine great art and hence to take a few giant steps up the Great Chain of Being; from would-be critics, encyclopaedic and often hyperbolic replies to Jefferson's disparaging generalizations. The critical responses included Thomas Clarkson's Prize Essay, written in Latin at Cambridge in 1785 and published as *An Essay on the Slavery and Commerce of the Human Species, Particularly the African* (1788), and the following, rather remarkable, volumes: Gilbert Imlay's *A Topographical Description of the Western Territory of North America* (1793); the Marquis de Bois-Robert's two-volume *The Negro Equalled by Few Europeans* (1791); Thomas Branagan's *Preliminary Essay on the Oppression of the Exiled Sons of Africa* (1804); The Abbé Grégoire's *An Enquiry concerning the Intellectual and Moral Faculties, and Literature of Negroes . . .* (1808); Samuel Stanhope Smith's *An Essay on the Causes of the Variety of the Human Complexion and Figure in the Human Species* (1810); Lydia Child's *An Appeal in Favor of That Class of Americans Called Africans* (1833); B. B. Thatcher's *Memoir of Phillis Wheatley, a Native American and a Slave* (1834); Abigail Mott's *Biographical Sketches and Interesting Anecdotes of Persons of Color* (1838); R. B. Lewis' *Light and Truth* (1844); Theodore Hally's *A Vindication of the Capacity of the Negro Race* (1851); R. T. Greener's urbane long essay in *The National Quarterly Review* (1880); Joseph Wilson's rather ambitious *Emancipation: Its Course and Progress from 1481 B.C. to A.D. 1875* (1882); William Simmon's *Men of Mark* (1887); Benjamin Brawley's *The Negro in Literature and Art* (1918) and Joel A. Rodgers' two-volume *The World's Great Men of Color* (1946).

Even more telling, for our purposes here, is that the almost quaint authenticating signatures and statements that prefaced Wheatley's book became, certainly through the period of Dunbar and Chesnutt and even until the middle of the Harlem Renaissance, fixed attestations of the "specimen" author's physical blackness. This sort of authenticating color description was so common to these prefaces that many late nineteenth- and early twentieth-century black reviewers, particularly in the *African Methodist Episcopal Church Review*, the *Southern Workman*, the *Voice of the Negro, Alexander's Magazine*, and *The Colored American*, adopted it as a political as well as rhetorical strategy to counter the intense and bitter allegations of African inferiority popularized by journalistic accounts and "colorations" of social Darwinism. Through an examination of a few of these prefaces, I propose to sketch an ironic circular thread of interpretation that commences in the eighteenth century but does not reach its fullest philosophical form until the decade between 1965 and 1975: the movement from blackness as a physical concept to blackness as a metaphysical concept. Indeed, this movement became the very text and pretext of the "Blackness" of the recent Black Arts movement, a solidly traced hermeneutical circle into which all of us find ourselves drawn.

II

Even before Jefferson allowed himself the outrageous remark that "the improvement of the blacks in body and mind, in the first instance of their mixture with the whites, has been observed by every one, and proves that their inferiority is not the effect merely of their condition of life,"[8] advocates of the unity of the human species had forged a union of literary tradition, individual talent, and innate racial capacity. Phillis Wheatley's "authenticators," for instance, announced that:

> We whose Names are under-written, do assure the world, that the POEMS specified in the following Page, were (as we verily believe) written by *Phillis*, a young Negro Girl, who was but a few years since, brought an uncultured Barbarian from Africa, and has ever since been and now is, under the Disadvantage of serving as a Slave of a Family in this Town. She has been examined by some of the best Judges, and is thought qualified to write them.[9]

Further, Wheatley herself asks indulgence of the critic, considering the occasion of her verse. "As her Attempts in Poetry are now sent into the World, it is hoped the critic will not severely censure their Defects; and we presume they have too much Merit to be cast aside with contempt, as worthless and trifling effusions." "With all their Imperfections," she concludes, "the poems are now humbly submitted to the Perusal of the Public."[10] Other than the tone of the author's preface, there was little here that was "humbly submitted" to Wheatley's public. Her volume garnered immense interest as to the nature of the African imagination. So compelling did evidence of the African's artistic abilities prove to be to Enlightenment speculation on the idea of progress and the scala naturae that just nine years after Wheatley's *Poems* appeared, over one thousand British lords and ladies subscribed to have published Ignatius Sancho's collected letters. Even more pertinent in our context, Joseph Jekyll, M.P., prefaced the volume with a full biographical account of the colorful Sancho's life, structured curiously about the received relation between "genius" and "species."

People were also fascinated by the "African mind" presented in the collected letters of Ignatius Sancho. Named "from a fancied resemblance to the Squire of Don Quixote,"[11] Sancho had his portrait painted by Gainsborough and engraved by Bartolozzi. He was a correspondent of Garrick and Sterne and, apparently, something of a poet as well: "A commerce with the Muses was supported amid the trivial and momentary interruptions of a shop," Jekyll writes. Indeed, not only were "the Poets studied, and even imitated with some success," but "two pieces were constructed for the stage." In addition to his creative endeavors, Sancho was a critic—perhaps the first African critic of the arts to write in English. His "theory of Music was discussed, published, and dedicated to the Princess Royal, and Painting was so much within the circle of Ignatius Sancho's judgment and criticism," Jekyll observes, "that several artists paid great *deference* to his opinion."

Jekyll's rather involved biography is a pretext to display the artifacts of the sable mind, as was the very publication of the *Letters* themselves. "Her motives for laying them before the publick were," the publisher admits, "the desire of showing that an untutored African may possess abilities equal to an European." Sancho was an "extraordinary Negro," his biographer relates, although he was a bit better for being a bit bad. "Freedom, riches, and leisure, naturally led to a disposition of African tendencies into indulgences; and that which dissipated the mind of Ignatius completely drained the purse," Jekyll puns. "In his attachment to women, he displayed a profuseness which not unusually characterizes the excess of the passion." "Cards had formerly seduced him," we are told, "but an unsuccessful contest at cribbage with a Jew, who won his cloaths, had determined to abjure the propensity which appears to be innate among his countrymen." Here, *again*, we see drawn the thread between phylogeny and ontogeny: "a French writer relates," Jekyll explains, "that in the kingdoms of Ardrah, Whydah, and Benin, a Negro will stake at play his fortune, his children, and his liberty." Thus driven to distraction, Sancho was "induced to consider the stage" since "his complexion suggested an offer to the manager of attempting Othello and Oroonoko; but a defective and incorrigible articulation rendered it abortive."

Colorful though Jekyll's anecdotes are, they are a mere pretext for the crux of his argument: a disquisition on cranial capacity, regional variation, skin color, and intelligence. The example of Sancho, made particularly human by the citation of his foibles, is meant to put to rest any suspicion as to the native abilities of the Negro:

Such was the man whose species philosophers and anatomists have endeavored to degrade as a deterioration of the human; and such was the man whom Fuller, with a benevolence and quaintness of phrase peculiarly his own, accounted "God's Image, though cut in Ebony." To the harsh definition of the naturalist, oppressions political and legislative have been added; and such are hourly aggravated towards this unhappy race of men by vulgar prejudice and popular insult. To combat these on commercial principles, has been the labour of [others]—such an effort here, [he concludes ironically] would be an impertinent digression.

That Sancho's attainments are not merely isolated exceptions to the general morass is indicated by the state of civilization on the African "slave-coast." Jekyll continues:

> Of those who have speculatively visited and described the slave-coast, there are not wanting some who extol the mental abilities of the natives. [Some] speak highly of their mechanical powers and indefatigable industry. [Another] does not scruple to affirm, that their ingenuity rivals the Chinese.

What is more, these marks of culture and capacity signify an even more telling body of data, since the logical extensions of mechanical powers and industry are sublime arts and stable polity:

> He who could penetrate the interior of Africa, might not improbably discover negro arts and polity, which could bear little analogy to the ignorance and grossness of slaves in the sugar-islands, expatriated in infamy; and brutalized under the whip and the task-master.

"And he," Jekyll summarizes, "who surveys the extent of intellect to which Ignatius Sancho had attained self-education, will perhaps conclude, that the perfection of the reasoning faculties does not depend on the colour of a common integument."[12]

Jekyll's preface became a touchstone for the literary anthropologists who saw in black art a categorical repository for the African's potential to deserve inclusion in the human community. Echoes of Jekyll's language resound throughout the prefaces to slave testimony. Gustavus Vassa's own claim in 1789 that the African's contacts with "liberal sentiments" and "the Christian religion" have "exalted human nature" is vouched for by more than one hundred Irish subscribers. Charles Ball's editor asserts in 1836 that Ball is "a common negro slave, embued by nature with a tolerable portion of intellectual capacity."[13] Both Garrison's and Phillip's prefaces to *The Narrative of the Life of Frederick Douglass* (1845) and James McCune Smith's introduction to Douglass' *My Bondage and My Freedom* (1855)[14] attest to Douglass' African heritage and former bestial status. McCune Smith proffers the additional claims for literary excellence demanded by the intensity of doubt toward the black African's mental abilities:

> the Negro, for the first time in the world's history brought in full contact with high civilization, must prove his title first to all that is demanded for him; in the teeth of unequal chances, he must prove himself equal to the mass of those who oppress him—therefore, absolutely superior to his apparent fate, and to their relative ability. And it is most cheering to the friends of freedom, to-day, that evidence of this equality is rapidly accumulating, not from the ranks of the half-freed colored people of the free states, but from the very depths of slavery itself; the indestructible equality of man to man is demonstrated by the ease with which black men, scarce one remove from barbarism—if slavery can be honored with such a distinction—vault into the high places of the most advanced and painfully acquired civilization.

What is more germane is a review of Douglass' *Narrative* that emphasizes the relevance of each "product" of the African mind almost as another primary argument in the abolitionists' brief against slavery:

> Considered merely as a narrative, we have never read one more simple, true, coherent, and warm with genuine feeling. It is an excellent piece of writing, and on that score to be prized as a specimen of the powers of the black race, which prejudice persists in disputing. We prize highly all evidence of this kind, and it is becoming more abundant.[15]

These readings of blackness discuss the very properties of property. In fact, what we discover here is a correlation between property and properties and between character and characteristics, which proved so pervasive in the latter half of the nineteenth century that Booker T. Washington's *Up from Slavery*, for example, becomes, after its seventh chapter, the autobiography of an institution, thereby detaching itself somewhat from the slave narrative tradition, where the structural movement was from institution and property to man.

This relation between essence and value, between ethics and aesthetics, became, at least as early as William Dean

Howells' 1896 review of Paul Laurence Dunbar's "Majors and Minors,"[16] a correlation between a metaphysical blackness and a physical blackness. Howells emphasizes almost immediately Dunbar's appearance:

> the face of a young negro, with the race's traits strangely accented: the black skin, the wooly hair, the thick, out-rolling lips, and the mild, soft eyes of the pure African type. One cannot be very sure, ever, about the age of those people, but I should have thought that this poet was about twenty years old; and I suppose that a generation ago he would have been worth, apart from his literary gift, twelve or fifteen hundred dollars, under the hammer.

Howells makes a subtle shift here from properties to property. Moreover, he outlines the still prevalent notion that treats art as artifact:

> He is, so far as I know, the first man of his color to study his race objectively, to analyze it to himself, and then to represent it in art as he felt it and found it to be; to represent it humorously, yet tenderly, and above all so faithfully that we know the portrait to be undeniably like. A race which has reached this effect in any of its members can no longer be held wholly uncivilized; and intellectually Mr. Dunbar makes a stronger claim for the negro than the negro yet has done.

Howells then makes that leap so crucial to this discussion, and so crucial to the aesthetics of the Black Arts movement:

> If his Minors [the dialect pieces] had been written by a white man, I should have been struck by their very uncommon quality; I should have said that they were wonderful divinations. But since they are expressions of a race-life from within the race, they seem to me infinitely more valuable and significant. I have sometimes fancied that perhaps the negroes *thought* black, and *felt* black: that they were racially so utterly alien and distinct from ourselves that there never could be common intellectual and emotional ground between us, and that whatever eternity might do to reconcile us, the end of time would find us far asunder as ever. But this little book, has given me pause in

my speculation. Here in the artistic effect at least, is white
thinking and white feeling in a black man, and perhaps the
human unity, and not the race unity, is the precious thing,
the divine thing, after all. God hath made of one blood all
nations of men: perhaps the proof of this saying is to appear in the arts, and our hostilities and prejudices are to
vanish in them.

Here in Howells we find suggestions of imperatives for
the cultural renaissance that Du Bois would outline in the
Crisis just fifteen years later. Here in Howells we find the
premise that would assume a shape in the fiction of a "New
Negro." Here we find the sustained apocalyptic notion of
the Negro arts, about which Carl Van Vechten and James
Weldon Johnson would correspond at length. Here we find
the supposition, elaborated on at length by Du Bois and
even William Stanley Braithwaite, by Langston Hughes and
Claude McKay, that, while blacks and whites are in essence
different, that difference can be mediated through the
media of art. The Black Christ would be a poetaster. And the
physical blackness to which would testify critics as unalike
as I. A. Richards at Cambridge and Max Eastman at the
Liberator, referred to in separate prefaces to different volumes by Claude McKay in 1919 and 1922, would resurface
in subtler form in Allen Tate and Irving Howe. Tate and
Howe, the ideological counterparts of Richards and Eastman, would in 1950 and 1963 reassert a metaphysical
blackness to which they were somehow privy, Tate's New
Critical "extrinsic" fallacies notwithstanding. Yet if we see
this remarkably persistent idea become Don L. Lee's per-
nicious preface to Gwendolyn Brooks's *Report from Part
One*, we can perhaps take comfort in Black Arts poet Larry
Neal's sensitive authenticating preface to Kimberly Ben-
ston's subtle readings of the plays of Imamu Baraka. As
blind men, we have traced the circle.

III

The confusion of realms, of art with propaganda,
plagued the Harlem Renaissance in the 1920s. A critical

determination—a mutation of principles set in motion by Matthew Arnold's *Culture and Anarchy*, simplified thirty years later into Booker Washington's "toothbrush and bar of soap," and derived from Victorian notions of "uplifting" spiritual and moral ideals that separated the savage (noble or not) from the realm of culture and the civilized mind— meant that only certain literary treatments of black people could escape community censure. The race against Social Darwinism and the psychological remnants of slavery meant that each piece of creative writing became a political statement. Each particular manifestation served as a polemic: "Another bombshell fired into the heart of bourgeois culture," as *The World Tomorrow* editorialized in 1921. "The black writer," said Richard Wright, "approached the critical community dressed in knee pants of servility, curtseying to show that the Negro was not inferior, that he was human, and that he had a gift comparable to other men."[17] As early as 1921, W. E. B. Du Bois wrote of this in the *Crisis*:

> Negro art is today plowing a difficult row. We want everything that is said about us to tell of the best and highest and noblest in us. We insist that our Art and Propaganda be one. We fear that evil in us will be called racial, while in others it is viewed as individual. We fear that our shortcomings are not merely human. . . .[18]

And, as late as 1925, even as sedate an observer as Heywood Broun argued that only through Art would the Negro gain his freedom: "A supremely great negro artist," he told the New York Urban League, "who could catch the imagination of the world, would do more than any other agency to remove the disabilities against which the negro now labors."[19] Further, Broun remarked that this artist-redeemer could come at any time, and he asked his audience to remain silent for ten seconds to imagine that coming! Ambiguity in language, then, and "feelings that are general" (argued for as early as 1861 by Frances E. W. Harper) garnered hostility and suspicion from the critical minority; ambiguity was a threat to "knowing the lines." The results on a growing black literature were disastrous, these perorations themselves dubious. Black literature came to be seen as a cultural artifact (the product of unique historical forces) or as a document and witness to the political and emotional tendencies of the Negro victim of white racism. Literary theory became the application of a social attitude.

By the apex of the Harlem Renaissance, then, certain latent assumptions about the relationships between "art" and "life" had become prescriptive canon. In 1925, Du Bois outlined what he called "the social compulsion" of black literature, built as it was, he contended, on "the sorrow and strain inherent in American slavery, on the difficulties that sprang from emancipation, on the feelings of revenge, despair, aspiration, and hatred which arose as the Negro struggled and fought his way upward."[20] Further, he made formal the mechanistic distinction between "method" and "content," the same distinction that allowed James Weldon Johnson to declare with glee that, sixty years after slavery, all that separated the black poet from the white was "mere technique!" Structure, by now, was atomized: "Form" was merely a surface for a reflection of the world, the "world" here being an attitude toward race; form was a repository for the disposal of ideas; message was not only meaning but value; poetic discourse was taken to be literal, or once removed; language lost its capacity to be metaphorical in the eyes of the critic; the poem approached the essay, with referents immediately perceivable; literalness precluded the view of life as "allegorical"; and black critics forgot that writers approached things through words, not the other way around. The functional and didactic aspects of formal discourse assumed primacy in normative analysis. The confusion of realms was complete: The critic became social reformer, and literature became an instrument for the social and ethical betterment of the black man.

So, while certain rather conservative notions of art and culture wove themselves into F. R. Leavis' *Scrutiny* in Cambridge in the 1930s, blacks borrowed whole the Marxist notion of base and superstructure and made of it, if you will, race and superstructure. Here, as in Wright's "Blueprint for Negro Literature," for example, "race" in American society was held to determine the social relations that determine consciousness, which, in turn, determines actual ideas and creative works. "In the beginning was the deed," said Trotsky in an attack on the Formalists; now, the deed was *black*.

This notion of race and superstructure became, during the 1940s and 1950s, in one form or another the mode of criticism of black literature. As would be expected, critics urged the supremacy of one extraliterary idea after another, as Ralph Ellison "challenged" Richard Wright on one front and James Baldwin on another. But race as the controlling "mechanism" in critical theory reached its zenith of influence and mystification when LeRoi Jones metamorphosed himself into Imamu Baraka, and his daishiki-clad, Swahili-named "harbari gani" disciples "discovered" they were black. With virtually no exceptions, black critics employed "blackness"-as-theme to forward one argument or another for the amelioration of the Afro-American's social dilemma. Yet, the critical activity altered little, whether that "message" was integration or whether it was militant separation. Message was the medium; message reigned supreme; form became a mere convenience or, worse, a contrivance.

The commonplace observation that black literature with very few exceptions has failed to match pace with a sublime black music stems in large measure from this concern with *statement*. Black music, by definition, could never utilize the schism between form and content, because of the nature of music. Black music, alone of the black arts, has developed free of the imperative, the compulsion, to make an explicit political statement. Black musicians, of course, had no choice: Music groups masses of nonrepresentational material into significant form; it is the audible embodiment of form. All this, however, requires a specific mastery of technique, which cannot be separated from "poetic insight." There could be no "knowing the lines" in the creation of black music, especially since the Afro-American listening audience had such a refined and critical aesthetic sense. Thus, Afro-America has a tradition of masters, from Bessie Smith through John Coltrane, unequalled, perhaps, in all of modern music. In literature, however, we have no similar development, no sustained poignancy in writing. In poetry, where the command of language is indispensable if only because poetry thickens language and thus draws attention from its referential aspect, we have seen the growth of what the poet Ted Joans calls the "Hand-Grenade" poets,[21] who concern themselves with futile attempts to make poetry preach, which poetry is not capable of doing so well. And the glorification of this poetry (especially the glorification of Baraka and Don Lee's largely insipid rhetoric), in which we feel the unrelenting vise of the poet's grip upon our shoulders, has become the principal activity of the "New Black" critic. The suppositions on which this theory of criticism rests are best explicated through a close reading of four texts that, conveniently, treat poetry, literary history, and the novel.

Stephen Henderson's *Understanding the New Black Poetry* is the first attempt at a quasi-formalistic analysis of black poetry.[22] It is of the utmost importance to the history of race and superstructure criticism because it attempts to map a black poetic landscape, identifying inductively those unique cultural *artifacts* that critics, "especially white critics," have "widely misunderstood, misinterpreted, and undervalued for a variety of reasons—aesthetic, cultural, and political." Henderson's work is seminal insofar as he is concerned with the uses of language, but in the course of his study he succumbs to the old idea of advancing specific ideological prerequisites.

Henderson readily admits his bias: He equates aesthetics and ethics. "Ultimately," he says, "the 'beautiful' is bound up with the truth of a people's history, as they perceive it themselves." This absolute of truth Henderson defines in his fifth definition of what "Black poetry is chiefly": "Poetry by any identifiably Black person whose ideological stance vis-à-vis the history and aspirations of his people since slavery [is] adjudged by them to be 'correct.' " Hence, an ideal of truth, which exists in fact for the black poet to "find," is a "Black" truth. And "Black" is integral to the poetic equation, since "if there is such a *commodity* as 'blackness' in literature (and I assume that there is), it should somehow be found in concentrated or in residual form in the poetry" (italics added).

Had Henderson elaborated on "residual form" in literary language, measured formally, structurally, or linguistically, he would have revolutionized black literary criticism and brought it into the twentieth century. But his theory of poetry is based on three sometimes jumbled "broad categories" that allow the *black* critic to define "norms" of "blackness." The first of these is an oversimplified conception of "theme": "that which is spoken of, whether the specific subject matter, the emotional response to it, or its intellectual formulation." The second is "structure," by which Henderson intends "chiefly some aspect of the poem such as diction, rhythm, figurative language, which goes into the total makeup." (At times, he notes, "I use the word in an extended sense to include what is usually called genre.") His third critical tool, the scale by which he measures the "commodity" he calls "Blackness," is "saturation." He means by this "several things, chiefly the communication of 'Blackness' and fidelity to the observed or intuited truth of the Black Experience in the United States."

Now, the textual critic has problems with Henderson's schema not only because it represents an artificial segmentation of poetic structure (which can never, in fact, be discussed as if one element existed independently of the rest) but also because that same schema tends to be defined in terms of itself, and hence is tautological. Henderson defines "theme," for example, as "perhaps the simplest and most apparent" of the three. By theme, however, he means a poem's paraphrased level of "meaning." To illustrate this, he contrasts a George Moses Horton quatrain with a couplet from Countée Cullen. The "ambiguity" of the former lines, he concludes, defined for us insofar as "it might evoke a sympathetic tear from the eye of a white [Jewish] New York professor meditating upon his people's enslavement in ancient Egypt, does make it a less precise kind of ['Black'] statement than Cullen's, because in the latter the irony cannot be appreciated without understanding the actual historical debasement of the African psyche in America." Thus, the principal corollary to the theorem of "black themes" is that the closer a "theme" approaches cultural exclusivity, the closer it comes to a higher "fidelity." Moreover, he allows himself to say, had Shakespeare's

Sonnet 130 "been written by an African at Elizabeth's court, would not the thematic meaning change?" That leap of logic is difficult to comprehend, for a poem is above all atemporal and must cohere at a symbolic level, if it coheres at all. In some fairness to Stephen Henderson, much of the poetry from which he is extracting his theory *is used* in the language game of *giving information*. Stephen Henderson's problem is, in short, the "poetry" prompting his theory; he has only followed that poetry's lead and in that way left himself open to Wittgenstein's remonstration: "Do not forget that a poem, even though it is composed in the language of information, is not used in the language of giving information."

The most promising of Henderson's categories is "structure," and yet it is perhaps the most disappointing. By "structure," he means that "Black poetry is most distinctively Black" whenever "it derives its form from two basic sources, Black speech and Black music." At first glance, this idea seems exciting, since it implies a unique, almost intangible use of language peculiar to Afro-Americans. On this one could build, nay one *must* build, that elusive "Black Aesthetic" the race and superstructure critics have sought in vain. But Henderson's understanding of speech as referent is not linguistic; he means a *literal* referent to non-poetic discourse and makes, unfortunately, no allowances for the manner in which poetic discourse differs from prosaic discourse or "instances" of speech. He provides us with an elaborate and complicated taxonomy of referents to speech and to music, yet unaccountably ignores the fact that the "meaning" of a word in a poem is derived from its context within that poem, as well as from its context in our actual, historical consciousness. But a taxonomy is a tool to knowledge, not knowledge itself. The use of language is not a stockpile of referents or forms, but an activity.

Henderson remarks with some astonishment that "Black speech in this country" is remarkable in that "certain words and constructions seem to carry an inordinate charge of emotional and psychological weight." These, he calls "mascon" words, borrowing the acronym from N.A.S.A., where it is employed to describe a "massive concentration" of matter beneath the lunar surface. What he is describing, of course, is not unique to black poetic discourse; it is common to all poetic uses of language in all literatures and is what helps to create ambiguity, paradox, and irony. This, of course, has been stated adamantly by the "practical critics" since the 1920s—those same "New" critics Henderson disparages. These usages, however, do make black poetic language unique and argue strongly for a compilation of a "black" dictionary of discrete examples of specific signification, where "Black English" departs from "general usage." They are not, I am afraid, found only in the language of black folks in this country. Had Henderson identified some criteria by which we could define an oral tradition in terms of the "grammar" it superimposes on nonliterary discourse, then shown how this comes to bear on literary discourse, and further shown such "grammars" to be distinctly black, then his contribution to our understanding of language and literature would have been no mean thing indeed.

His final category, "saturation," is the ultimate tautology: Poetry is "Black" when it communicates "Blackness." The more a text is "saturated," the "Blacker" the text. One imagines a daishiki-clad Dionysus weighing the saturated, mascon lines of Countée Cullen against those of Langston Hughes, as Paul Laurence Dunbar and Jean Toomer are silhouetted by the flames of Nigger Hell. The blacker the berry, the sweeter the juice.

Should it appear that I have belabored my reading of this theory, it is not because it is the weakest of the three theories of black literature. In fact, as I will try to show, Henderson's is by far the most imaginative of the three and has, at least, touched on areas critical to the explication of black literature. His examination of form is the first in a "race and superstructure" study and will most certainly give birth to more systematic and less polemical studies. But the notions implicit and explicit in Henderson's ideas are shared by Houston A. Baker, Jr., and Addison Gayle as well.

In the first essay of *Long Black Song, Essays in Black American Literature and Culture*,[23] Houston Baker proffers the considerable claim that black culture, particularly as "measured" through black folklore and literature, serves in intent and effect as an "index" of repudiation not only of white Western values and white Western culture but of white Western literature as well. "In fact," he writes, "it is to a great extent the culture theorizing of whites that has made for a separate and distinctive black American culture. That is to say, one index of the distinctiveness of black American culture is the extent to which it repudiates the culture theorizing of the white Western world." Repudiation, he continues, "is characteristic of black American folklore; and this is one of the most important factors in setting black American literature apart from white American literature." Further, "Black folklore and the black American literary tradition that grew out of it reflect a culture that is distinctive both of white American and of African culture, and therefore neither can provide valid standards by which black American folklore and literature may be judged." A text becomes "blacker," it surely follows, to the extent that it serves as an "index of repudiation." Here we find an ironic response to Harold Bloom's *Anxiety of Influence* in what we could characterize as an "Animosity of Influence."

Baker discusses this notion of influence between black and white American culture at length. "Call it black, Afro-American, Negro," he writes, "the fact remains that there is a fundamental, qualitative difference between it and white American culture." The bases of this "fundamental, qualitative difference" are, first, that "black American culture was developed orally or musically for many years"; second, that "black American culture was never characterized by a collective ethos"; and, finally, that "one of [black American culture's] most salient characteristics is an index of repudiation." Oral, collectivistic, and repudiative, he concludes, "each of these aspects helps to distinguish black American culture from white American culture."

These tenets suggest that there must be an arbitrary relation between a sign and its referent; indeed, that all meaning is culture-bound. Yet what we find elaborated here are rather oversimplified, basically political, criteria, which are difficult to verify, partly because they are not subject to *verbal* analysis (that is, can this sense of *difference* be measured through the literary uses of language?), partly because the *thematic* analytical tools employed seem to be useful primarily for black naturalist novels or for the mere paraphrasing of poetry, partly because the matter of influence is almost certainly too subtle to be traced in other than close textual readings, and finally because his three bases of "fundamental, qualitative difference" seem to me too unqualified. There is so much more to Jean Toomer, Zora Hurston, Langston Hughes, Sterling Brown, Ralph Ellison, Leon Forrest, Ishmael Reed, Toni Morrison, and Alice Walker than their "index of repudiation," whatever that is. Besides, at least Toomer, Ellison, and Reed have taken care to discuss the complex matter of literary ancestry, in print and without. It is one of the ironies of the study of black literature that our critical activity is, almost by definition, a comparative one, since many of our writers seem to be influenced by Western masters, writing in English as well as outside it, as they are by indigenous, Afro-American oral or even written forms. That the base for our literature is an oral one is certainly true; but, as Millman Parry and Albert Lord have amply demonstrated,[24] so is the base of the whole of Western literature, commencing with the Hebrews and the Greeks. Nevertheless, Baker does not suggest any critical tools for explicating the oral tradition in our literature, such as the formulaic studies so common to the subject. Nor does he suggest how folklore is displaced in literature, even though, like Henderson, he does see it at "the base of the black literary tradition." That black culture is characterized by a collective ethos most definitely demands some qualification, since our history, literary and extraliterary, often turns on a tension, a dialectic, between the private perceptions of the individual and the white public perceptions of that same individual.

Nor does Baker's thought-provoking contention of the deprivation of the American frontier stand to prove this thesis:

> When the black American reads Frederick Jackson Turner's *The Frontier in American History*, he feels no regret over the end of the Western frontier. To black America, *frontier* is an alien word; for, in essence, all frontiers established by the white psyche have been closed to the black man.

Heretofore, later, few have been willing to look steadily at America's past and acknowledge that the black man was denied his part in the frontier and his share of the nation's wealth.

Yet, at least Ralph Ellison has written extensively on the fact of the frontier (physical and metaphysical) and its centrality to his sensibility. Further, Ishmael Reed uses the frontier again and again as a central trope.

Part of the problem here is not only Baker's exclusive use of thematic analysis to attempt to delineate a literary tradition but also his implicit stance that literature functions primarily as a cultural artifact, as a repository for ideas. "It is impossible to comprehend the process of transcribing cultural values," he says (in his essay "Racial Wisdom and Richard Wright's *Native Son*"), "without an understanding of the changes that have characterized both the culture as a whole and the lives of its individual transcribers." Further, "Black American literature has a human immediacy and a pointed relevance which are obscured by the overingenious methods of the New Criticism, or any other school that attempts to talk of works of art as though they had no creators or of sociohistorical factors as though they did not filter through the lives of individual human beings." Here we find the implicit thesis in *Long Black Song*, the rather Herderian notion of literature as primarily the reflection of ideas and experiences outside of it. It is not, of course, that literature is unrelated to culture, to other disciplines, or even to other arts; it is not that words and usage somehow exist in a vacuum or that the literary work of art occupies an ideal or reified, privileged status, the province of some elite cult of culture. It is just that the literary work of art is a system of signs that may be decoded with various methods, all of which assume the fundamental unity of form and content and all of which demand close reading. Only the rare critic, such as Michael G. Cooke, Nathan A. Scott, or Sherley Williams, has made of thematic analysis the subtle tool that intelligent, sensitive reading requires. Baker seems to be reading black texts in a particular fashion for other than literary purposes. In *Singers of Daybreak: Studies in Black American Literature*,[25] he suggests these purposes. "What lies behind the neglect of black American literature," he asserts, "is not a supportable body of critical criteria that includes a meaningful definition of *utile* and *dulce*, but a refusal to believe that blacks possess the humanity requisite for the production of works of art." Baker finds himself shadowboxing with the ghostly judgments of Jefferson on Phillis Wheatley and Ignatius Sancho; his blows are often telling, but his opponent's feint is deadly.

If Houston Baker's criticism teaches us more about his attitude toward being black in white America than it does about black literature, then Addison Gayle, Jr.'s *The Way of the New World* teaches us even less.[26] Gayle makes no bones about his premises:

> To evaluate the life and culture of black people, it is necessary that one live the black experience in a world where substance is more important than form, where the social takes precedence over the aesthetic, where each act, gesture, and movement is political, and where continual rebellion separates the insane from the sane, the robot from the revolutionary.

Gayle's view of America, and of the critic, means that he can base his "literary judgments" on some measure of ideology; and he does. Regrettably, he accuses James Baldwin of "ignorance of black culture." His praise of John A. Williams seems predicated on an affinity of ideology. He praises John Killens' *And Then We Heard the Thunder* because he "creates no images of racial degradation." For him, the "central flaw" of the protagonist in *Invisible Man* ("an otherwise superb novel") is "attributable more to Ellison's political beliefs than to artistic deficiency." In Addison Gayle, we see race and superstructure criticism at its basest: Not only is his approach to literature deterministic, but his treatment of the critical activity itself demonstrates an alarming disrespect for qualified scholarship.

What is wrong with employing race and superstructure as critical premises? This critical activity sees language and literature as reflections of "Blackness." It postulates "Blackness" as an entity, rather than as metaphor or sign.

Thus, the notion of a signified *black* element in literature retains a certain impressiveness insofar as it exists in some mystical kingdom halfway between a fusion of psychology and religion on the one hand and the Platonic Theory of Ideas on the other. Reflections of this "Blackness" are more or less "literary" according to the ideological posture of the critic. Content is primary over form and indeed is either divorced completely from form, in terms of genesis and normative value, or else is merely facilitated by form as a means to an end. In this criticism, rhetorical value judgments are closely related to social values. This method reconstitutes "message," when what is demanded is a deconstruction of a literary system.

The race and superstructure critics would have us believe that the function of the critic is to achieve an intimate knowledge of a literary text by re-creating it from the inside: Critical thought must become the thought criticized. Only a black man, therefore, can think (hence, rethink) a "black thought." Consciousness is predetermined by culture and color. These critics, in Todorov's phrase, "re-create" a text either by repeating its own words in their own order or by establishing a relationship between the work and some system of ideas outside it. They leave no room for the idea of literature as a system. Normative judgments stem from how readily a text yields its secrets or is made to confess falsely on the rack of "black reality."

Yet, perceptions of reality are in no sense absolute; reality is a function of our senses. Writers present models of reality, rather than a description of it, though obviously the two may be related variously. In fact, fiction often contributes to cognition by providing models that highlight the nature of things precisely by their failure to coincide with it. Such, certainly, is the case in science fiction. Too, the thematic studies so common to black criticism suffer from a similar fallacy. Themes in poetry, for instance, are rarely reducible to literal statement; literature approaches its richest development when its "presentational symbolism" (as opposed by Suzanne Langer to its "literal discourse") cannot be reduced to the form of a literal proposition. Passages for creative discourse cannot be excerpted and their "meaning" presented independent of context. For Ralph

Ellison, invisibility was not a matter of being seen but rather a refusal to run the gamut of one's own humanity.

"Blackness," as these critics understand it, is weak in just the decisive area where practical criticism is strong: in its capacity to give precise accounts of actual consciousness, rather than a scheme or a generalization. And the reason for the corresponding weakness is not difficult to find: It lies in the received formula of race and superstructure, which converts far too readily to the simple repetition of ideology. The critical method, then, is reductionist; literary discourse is described mechanically by classifications that find their ultimate meaning and significance somewhere else.

Ultimately, black literature is a verbal art like other verbal arts. "Blackness" is not a material object or an event but a metaphor; it does not have an "essence" as such but is defined by a network of relations that form a particular aesthetic unity. Even the slave narratives offer the text as a world, as a system of signs. The black writer is the point of consciousness of his language. If he does embody a "Black Aesthetic," then it can be measured not by "content," but by a complex structure of meanings. The correspondence of content between a writer and his world is less significant to literary criticism than is a correspondence of organization or structure, for a relation of content may be a mere reflection of prescriptive, scriptural canon, such as those argued for by Baker, Gayle, and Henderson. A relation of structure, on the other hand, according to Raymond Williams, "can show us the organizing principles by which a particular view of the world, and from that the coherence of the social group which maintains it, really operates in consciousness."[27] If there is a relationship between social and literary "facts," it must be found here.

To paraphrase René Wellek, black literature may well be dark, mysterious, and foreboding, but it is certainly not beyond careful scrutiny and fuller understanding. The tendency toward thematic criticism implies a marked inferiority complex: Afraid that our literature cannot sustain sophisticated verbal analysis, we view it from the surface merely and treat it as if it were a Chinese lantern with an elaborately wrought surface, parchment-thin but full of hot air. Black critics have enjoyed such freedom in their "discipline" that we find ourselves with no discipline at all. The present set of preconceptions has brought readers and writers into a blind alley. Literary images, even black ones, are combinations of words, not of absolute or fixed things. The tendency of black criticism toward an ideological absolutism, with its attendant Inquisition, must come to an end. A literary text is a linguistic event; its explication must be an activity of close textual analysis. Simply because Bigger Thomas kills Mary Dalton and tosses her body into a furnace, *Native Son* is not necessarily a "blacker" novel than *Invisible Man*—Gayle notwithstanding. We urgently need to direct our attention to the nature of black figurative language, to the nature of black narrative forms, to the history and theory of Afro-American literary criticism, to the fundamental unity and form of content, and to the arbitrary relations between the sign and its referent. Finally, we must begin to understand the nature of intertextuality, that is, the nonthematic manner by which texts—poems and novels—respond to other texts. All cats may be black at night, but not to other cats.

Notes

[1] Briton Hammon, *A Narrative of the Uncommon Sufferings and Surprising Deliverance of Briton Hammon, a Negro Man* (Boston, 1760).

[2] William Wimsatt and Cleanth Brooks, *Literary Criticism: A Short History* (New York: Knopf, 1969), p. 366.

[3] Phillis Wheatley, *Poems* (Philadelphia: A. Bell, 1773), p. vii.

[4] *De la littérature des nègres, ou recherches sur leurs facultés intellectuelles, leurs qualités morales, et leur littérature* (Paris: Maradan, 1808), p. 140.

[5] Eugene Parker Chase, *Our Revolutionary Forefathers, The Letters of François, Marquis de Barbé-Marbois during His Residence in the United States as Secretary of the French Legation, 1779–1884* (New York: Duffield, 1929), pp. 84–85.

[6] *Letters of the Late Ignatius Sancho, an African* (London: J. Nichols and C. Dilly, 1783), p. vi.

[7] *Notes on the State of Virginia* (London: Stockdale, 1787), Bk. II, p. 196.

[8] Jefferson, p. 196.

[9] Wheatley, p. vii.

[10] Wheatley, p. vi.

[11] Sancho, p. vi.

[12] Sancho, pp. xiv–xvi.

13 Charles Ball, *Fifty Years in Chains; Or, The Life of an American Slave* (New York: H. Dayton, 1858), p. 3.

14 Introd., *My Bondage and My Freedom* (New York: Miller, Orton, and Mulligan, 1855), pp. xvii–xxxi.

15 *New York Tribune*, 10 June 1845, p. 1, col. 1. Rpt. in *Liberator*, 30 May 1845, p. 97.

16 "Majors and Minors," *North American Review*, 27 June 1896, p. 630.

17 "Blueprint for Negro Writing," *New Challenge*, 2 (Fall 1937), 55.

18 "Negro Art," *Crisis*, 22 (June 1921), 55–56.

19 *New York Times*, 26 Jan. 1925, p. 3.

20 "The Social Origins of American Negro Art," *Modern Quarterly*, 3 (Autumn 1925), 53.

21 "Ted Joans: Tri-Continental Poet," *Transition*, 48 (1975), 4–12.

22 *Understanding the New Black Poetry* (New York: Morrow, 1972). All subsequent quotes are from pp. 3–69.

23 *Long Black Song* (Charlottesville: Univ. of Virginia Press, 1972).

24 Lord, *The Singer of Tales* (Cambridge: Harvard Univ. Press, 1960).

25 *Singers of Daybreak: Studies in Black American Literature* (Washington, D.C.: Howard Univ. Press, 1974).

26 *The Way of the New World* (Garden City, N.Y.: Doubleday, 1975).

27 "Base and Superstructure in Marxist Cultural Theory," *New Left Review*, 82 (Dec., 1973), 3–16.

Black
Figurative
Language

The Blues Roots of Contemporary Afro-American Poetry

Sherley Anne Williams

Ethnopoetics is for me the study of the new forms of poetry that develop as a result of the interfaces or confrontations between different cultures. The spirituals, play and work songs, cakewalks and hoe-downs, and the blues are the first recorded artifacts to grow out of the complex relationship between Africans and Europeans on the North American continent. Afro-American oral tradition, of which these lyric forms are a part, combines with white American literature, whose traditions are rooted more in the literate cultures of the West than in the oral traditions, either indigenous or transplanted, of the New World. Afro-American literature is thus created within the framework of multiple relationships, and the tension between the white literary and the black oral traditions informs and influences the best contemporary Afro-American poetry at the level of structure as well as of theme. The themes of the poetry are usually accessible to nonblack audiences, but the poets' attempts to own the traditions to which they are heir create technical transformations that cannot be analyzed, much less evaluated, solely within the context of their European roots. Most critics pay lip service to the idea that Afro-American music, speech, and life-styles influence the form and structure of Afro-American writing. Thus Stephen Henderson's discussion, in *Understanding the New Black Poetry* (1973), of some of the techniques of Afro-American speech and singing that have been carried over virtually unchanged into Afro-American poetry is rare in its concrete descriptions of these devices. This paper builds on his work, concentrating on the transformations that result when the blues of Afro-American oral tradition interfaces with the "poetry" of European literary tradition.

Blues is essentially an oral form, meant to be heard rather than read; and the techniques and structures used to such powerful purpose in the songs cannot always be transferred directly to the literary traditions within which, by definition, Afro-American poets write. Blues is viewed here as a verbal—as distinct from a musical—genre that developed out of the statement (or call) and response patterns of collective work groups. Blues culminated in a "classic" form (heard most consistently in the early blues recordings of Bessie Smith, Ma Rainey, and the other "classic blues" singers) that embodies the distinctive features of Afro-American song forms in a standardized structure. In some contemporary Afro-American poetry, the devices and structures of the classic blues form are transformed, thus allowing the poetry to function in much the same way as blues forms once functioned within the black communities across the country.

I. Function

Afro-American music still functions to some extent as a reflector of a wide range of values in the national black community and often serves as a catalyst for discussions, reviews, and revisions of these values. The immediacy of this process has been diminished by the advent of huge impersonal concerts, but records and local "soul" stations keep alive this supra-entertainment function of the music. The professional songwriter had modified what used to be a very close and personal relationship among singer, song, and the group tradition, on which all depended for the act of creation and which the act of creation affirms and extends. In an age where almost everyone is singing someone else's song, performance has to some extent taken the place of authorship. Thus Otis Redding's version of "Respect," while very popular, was never made into the metaphor of Black Man/Black Woman or, just as importantly, Black/White relationships that Aretha Franklin's version became.

Of course, Aretha was right on time, but there was also something about the way Aretha characterized respect as something given with force and great effort and cost. And when she even went so far as to spell the word "respect," we just knew that this sister wasn't playing around about getting Respect and keeping it. Early blues singers and their growing repertoire of songs probably helped to solidify community values and heighten community morale in the late nineteenth and early twentieth century. The singers provided welcome entertainment and a necessary reminder that there had to be more to the lives of the audience than the struggle for material subsistence—if they were ever to achieve and enjoy the day the sun would shine in their back door. Michael S. Harper, in his liner notes to the album *John Coltrane*, alludes to the communal nature of the relationship between blues singer and blues audience when he speaks of the audience that assumes "we" even though the blues singer sings "I." Blues singers have also been aware of this function of their art, for as Henry Townsend said in an interview with Samuel B. Charters (*The Poetry of the Blues*, 1963):

> You know I'm going to put this a little blunt. I don't know if I should say it or not, because it might hurt the religious type of people, but when I sing the blues, I sing the truth. The religious type of people may not believe that it's good, because they think the blues is not the truth; but the blues, from a point of explaining yourself as facts, is the truth and I don't feel that the truth should be condemned. . . .

Unlike sacred music, the blues deals with a world where the inability to solve a problem does not necessarily mean that one can, or ought to, transcend it. The internal strategy of the blues is action, rather than contemplation, for the song itself is the creation of reflection. And while not all blues actions achieve the desired result, the impulse to action is inherent in any blues that functions out of a collective purpose. But while the gospels, for example, are created for the purpose of preparing the congregation to receive the Holy Spirit and become possessed by it, the blues singer strives to create an atmosphere in which analysis can take place. This necessary analytic distance is achieved through the use of verbal and musical irony seldom found in the singing of the spirituals or the gospels. Thus Billie Holiday, in "Fine and Mellow," concludes the recital of the wrongs her man has done her with the mocking observation that

> Love is like a faucet
> it turns off and on
> Sometimes when you think it's on, baby
> it have turned off and gone.

The persona pointedly reminds her man that her patience with his trifling ways has its limits at the same time that she suggests that she might be in her present difficulties because he wasn't alert to the signs that her well was going dry. The self-mockery and irony of the blues pull one away from a total surrender to the emotions generated by the concreteness of the experiences and situations described in the song. Even where the verbal content of the song is straightforward and taken at face value, the singer has musical techniques that create ironic effects.

The vocal techniques of Afro-American music—melisma, intentional stutters and hesitations, repetitions of words and phrases, and the interjection of exclamatory phrases and sounds—are used in the spirituals and gospels to facilitate emotional involvement. In blues singing, however, these same devices are often used in a deliberately random manner, which emphasizes unimportant phrases or words as often as it does key ones. The devices themselves, especially melisma and changes in stress, have become standardized enough to have formed a substantial part of the artistry of Billie Holiday. At their worst, the devices become no more than meaningless vocal calisthenics, but at their best they disengage meaning from feeling. Put another way, the singer objectifies, almost symbolizes, the emotional content of the song through the use of melisma, stuttering, and variations in stress and, in so doing, places the situation in stark relief as an object for discussion. Thus, a member of the blues audience shouts "Tell it like it is" rather than "Amen" or "Yes, Jesus" as a response to a particularly pungent or witty truth, for the emphasis is on thinking, not tripping.

Charles Keil's analysis (*The Urban Blues*, 1966) of a Bobby Blue Bland performance illustrates how even the selection of songs in a blues performance underscores the relationship of singer and audience and the manner in which communal values are incorporated into the presentation of the blues performer's act. Many contemporary Afro-American poets consciously assume the role of people's voices—see, for example, Marvin X's second volume of poetry, *The Son of Man*—and ask black people (rather than whites) to affirm their stance. That initial gesture may have grown out of the learned intellectual model provided by Marx and Herskovits; once having made it, however, it became real for many poets, at more than just the level of rhetoric and "kill the honkey" poems. We witness this realness in the increasing sureness with which Afro-American poets challenge the primacy of European forms.

II. Structure

A number of Afro-American poets have written poems based on the less structured blues forms; few, however, have attempted to utilize the deceptively simple classic blues structure. Langston Hughes is an exception. The sophistication of meaning and form that characterizes Hughes's poem "Young Gal's Blues" is, of course, characteristic of classic blues at its best, and the literary sophistication is in fact made possible by the existence of such songs as "Backwater Blues" or the more contemporary variation on the classic form "Your Friends." "Young Gal's Blues," in which a young woman tries to fortify herself against the prospect of death (which can come at any time) and the loneliness of old age (which will certainly catch her if death don't do it first), is an example of an oral form moving unchanged into literary tradition:

> I'm gonna walk to the graveyard
> 'Hind ma friend, Miss Cora Lee

> Gonna walk to de graveyard
> 'Hind ma dear friend Cora Lee
>
> Cause when I'm dead some
> Body'll have to walk behind me.

Hughes worries the first line by dropping "I'm" in the repetition of the first half line and adding "dear" when he repeats the second half-line. Repetition in blues is seldom word for word and the definition of worrying the line includes changes in stress and pitch, the addition of exclamatory phrases, changes in word order, repetitions of phrases within the line itself, and the wordless blues cries that often punctuate the performance of the songs. The response to this opening statement repeats and broadens the idea of death even as it justifies and explains the blues persona's action. Ideally, each half line is a complete phrase or clause; but Hughes, even in breaking the line between "some" and "body" rather than after dead, keeps within the convention of half lines on which the classic structure is based. The stanza is a closed unit without run-over lines or run-over thoughts; and the same pattern, response justifying the statement, is followed in the second stanza in which the persona tells of her determination to visit old Aunt Clew in "de po' house" because "When I'm old an' ugly/I'll want to see somebody, too." The "po' house" evokes the known social and political conditions rather than stating them directly.

In evoking rather than stating these conditions, Hughes makes the same assumption about his audience that a blues singer makes: poet (singer) and audience share the same reality. The lives of the audience are bound by the same grim social reality in which one faces an old age characterized by the same grinding poverty that destroys youth before it can flower and that makes work still necessary even when one is no longer capable of doing it—the only distinction between middle and old age. The particularized, individual experience rooted in a common reality is the primary thematic characteristic of all blues songs no matter what their structure. The classic song form itself internalizes and echoes, through the statement/response pattern, the thematic relationship between individual and group ex-

perience that is implied in these evocations of social and
political reality.

> De po' house is lonely
> an' de grave is cold.
> O, de po' house is lonely
> De grave is cold.
> But I'd rather be dead than to
> be ugly and old

The statement in this stanza is more general than the
statement in either of the first two stanzas, and while the
stanza is self-contained, it places the personal reflection of
the preceding stanza within a larger context. The response
returns to the first person, the subjective testimony, as the
persona says quite frankly that she would rather die than be
ugly. It is also Hughes's definition of what it is to be young:
to care more for the quality of one's life than the fact of life
itself. Thus the response in this stanza makes explicit the
persona's choices in life. But neither choice, death at an
early age or an old age endured in poverty and loneliness,
is particularly happy, and the persona, recognizing that
love is one of the few things that make any life bearable,
concludes the fourth stanza and the poem with the plea
"Keep on a-lovin me, daddy/Cause I don't want to be
blue."

The response can also be the antithesis of the statement,
as in the opening stanza of "Billie's Blues,"

> I love my man
> I'm a lie if I say I don't
> But I'll quit my man
> I'm a lie if I say I won't.

where the paradox also provides the frame for the distinctions that the persona later makes between being a slave,
which she is quite prepared to be for her man, and a "dog,"
which she refuses to become, between mere good looks
typified by white features ("I ain't good looking and my
hair ain't curled") and the confidence, the affirmation of
self necessary to get one through the world.

The change in focus from individual to communal reality may be done as in the Hughes poem or through simply worrying the line as in the blues standard "The Things I Used to Do": "The things I used to do/I won't do no more./Lawd the things I used to *I'm tryna tell yo' all*/I won't do no more," where the singer appeals directly to the audience to witness his situation and, in effect, to affirm his solution to his problem. The abrupt change of subject or theme as in "Sweet Sixteen" serves the same purpose. The persona describes his love for a flighty, headstrong young girl who has run away from her home and now wants to "run away from old me, too." The persona is now desperate, and the song is really a plea to the woman to do right, love him as he loves her. The third stanza ends with the line "Seems like everything I do [to try and keep you with me] is in vain."

Then, in a dramatic shift in subject and perspective:

> My brother's in Korea
>   My sister's down in New Orleans
> You know I'm having so much trouble, people
>   I wonder what in the world's gonna happen to me.

At the level of the love theme, the absence of family ties underscores the persona's loneliness; hence his dependence on this relationship. His scattered family exists within the framework of the ruptured family relationships, caused by the oppressive and repressive system of the country, which characterizes too much of the Afro-American experience. The response to this statement of loneliness is one of complete despair, addressed to "people," the audience whose private pains are set within the same kind of collective experience. The next stanza is again addressed to the woman and reiterates, at the level of their personal relationship, the persona's realization that he has lost pride, dignity, and a necessary sense of himself as a result of this relationship:

> Treat me mean, baby,
>   but I'll keep on loving you anyway
> But one of these old days, baby,
>   you're gonna give a lot of money to hear someone call my
>   name.

Billie Pierce's version of "Married Man Blues," recorded by Samuel B. Charters in New Orleans in 1954, uses what had become a traditional statement/response description of the problems of loving a married man to place the song within a more universal context. The persona has loved only one man, a married man, in her life. And despite the fact that she "stole him from his wife" she is still in trouble because she has stolen only his affection, not his continued presence. The traditional verse is used to summarize her situation:

> Girls it's awful hard
> to love another woman's man
> Cause you can't get him when you wanna
> have to catch catch as catch's can.

The last half-line in the response is Billie's personal variation on the standardized wording, "Got to catch him when you can," and the rhythmical variation plays nicely against the established rhythm of the statement. The stanza, in addition, serves as a transition, tying together the fictive first person experiences and the more "real" first person admonitions of the last part of the song.

The second portion of the song opens with an assertion of individuality: "My first name is Billie/and my last name is Pierce." The assertion of individuality and the implied assertion—as action, not mere verbal statement—of self are an important dimension of the blues. Janhienz Jahn (*Neo-African Literature*, 1968) is essentially correct when he describes the blues in terms of this assertion of life-force rather than the usual ones of melancholy and pain. The assertion of self usually comes at the end of the blues song after the description/analysis of the situation or problem and is often the only solution to that problem or situation. In "Married Man Blues," Billie's assertive stance is underscored in successive stanzas that imply some of the values inherent in a good love relationship:

> Aw, you want me to do right there, Little Dee Dee
> And you ain't doing right yourself
> Well you get yourself another woman

And I'll get me somebody else.
Well, at my first time leaving you, baby
  Crying ain't gone make me stay
Cause the more you cry Dee Dee, baby
  Well the more you gonna drive little Billie away.

The sting of the stanzas is balanced by the fact that they are part of the anonymous oral tradition, and Billie Pierce was a master at combining such traditional verses with written songs ("Saint Louis Woman," "Careless Love," for example) to create her own personal versions of these songs. Here, she also underscores the closeness of her musical relationship with her husband, Dee Dee Pierce, who accompanies her on trumpet, by the encouragements spoken throughout this portion of the song to, "Play it nice, play it the way I like it Dee Dee, baby."

This complex interweaving of general and specific, individual and group, finds no direct correspondence in Afro-American literature except in the literary blues. But the evocation of certain first person experiences and the extensive use of multiple voices in Afro-American poetry may be, at least in part, an outgrowth from this characteristic of the blues. Nikki Giovanni's "The Great Pax Whitey," which seems a rather pedestrian and undigested patchwork of folk and personal legend and black nationalist philosophy, becomes, when viewed (or better yet, read) as a poem in which a congregation of voices speaks, a brilliant literary approximation of the kind of collective dialogue that has been going on underground in the black community at least since the nineteenth century and of which the blues in its various forms was an important part.

III. Transformation

Blues songs are almost always literal, seldom metaphoric or symbolic except in sexual and physical terms. And, while similes are used extensively, much of the verbal strength of the blues resides in the directness with which the songs confront experience and in what Stephen Henderson identifies as "mascon images," Afro-American archetypes that represent "a massive concentration of black experiential energy." Often the mascons are not really images in the literary sense of the word; rather, they are verbal expressions that evoke a powerful response in the listener because of their direct relationship to concepts and events in the collective experience. Thus the graveyard and the po'house in "Young Gal's Blues" might be described as universal archetypes or mascons, while the calling of the names in "Sweet Sixteen" is a specifically black one. The latter expression grows directly out of traditional peoples' belief in the strong relationship between name and personal essence and the corresponding Afro-American preoccupation with titles (Miss, Mr., Mrs. and, with great deliberation and care, Ms.), with the naming of children and the acquisition of nicknames and sobriquets—and who may use them. In such an atmosphere, to call someone out of his name, as the Monkey tells the Lion that the Elephant has done him in the "Signifying Monkey," is punishable, in children, by a beating. And the changing of one's names as most blacks did after emancipation and many more did during the sixties takes on an added significance.

Very often, the meanings of mascons cut across areas of experience usually thought of as separate but in Afro-American experiences not mutually exclusive. Thus the term "jelly roll," as Henderson illustrates, moves at a number of different levels, while the expressions centered in the concept of "home" move at both a spiritual and a material level, and "The Streets," which has developed into a mascon as a result of the Afro-American urban experience, involves both pleasure and pain. Despite the fact that these expressions are used over and over again by blacks in everyday conversations as well as in more self-conscious verbal events, they escape being clichés because their meanings are deeply rooted in a constantly renewed and thus *living* reality. They are distinguished from the vernacular vocabulary of black speech in that the vernacular rests on the idea that the standard English version of a word, say "bad" or "dig," has one meaning, and the standard black version has another, often contradictory, meaning: excellent and understand. Mascons, on the contrary, concentrate their massive force within the frame of the literal meaning of the standard English word. And it is this literal yet figuratively complex relationship that makes the response in the final stanza of "Sweet Sixteen" such a powerful climax to the song. But one of these old days, the persona tells his woman, you would even get up off some money, just to have back the man I was when I met you, the man that loving you destroyed. Thus mascons are a compression, as well as a concentration, whose power is released through the first person experience.

When Harriet Tubman, in Robert Hayden's "Runagate Runagate Runagate," invites us to "ride my train," it is not merely the thought of the Underground Railroad to which blacks respond. Harriet's "train" is also the train whose tracks throughout the South were laid by black men who also worked on them as cooks, porters, and red caps and that many blacks rode to the promised land of the North. And despite the fact that trains are no longer a significant part of our day-to-day reality, they live on in the metaphors of the "Gospel Train," which many plan to ride to glory, and the "Soul Trains," which proclaim the black musical presence in the world. It is the stored energy of this mascon that enables Afro-American poets to play so lovingly and meaningfully with John Coltrane's name, and they capture something of his function as an artist in their use of his nickname, Trane.

Many Afro-American poets have used techniques that approximate or parallel various blues devices, and Lucille Clifton, in her first volume of poems, *Good Times*, uses these transformations consistently and successfully. Like the blues, her poems are firmly based in a living black reality that is more concerned with itself than with direct confrontations with white society and its values. There are several poems about whites in the volume, but even here, the impression is of a black person, involved in a conversation with other blacks, who occasionally tosses a comment to the white man she knows is waiting in the wings. His presence does not cause her to bite her tongue, however, and the opening poem, "in the inner city," is addressed as much to the white man in the wings as it is to the black audience.

in the inner city
or
like we call it
home
we think a lot about uptown
and the silent nights
and the houses straight as
dead men
and the pastel lights
and we hang on to our no place
happy to be alive
and in the inner city
or
like we call it
home

Clifton's poems are created out of the collective experience that culminates in, and is transformed by, the inner city. Those experiences in their broader outlines are evoked rather than stated, through vignettes told in the first person; and the individual experience plays against the assumed knowledge of that collective history in much the same way that the communal pattern of statement and response plays against the individual experience expressed in the blues. The inner city of which Clifton speaks is neither that of the "deviants" who inhabit most sociological studies about blacks nor the statistics politicians manipulate so skillfully for their own gains; it is the community, home. "Inner city" becomes both the literal ghetto and the metaphoric inner landscape of black hearts, which has seldom been explored so sensitively and revealingly as in Clifton's *Good Times*.

The spareness of Clifton's poetry depends in part on mascon images. "Pushing," a mascon of enormous contemporary force, is used to climax "For deLawd," Clifton's tribute to the long "line/of black and going on women" from which she comes. Grief for murdered brothers, murdered husbands, murdered sons has kept on pushing them, kept them "for their still alive sons/for their sons coming/ for their sons gone/just pushing." And pushing Is both the will to struggle on toward a long sought goal, even in the face of enormous odds (as Curtis Mayfield and The Impressions exhort us to do in "Keep on Pushing"), and the double consciousness blacks have of this country and its institutions—a consciousness that many would rather not have for it often highlights the futility of trying to "make it" in America (the expression "I'm so pushed" is used interchangeably with "I'm hipped"). And this reading of "pushing" complements the ironic use of "making it." For it is against the background of the collective experience of "making it through . . . sons" murdered literally and figuratively by the society and the individual prospect of what can happen to her sons that the persona knowingly goes on about her business. The ability to keep on pushing, to keep on keeping on, to go on about one's business, is the lifeforce, the assertion of self amidst collective and individual destruction that comes directly out of the blues tradition. This is what the persona's mother in "Billie's Blues" passes on to her daughter and what makes the closing of that song so delightful:

> Some men call me honey
> Some think that I've got money
> Some men like me cause I'm snappy
> Some because I'm happy
> Some men tell me, Billie
> Baby, you're built for speed
> Now when you put that all together
> It makes me everything a good man need.

The loss of that sense of vitality makes the persona in "Sweet Sixteen" a tragic figure. Clifton expresses this life force again and again, and it provides a continuing frame for and necessary counterpoint to the often-fatal despair that also stalks the inner city.

The power of first person experiences is balanced by distancing techniques—shifts in diction, voice, and focus—that parallel the ways in which distance is achieved in the blues. After a series of first person poems whose diction hovers marvelously between the standard and the black dialects (and thus embodies both), Clifton will place a poem written from a third person perspective in precise standard diction. The shift in viewpoint immediately makes the subject of the poem its object.

Robert

was born obedient
without questions

did a dance called
picking grapes
sticking his butt out
for pennies

married a master
who whipped his mind
until he died

until he died
the color of his life
was nigger

"Robert" as both poem and person is such an object and
comes after a series of poems in which a female persona
talks about members of her immediate and extended family
who have lost the battle for psychic survival in the society.
The focus within this series of four poems (which begin
with "My mamma moved among the days") shifts from the
destruction of these others to the survival of the persona,
and the series ends with the lines "I stand up/through your
destruction/I stand up." The reference is not only to the
destruction of Miss Rosie, who is the subject of this poem,
but to the persona's mother, father, and sister, who have
each appeared in previous poems. Clifton implies that the
only thing that makes the destruction of these others somewhat bearable is the persona's ability to stand up, to affirm
herself because these others have died that she might live.
Robert is an immediate contrast to the lives sketched in
these miniportraits for he begins his existence in defeat and
"until he died/the color of his life/was nigger." This poem
further enlarges the context in which each poem in the
series exists, and its impersonal, objective stance returns, at
a more abstract level, to the general/collective tone of "in
the inner city," the poem that serves as introduction to this
sequence and to the volume as a whole. The shift from first
to third person perspective provides both an inner and
outer view of the inner city and creates an atmosphere that
encourages one to enter into and understand the experi-

ences presented in the poems at both an emotional and analytic level. Sequences of poems are used to develop themes beyond the limits of a single poem; and individual poems come, in fact, to function in much the same way that individual classic blues stanzas function within the classic song. The individual expression is always seen within the context of the collective experience.

Lucille Clifton and other poets who work or even attempt to work in a similar mode extend the verbal traditions of the blues in the same way that the Swing of Count Basie and the bebop of Charlie Parker extend the instrumental traditions of the blues, making those traditions "classic" in a recognizably Western sense while remaining true to the black experiences and black perceptions that are their most important sources. But unlike the oral lyrics, which, of necessity, preserve their group traditions only in their forms or structures and need a separate history to preserve a concrete sense of the collective life styles, values, and experiences they represent, poetry, as a written form, carries with it the possibility of functioning simultaneously on both levels. Thus, while B. B. King in "Sweet Sixteen" can allude to, even symbolize, collective experiences or internalize the necessary and sustaining relationship between group and individual in the statement/response pattern and structures, Clifton, in her poetry, incorporates elements of the older oral traditions, reasserts the collective at concrete levels even as she deals, through subjective testimony, with individual experiences. And this is the beginning of a new tradition built on a synthesis of black oral traditions and Western literate forms.

Dis and Dat: Dialect and the Descent

Henry-Louis Gates, Jr.

> Singing a different stave, or closely hidden,
> Oh there is a precedent, legal tradition,
> To sing one thing when your song means another.
> —Ezra Pound, *Near Perigord*

> With torn and bleeding hearts we smile,
> And mouth with myriad subtleties.
> Nay, let them only see us, while we wear the mask.
> —Paul Laurence Dunbar, *We Wear the Mask*

I

Of all the artifacts out of Africa, it is indeed the mask that most compels. The principal artistic attraction at the 1897 Exposition in Brussels was a magnificent collection of African masks and sculptures. Vlaminck, Matisse, Derain, Braque, and Picasso all owned a number of African masks. It is a commonplace by now that the galleries of the old Trocadero and the studio of Paul Guillaume impressed French artists to such an extent that the concepts of movement, rhythm, and self-contained interiority that gave rise to cubism and dadaism arose from a transformation of the African mask. Still, it is the mask that attracts us to blackness, and rightly so. For therein is contained, as well as reflected, a coded, secret, hermetic world, a world discovered only by the initiate.

Obatala, the Yoruba sculptural god, is not the artist of

Apollonian illusion; he is the artist of inner essence. The Yoruba mask remains only a piece of carved wood, *Omolangidi ni i* ("He is nothing but a doll in wood," as Denrele Obasa writes in *Awan Akewi*), without *iwa*, or "character"—in non-Yoruba terms, without the artist who bears it before his choral-audience. In all African art, the audience is the chorus, and the mask is wood until it becomes the mask-in-motion. The Western concept of "mask" is meaningless to, say, the Yoruba. Precisely because the "doll in wood" cannot of itself signify; once in motion, once the signification is effected, the misnomer "mask" becomes "mask-in-motion," or what "mask" itself implies to the Yoruba. Mask becomes functional—indeed, becomes—only in motion. (It is obvious that language fails us here, in part because our concepts presuppose the world in which we take them to apply. We are reminded here of Wittgenstein's latter doctrine of the inseparability of meaning and belief.)

Once effected, the mask is a vehicle for the primary evocation of a complete hermetic universe, one of force or being, a world autonomous, marked both by a demonstrably interior cohesion and by a complete neutrality to exterior mores or norms. This internal cogency makes it impervious to the accident of place or time. The mask, with its immobilized features all the while mobile, itself is a metaphor for dialectic—specifically, a dialectic or binary opposition embracing unresolved or potentially unresolvable social forms, notions of origins, or complex issues of value. Mask is the essence of immobility fused with the essence of mobility; fixity with transience; order with chaos; permanence with the transitory; the substantial with the evanescent. Through the mask, a code of meanings is established through the media of rhythm, movement, and tonal-specific harmonies that instantly, and in their turn, create further their own rhythm. In a collective as well as a functional sense, the mask effects the "spiritual consolidation" of the race, in an especial universe governed only by laws of cohesive interiority. Mask enmeshes "the day to day awareness of a people," surely a fundamental aesthetic value in all of African art.

Denrele Obasa's metaphor for "mask"—that it is nothing but a "doll" in wood—is, interestingly enough, etymologically sound in English.[1] The word "mask," from the Late Latin *mascus, masca,* has its origin in the Arabic *maschara,* denoting the masked person, like a clown or buffoon—thus a live doll. This Arabic loan word was not understood properly by the Roman people, who adopted it as *masca,* and we may surmise that they assimilated the foreign word to their own verbal resources. At least the first part of the compound sounded familiar to the Roman ear. The Latin *mas* or *mas, maris,* properly denotes the "little man," hence "doll" and "puppet." We see the literal correspondence.

And on another level—that is, the level of connotation—there is another correspondence that will come to bear on our notion of dialect as a verbal mask. Linguists also identify the Teutonic word *maskwo* as a progenitor of the English word "mask." The word meant "net." And it is certain that as early as the ninth century, *max* was used in the sense of "mesh." And if the Late Latin *mascha* is indeed the modern word's antecedent, then our connotative connection is clearer still. For *mascha* was used as early as c. 680 by Adlheim in association with *larva,* which had the senses "mask" and "specter," and *masca* occurs in the Lombard Laws c. 800 with the sense "witch." Already we begin to see a ritual connection. And as late as 1814, "mask" could be used to mean "to infuse." Surely these meanings lurk in our consciousness; certainly these resonances inform our usage. To net meanings not obvious; to enmesh a meaning somehow obscured; to re-member, in this very act of decoding these subtle inferences now buried in artifice; to infuse with the newly translated or interpreted meaning—we imply all these when we speak of "the mask." And this analogue in English we employ to describe an African concept we have come to call "the mask," which in Yoruba ritual is essential to the art of "re-covering,"—that is, covering the human face with an-other, second surface—to re-cover, in an almost mystical sense, a self-contained, virtually autonomous world. It is a world not readily habitable—perhaps not even approachable—through any other means of transmission.

The African mask in the drama invokes as well as

evokes a habit of mind, a state of being separate and distinct from the mundanity of everyday life. The mask—the "mask-in-motion"—transubstantiates the motley, disarrayed audience into the unified, homogeneous, choral community. The mask evokes a view of reality, of human experience, in the truest sense of a "theatrical presence." With the mask, the choral world view is again organic, the creative act becomes collective, artistic expression becomes functional, and the scene is set for transition into the Fourth Stage—that nebulous, singular arena where God and man can interact to lament their primal severance. All this through the mask.

Dionysus, whom Wole Soyinka invokes as a quasi-counterpart to Ogun, was "the god of masks" and of theater as well. Our root words referring to mask indicate that the holes of the mask—the openings of the mouth and the eyes—appear as the characteristic feature of the object "mask." These holes, if you will, permit an in-sight into the true identity of the bearer. Our languages distinguish two kinds of mask: the oral mask and the ocular mask. On the oral level, the mouth is considered to be the aperture through which one can look behind the mask and gain an insight into the hidden secrets or meanings. Since the word *per-sona* is of Latin origin, it also refers to the oral mask, which permits "per-sound" to discover the true identity of the actor hidden behind the mask.

The ocular mask derives its name from the eyeholes. The Greek *ope* means "opening, hole"; *omma*, from *op-ma*, means "eye"; *pros-opon* means "face, visage, countenance." And *pros-opeion* means "mask." It is a conspicuous phenomenon of many languages that they denote the "face" with reference to "seeing" or "eye." So the Greek *ops* means "eye, face, countenance"; the same holds true for the French *visage*. The psychological reason for this identification of "face" and "seeing," however, is not, as generally supposed, that the "look" is most characteristic of the "face" but that the face is considered to be a living, ocular mask, as suggested also by the above Greek instances. Even the word "face," from the Latin *facies*, refers to the artificial "making up," from the verb *facio*, "to make." Much like the Greek *pros-opon* or the Latin *superficies*, "surface," it refers to the outer sur-face in contradistinction to the inside essence. Some people dream that they have lost their face. The "loss of face" refers primarily to the loss of the hiding mask and thus to being exposed, or unmasked; being unmasked brings about a feeling of shame and the desire to be invisible. Hence, the genius of Ralph Ellison's archetypal confrontation between Invisible Man—who is face-less, who exists for us as a voice alone—and Rinehart, who dwells in that Chaos of ever-shifting masks; thus the urge to disappear in invisibility once Rinehart's masks are discarded.

Ellison provided a metaphor for the very nature of language and for the confrontation between Genius and *genius loci*. Derek Walcott has said that all language is metaphor, and hence words mask or "stand between" us and the thing language "describes." We communicate through this peculiar sense of metaphoric transfer. Yet, if to communicate is an essential and social function of all language, so is to conceal, to leave unspoken, to mask. Languages conceal and internalize more, perhaps, than they convey outwardly. The element of privacy in language makes possible this crucial linguistic function. All "reality" is encoded in a distinctive idiom. Insofar as language is a mirror of, or even a counterstatement to, the world, it changes as rapidly and in as many ways as does "reality" or human experience itself. A culture is imprisoned in a linguistic contour that no longer matches—or matches only at certain ritual, arbitrary points—the changing landscape of fact. (Thus the need for another poetic diction in that space between our debased dialect poetry at the turn of the century and the dialect of Langston Hughes and Sterling Brown; or, if you will, thus that oddly short chronological space between the rhetorical stance of Booker T. Washington, who uses dependent clauses to qualify and hence whitewash the slave past, and the rhetorical stance of Du Bois, who somehow saw that without our own fiction of history, without the unbroken animation of a *chosen* past, we become flat shadows.) No two historical epochs, no two social classes, no two localities use words and syntax to signify identical signals of value and inference. Neither, in fact, do two human beings. Each person draws on two sources of linguistic supply: the current usage that corresponds to his particular level of literacy as well as a private thesaurus. This latter is inextricably a part of his subconscious, of his memories so far as they may be verbalized, and of his regular identity. Each communication act has a private residue. The "personal lexicon" in each of us inevitably qualifies the definitions, connotations, and denotations in public discourse. Even the concept of standard usage is a fiction, a statistical average. The language of a community, however uniform its social contour, is an inexhaustibly multiple aggregate of finally irreducible meanings. This is what I call the notion of privacy in language, and this element of privacy makes it possible to use language to mask.

We can misinform, for instance, in numerous ways, such as down-right lying or remaining completely silent. The "aside" was used in Afro-American melodrama so that the speaker could communicate to himself (and thus to his audience) all that his overt statement to another character left unsaid. As we grow intimate with other men or women, we often "hear," in the slightly altered cadence, rhythm, beat, or intonation of whatever they are saying to us, the true movement of articulate but unvoiced intent. Desdemona asks of Othello, in the first, scarcely realized instant of shaken trust: "why is your speech so faint?"

Thus the human being performs an act of translation, in the full sense of the word, when receiving a speech-message from any other human being. Time, disparities in outlook, and distance make this translation even more difficult. In literature this same principle of individuation (at once cultural and temporal-specific as well as personal) requires that any thorough reading of a text out of the past of one's own language and literature is a manifold act of interpretation. That we do not usually realize this helps to explain how easily we can misread Phillis Wheatley's poetry or Frederick Douglass' narrative or, especially, dialect poetry.

The use of dialect in Afro-American poetry itself was a form of masking, a verbal descent underground to the Great Dis. In one sense, the poet masks a political act by sacrificing on the altar of his own muses, often sable as well

as white. Each muse speaks one language and demands
that the poet hold the nature of that language sacred. The
poet, however, as Derek Walcott writes, "is the mulatto of
style."[2] He has in this mutation—this dialect—an accessible linguistic system that turns the literate language
upon itself, that exploits the metaphor against its master.
Afro-American dialects exist between two poles, one English and one "lost" in some "mythical" linguistic kingdom
now irrecoverable. Dialect is our only key to that unknown
tongue; and in its obvious relation and reaction to English,
it contains, as does the Yoruban mask, a verbal dialectic:
that is, a dialectic between some form of an African antithesis all the while obviating the English thesis. This dialectic, in turn, establishes a new set of oppositions that plague
the writer "dedicated to purifying the language of the
tribe." That writer is the bastard son rejected, it seems, by
both parents; he is the *griot* accused, misused, and generally abused, "jumped on by both sides for pretentious-
ness or playing white," for pandering to humor and pathos.
Yet in dialect he is able to contain a hermetic, closed world.
As Walcott concludes:

> What would deliver [the New World Negro] from servitude
> was the forging of a language that went beyond mimicry,
> a dialect which had the force of a revelation as it invented
> names for things, one which finally settled on its own mode
> of inflection, and which began to create an oral culture of
> chants, jokes, fall-songs, and fables; this, not merely the
> debt of history was his proper claim to the New World. . . .
>
> So the people, like the actors, awaited a language. They
> confronted a variety of styles and masks, but because they
> were casual about commitment, ashamed of their speech,
> they were moved only by the tragic-comic and farcical.
> The tragic-comic was another form of contempt. They con-
> sidered tragedy to be, like English, an attribute beyond
> them.

James A. Harrison, in *Anglia*, the German-English
journal of philology, implied this potential of Negro speech
as early as 1884.[3] In an article called "Negro English," he
outlines specific characteristics of the independent language Negroes speak:

much of his talk is baby-talk, of an exceedingly attractive sort to those to the manner born; he deals in hyperbole, in rhythm, in picture-words, like the poet; the slang which is an ingrained part of his being as deep-dyed as his skin, is, with him, not mere word-distortion; it is his verbal breath of life caught from his surroundings and wrought up by him unto the wonderful figure-speech specimens of which will be given later under the head of Negroisms.

Harrison emphasizes the highly metaphorical nature of "Negro English," which makes it a ready conduit for figurative language or "picture-words." Further, Harrison suggests that what is considered generally to be "slang" or "mere word-distortion" is in fact the hallmark of this new language, its capacity to create itself out of a standard English antecedent, which Harrison cannot name but the function of which he can describe in an uncharacteristically mystical manner:

[the Negro] reproduces in words that imitate, often strikingly, the poetic and multiform messages which nature sends him through his auditory nerve. . . . Negro English is an ear-language altogether.

Negro English is, then, a mythopoeic language that is the product both of "a total abstraction of all means of self-cultivation from the field of negro life" and of a peculiar habit of mind that oddly insists on "mis-hearing":

The humorous and proverbial character of many of these expressions shows a distinct feature of the Negro mind. The talk of the African abounds in metaphors, figures, similes, imaginative flights, humorous delineations and designations, saws and sayings. These have so interwoven themselves in his daily speech as to have become an unconscious and essential part of it.

Although he cites in detail the principles by which "Negro" language formation occurs, Harrison insists on an explanation that is essentially sociological rather than linguistic. Thus, even though he persists in identifying this speech with "the talk of the African," he also implies that "cultivation" would make this language a mere relic of the slave past. At the same time, he charts this mythopoeic quality of the Negro linguistic code and its cultural "correlatives" as features of a "black" habit of mind:

> The Negro passion for music and for rhythmic utterance has often been remarked; a Negro sermon nearly always rises to a pitch of exaltation at which ordinary prose accent, intonation, word-order are too tame to express the streaming emotion within; the sermon becomes a cry, a poem, an improvisation; it is intoned with melodious energy; it is full of scraps of Scripture in poem-form, and to say that it becomes an orgy of figures and metaphors sobbed or shouted out with the voice of Boanerges is hardly going at all too far.

This propensity for passionate rhythmic utterance has a secular dimension as well as the sacred one found in the sermon:

> The sermon style naturally exerts a powerful influence on the style of ordinary life; so that it is not remarkable if the utterance and language of the household and the street are largely cast in a rhythmic mould. Nearly every Negro above the average is a hymn-maker. . . . He invents his own airs and tunes, which are often profoundly touching and musical. . . .

Above all, it is the well-developed sense of visual imagery and concrete metaphor to which Harrison is drawn, and which he sees as permeating almost the whole of Negro cultural expression because of the nature of "Negro language." This precise "feel" for the apt metaphor, which virtually creates a thing through its naming but which equally allows a verbal image to stand for a thing, is a kind of verbal "masking" and is, Harrison concludes, the fundamental hallmark of "the Negro mind," a term replete with implications for a literary tradition. It is this capacity for metaphor that is contained so strikingly in the language of the spirituals but that is most often as strikingly absent from the body of dialect poetry.

The mask is a common motif in Afro-American poetry;

common, yet carefully veiled in the main. Of course, with slavery and the evolution of the "slave songs" into the "spirituals," the mask was utilized in a political context— indeed, as a matter of personal safety—to say one thing, all the while meaning another, usually under the guise of religious expression. The spiritual *Go Down Moses* is a classic example. The hymn beseeches a prototypic "Moses" to seek out ole "Pharaoh" and demand of him with all the weight of the wrath of Jehovah Himself "to let my people go." Anyone who has heard this sung with the force and command of, say, a Paul Robeson, not only knows but feels the signification. The usage in this context is common; too, it is obvious. That the mythical Pharaoh "way down in Egypt land" was no further divorced from the slave quarters than the distance from the "big house" to the "field shanty" is by now familiar.

> Go down, Moses,
> Way down to Egypt land,
> Tell ole Pharaoh,
> To let my people go.

The stanza itself became, as we shall see, a reference point for much of black poetry, as did nearly all of the spirituals. The spirituals are of such import to black poetic language that when they surface as referents in the poetry—be that poetry spoken, sung, or "danced speech"—they cannot but bear the full emotional and structural import of another lurking but not lost hermetic universe. Scores of reviews compared Paul Laurence Dunbar's "lyrics" with songs (as did Dunbar). Spirituals as referents give black poetry an opulence of meaning—one translated through time and space by an oral tradition of over three and a half centuries —not readily available to exterior exploration.

This assumption of especial meaning to the initiated becomes more than simply "knowing the lines." An academic exercise of chasing down poetic allusions, while intellectually gratifying, cannot even begin to translate the "organic world view" that that allusion, that especial usage, suggests. That, of course, is our problem when reading, say, a poet in translation, since the best of poetic expression is essentially untranslatable; but it is also our problem when faced with "understanding" a poet in our own language whose universe underwent essential alterations in perception subsequent to his writing. In many instances, the gap is unbridgeable. This usage is, of course, obvious to us all—but there is another, far more subtle rendering.

It has been the traditional role of the black poet—again, given the nature of his oral tradition—to be the point of consciousness, or superconsciousness, of his people: It is he who bridges the gap in tradition, he who modifies tradition when experience demands it, he who translates experience into meaning, meaning into belief. More often than not, however, this point of consciousness in Afro-American art has been the role of the musician, rather than the writer. The reasons for this, we suspect, are not only socio-historical but also linguistic. The poet, and the musician-as-poet, through the process of translation of meaning into belief, has had to serve a mythopoeic function—a function of incorporating experience into a people's pantheon of value, a process more integral to the stability of society than would be one of incorporating experience into belief. As Anthony Appiah notes, "The distinctively moral features of a way of life have to do with our relations to others, to the community. Ultimately in determining our goals we are faced simply with a decision. It is a matter of preference. This mistake that Kierkegaard made in presenting the issue was to see the choice as being about what one should believe. The real choice is about what one should value."[4] Unlike that of the Western scientist, the black poet's mythopoeic function has never been to look plainly at the world through its veils; it has been to re-create in metaphor an outer world and in metonym an inner world in the image of a people, in terms where any opposition between these two is resolved. Thus, his primary task has been to create, by definition, reality for the members of his community, to allow them to perceive their universe in a distinctively new way. This "new way" is built on tradition, only now reformed to be valued anew. This is the black poet's mythopoeic role: to "predict" our future through his sensitivity to our past coupled with his acute, almost intuitive awareness of the present. "Present life for him," writes Wole Soyinka, "must contain within it manifestations of ancestor, the living, and the unborn."[5] By forging value, by solidifying meaning, he, in his own way, forges myth. The importance of myth, of course, is not whether it is believed, or even verifiable; the importance of myth is whether or not it is valued. When no longer valued, myth is disposed of or modified into a new myth, often a mutation of that which it displaced. Both through nonverbal musical expression and through verbal manifestations of mutated meaning, this step-by-step evolution is traceable structurally.

Why do we argue that the poet-musician has served this function more than the writer? Primarily because the evocation of a "theatrical" or hermetic universe where only truth could be conveyed is for the black artisan bound to his language, a language inextricably interwoven with music. The medium of music itself carries with it its own value and its own tradition, again of a historically mutated meaning-into-value. It would be as idle to attempt to utter poetry without syllables as it is for a black poet, functioning mythopoeically, to utter poetry without music. Here again, language fails us. We must state this in a different manner: There can be no "poetry" in this context without music and myth. Indeed, "poetry" implies music and myth. The nature of black music is the nature of black speech, and conversely. Not only is it "unmusical" to separate these, it is simply not poetic. "Nonverbal" music itself contains the language, indeed the coded value, of hermetic tradition. To quote Soyinka from a slightly different context: "Only the battle of the will is thus primarily creative, from its spiritual stress springs the soul's despairing cry which proves its own solace, which alone reverberating within the cosmic vaults usurps (at least, and however briefly) the powers of the abyss. At the charged climax of the tragic rites we understand how music came to contain, the sole art form which does contain, tragic reality." This is certainly true for black poetry as well. For, where language is not only another dimension of nonverbal music but also an elaborator on that medium and where "language still is the embryo of thought" and music a "daily companion," then "poetry"—again, poetry-music-myth—is by definition continuously mythopoeic. It can be nothing else.

Because of the nature, then, of black poetic expression, the black poet is far more than a mere point of consciousness of the community. He is a point of consciousness of the *language*. In the former role—especially in black America—one is often bogged down by far too many political considerations. The latter role, however, though based in part on political reality, allows the poet to transcend his "political" reality and arrive at the core of his community's values and way of life. It is debilitating to a people's art to be tied merely to its immediate political reality. That which individuates a way of life is not only the set of principal goals a people hold, but, more important, their central beliefs about human happiness and suffering (above all, about death), which play their part in determining choice and motivating action—indeed, in determining value. It seems an insufferable tense between the future perfect promise for dialect poetry that Harrison's essay holds and the still imperfect preserve of nineteenth-century dialect poetry. In most cases, efforts to employ a weak rhetorical art in acts of "liberation" from an oppressive political reality disrupt the poet's mythopoeic function. These disruptions—which usually result in the disintegration of the bond between black written art and music—debilitated the tradition of dialect poetry.

II

In 1931, James Weldon Johnson could assert assuredly that "the passing of traditional dialect as a medium for Negro poets is complete."[6] There is a ring of victory, both aesthetic and political, in Johnson's tone. In his first Preface to *The Book of American Negro Poetry* (1922),[7] Johnson had described the necessarily urgent preoccupation of the emerging "New Negro" poet to be the "break away from, not Negro dialect itself, but the limitations on Negro dialect imposed by the fixing effects of long convention." And that convention, argued Johnson, was an unrealistic—indeed, insidious—archetypal portraiture of the black man as a head-scratching, feet-shuffling, happy-go-lucky fool. The use of dialect in black poetry, then, could only reinforce that convention; dialect, therefore, was a trap: "*naturally* and by long association [dialect has been] the exact instrument for voicing this phase of Negro life; and by that very exactness it is an instrument with but two full stops, humor and pathos" (emphasis added). Form had come to determine sense, or worse, he implied, to delimit sense, to mold it into a too familiar stock response. Thus, because of the peculiar artistic treatment accorded "the black image" through the exploitation of black dialect, by both black and nonblack poets, Johnson argued, "there are phases of Negro life in the United States which cannot be treated in the dialect either adequately or artistically." This almost ideal, imposed limitation of the medium, continued Johnson, renders it useless to the new black poet, precisely because the would-be poet is almost psychologically bound to the weight of tradition and is thus unable to use dialect as effectively as, say, Claude McKay could do using the Jamaican patois. This because of the entrapment of usage.

Although Johnson acknowledged that Paul Laurence Dunbar used dialect "as a medium for the true interpretation of Negro character and psychology" and that the passage of "this quaint and musical folk speech as a medium of expression" would be a distinct loss, he mistakenly assumed that the "poetic" uses of dialect gave to it "the humble speech of [the] people," an order and form beyond the potential of the dialect itself. "In it," wrote Johnson, Dunbar "wrought music." The distinction here, I would suggest, is crucial. For where Dunbar used dialect successfully, he managed to contain a musicality inherent in the form itself, significantly an *oral* form, in a stylized, literate, written form. It is not that Dunbar "wrought music" in dialect; dialect "wrought music" in Dunbar's best poetry. The distinction, again, is crucial, particularly when we compare Dunbar's "literate" verse with his dialect.

Himself a musician and a poet, Johnson knew that dialect itself—beyond convention, if such an aesthetic realm exists in a social context where every manifestation of poetic sensibility was by definition a political act—could contain the sublime, especially in the spirituals. "That this shortcoming [of the two full stops, humor and pathos] is not a shortcoming inherent in the dialect as dialect," Johnson argued, "is demonstrated by the wide compass it displays in its use in the folk creations." But because the use of dialect in minstrelsy—a white parody of black sentiment —was firmly rooted in the "slough of sentimentality" and because "these conventions were not broken for the simple reason that the individual writer wrote chiefly to entertain an outside audience," the black poet never managed to make the form *his*, an especially odd anomaly considering that the form from the beginning "borrowed" from the black man's verbal store. This line of thinking is even stranger when one considers that the black poet did not have to retreat to some mythic Western Isles to experience the poignancy of dialect; he had only to step out into the field, or by this time into the street, and listen.

That dialect ceased to be a major form in the Harlem Renaissance (although Jean Toomer, Langston Hughes, and especially Sterling Brown would, most effectively, move against the grain) was of paramount importance to that literary movement's lifeblood, but not for the reasons Johnson so longingly wished. His mistake, a common mistake of post-Renaissance writers, was to confuse the absence of dialect in poetry with a new and seminal relationship among the poet and his audience, his possible subject matter, and *attitude*. Much has been made of the notion that, for the first time in their aesthetic history, the black poets of the Renaissance turned to their own separate and unique experience as Afro-American people to celebrate that which was essentially and especially *theirs*. The change, argued Alain Locke in *The New Negro*, heralded a new era's racial consciousness of itself and of the artist's relationship to his material and his medium. The artistic end of this, Locke contended, would be Art, would be the black man's entry into the realm of the secret and the sublime. The result, of course, would be a political liberation of the most subtle yet profound sort.

Johnson was correct in asserting that the limitations of dialect were brought about because "the individual writers wrote chiefly to entertain an outside audience, and in accord with its stereotyped ideas about the Negro." But he failed to see the ramifications of his own contention that "herein lies the vital distinction between [the poets] and the folk creators, who wrote solely to please and express themselves." For, with the passage of dialect went, in the main, the potential for the expression of that which was hermetic and singular about the black in America. With the passage of dialect went a peculiar sensitivity to black speech as music, poetry, and a distinct means of artistic discourse on the printed page.

This notion had been William Stanley Braithwaite's just four years before Johnson's first Preface, in an essay called "Some Contemporary Poets of the Negro Race."[8] "Dialect," he argued strongly enough to force Johnson to address the matter in his Preface,

> may be employed as the *langue d'oc* of Frederic Mistral's Provençal poems, as a preserved tongue, the only adequate medium of rendering the psychology of character, and of describing the background of the people whose lives and experience are kept within the environment where the dialect survives as the universal speech; or it may be employed as a special mark of emphasis upon the peculiar characteristic and temperamental traits of a people whose action and experiences are given in contact and relationship with a dominant language, and are set in a literary fabric of which they are but one strand of man in the weaving.

Dialect, Braithwaite continued, had been the language of the spirituals, the first black American poetry, at once "impassioned and symbolic," "the poetry of an ancient race passing through the throes of an enforced re-birth into the epoch of an alien and dominating civilization." Yet dialect as a written form of discourse had begun and culminated with the poetry of Dunbar: "it was a finale, in a rather conscious manner, of centuries of spiritual isolation, of a detached brooding and yearning for self-realization in the universal human scale, and in a childish gayety in eating the fruits of a freedom so suddenly possessed and difficult to realize." Dunbar, Braithwaite admitted, wrestled the language from the exploitation of the minstrel parody. But he was 'the end of a regime," as well as its beginning, because "he never ventured into the abstract intricacies and wrung from the elements of rhythmic principles the subtle and most haunting forms of expression," in the main and precisely because "he did not have the deep and indignant and impassioned vision, or the subtle and enchanting art to sustain" the consciousness of the race.

With very few exceptions, notably Sterling Brown and Langston Hughes, two examples to which we shall turn again and again, poetic expression, and hence poetic image, became a stylized, literate experience for the printed page and the outside reader. And because of this, black poetry—that is, the oral component of black poetry, which even the formalized abuse of black language in its parodies failed to smother completely—was sacrificed on the Altar of the Universal to the Spirit of Western Art. Too, the "triumph" over dialect drove these poets to the opposite extreme; they became self-conscious of displaying their experience, and hence their art, as just another in the human community made distinct, where distinct, by social context, by imposed forms.[9] Art for the black poet, in a very real sense, was functional; but it could not remain collective.

Weldon Johnson concluded his section on dialect by saying that "if he addressed himself to the task, the Aframerican poet might in time break the old conventional mold; but I don't think he will do it, because I don't think he considers it now worth the effort." Because that task was not "worth the effort," much of the poetry of the Harlem Renaissance was destined to remain minor and was to pale by comparison with the independent and collateral evolution of black music.

Part of this confusion as to the potential poetic uses of dialect can be demonstrated to be rooted in the social role of the black artist in the first quarter of this century. "The colored poet," Johnson lamented, "labors within limitations which he cannot easily pass over. He is always on the defensive or the offensive. These conditions are suffocating to breadth and to real art in poetry." The question of just what Johnson implied by "real art in poetry" notwithstanding, these "political" considerations of the black poet made the value of dialect especially dubious to the "New Negro," for dialect was an oral remnant of slavery[10] and it was that degradation to the dignity of a proud people that these artists, both consciously and unconsciously, intended to abolish. Abolish dialect they did, and with the bathwater went the baby.

There is nothing intrinsically limiting about the use of dialect in poetry, as Sterling Brown proved, as long as dialect is not seen to be mere "misspellings" of "mispronounced" words—in Johnson's words, "the mere mutilation of English spelling and pronunciation." True and dynamic dialect contains what Roman Jakobson calls "instances"—the speech-segment of natural language. And that speech-segment must be seen to be, in Hugh Kenner's phrase, "a broken mirror of memory," be that race- or linguistic-memory, if not both. The form of dialect carried a distinct, often independent meaning from the language from which it arose. Because dialect was an independent form, it could carry "independent" meaning—if you will, a distinctively "black" meaning. Here, perhaps, Richard Ohmann's argument applies: "Each writer tends to exploit deep linguistic resources in characteristic ways—that is style, in other words, rests in syntactic options within sentences—and that these syntactic preferences correlate with habits of meaning that tell us something about this mode of conceiving experience."[11] Ohmann's argument is concerned with prose, but the relationship between form and meaning holds even more for poetry. Style and structure reflect understanding and meaning implicit in the use of language, in fact in the very use of style and structure. One would be tempted to add that, if a "meaning" is in fact an independent one, then the form that "contains" it must of necessity be independent as well. Thus when a people see their communal experience as a unique one, it is the poet who becomes the representative of the only vehicle they might have to convey this especial meaning or value in a verbal way. And that vehicle, of course, is their language.

If there was nothing intrinsically limiting about dialect in poetry, then why did most dialect poems, as Johnson, Braithwaite, and Countée Cullen[12] rightly observed, fail? Johnson's own answer, again from the Preface, given in an alarmingly off-handed manner is: "mere technique." This is an important statement, one crucial to understanding the state of black poetry today. Black poetry during the Renaissance and the period surrounding it was marked by what Stephen Henderson calls "urgency," a seemingly overwhelming sense of political purpose. Each poem penned during the Renaissance, jested Wallace Thurman, was "another bombshell fired at American Kulchur." And "political" in this sense must be seen as having at least two connotations. Claude McKay's *If We Must Die* (1919) is a "political" poem of the first order:

> If we must die—let it not be like hogs
> Hunted and penned in

Regardless of an evaluation of the sentiment, this sonnet could not help but be "political"—in a very obvious sense —in a post-war America. Yet, there was still another sense of "political," one not so obvious at all.

For the Renaissance poets, the act of writing itself was an act of definition, not only of a personal, poetic sensibility but also of a "people-hood" through the "exemplars" of "the race"—Du Bois' "talented tenth," Braithwaite's "cultured few." Johnson himself saw this inherent "intent" of black poetics and said as much in his Preface:

> A people may become great through many means, but there is only one measure by which its greatness is recognized and acknowledged. The final measure of the greatness of all peoples is the amount and standard of the literature and art they have produced. The world does not know that a people is great until that people produces great literature and art. No people that has produced great literature and art has ever been looked upon by the world as distinctly inferior.

The act of poetic creation was both collective and functional, but "collective" and "functional" as defined by the larger, largely white outside world. True, these are two canons of African poetics, as old as Kilimanjaro and just as enduring. But the sense of "function" here implied by the Victorian deans of the Renaissance—Johnson, Locke, Braithwaite, Du Bois—was to "elevate the race"[13] in the eyes of an incredulous, white world; internal function, hence, could be only secondary. Here is to be found the distinction between African poetics and the poetics espoused during the Renaissance: The overriding requisite of black art was that it ennoble the race's image-qua-culture bearers in the pantheon of Western people's arts. This was the first and foremost function; it was a trap.

This sense of "urgency" had many ramifications for the poetry of the Renaissance, none of which proved productive. Although this is not a popular view, many of these writers were not primarily "poets," either in the traditional West African sense of the *griot* or in the Western sense. They were polemicists, concerned with making an almost literal statement.[14] Their concern was with the basic "what" and not the basic "how." Too, many of these poets borrowed with very little modification the forms of white poetry. Far too often, their models were not of the first order; these black "mockingbirds" did not supersede the creations of their borrowed forms. Nor, upon reflection, could they have been expected to, considering their conception of poetic priority. They produced second-rate poetry, and the result was self-defeating: mediocre poetry, it was said, from a mediocre intellect.[15]

Johnson knew this: "The pressure upon [the colored poet] to be propagandic [sic] is well-nigh irresistible. . . . These conditions are suffocating to breadth and to real art in poetry." And yet, he argued elsewhere in the Preface, the "best" of black poetry dealt thematically with "race": "I have," he declared, "no intention of depreciating the poetry not stimulated by a sense of race that Aframerican poets have written; much of it is as high as the *average standard* of American poetry and some of it higher; but not in all of it do I find a single poem possessing the power and artistic finality found in the best of the poems rising out of racial conflict and contact" (emphasis added). "Race" contained and sustained a dynamic and a sense of the language not otherwise found in "nonracial" poetry. "All of which," Johnson concluded, "is merely a confirmation of the axiom that an artist accomplishes his best when working at his best with materials he knows best."

Aesthetic theories of the period were punctuated by this term "race." In fact, for Johnson and his contemporaries, "race" was used as a blanket concept to denote two very divergent significations; rarely, though, is the distinction drawn in Johnson's argument. "Race," to Johnson, meant the political oppression of Negro Americans vis-à-vis white Americans. Yet, the notion of "race" as descriptive of a sensibility outside of a political context, beyond time and space, escaped Johnson, as it did most of his contemporary poets. It was an oversight. Johnson said of race that "up to this time, at least, [it] is perforce the thing the American Negro knows best. Assuredly, the time will come when he will know other things as well as he now knows 'race,' and will, perhaps, feel them as deeply; or, to state this another way, the time should come when he will not have to know 'race' so well and feel it so deeply." There is something fundamentally wrong with this notion of the poet turning outside of himself for meaning and for value. While we can understand Johnson's anxiety and desire to see the black artist escape the confinements of protest, to escape, in effect, from "the race problem," there is in his argument a not-so-latent urge to the "universal," which "universal," in practice at least, tended to demand the sacrifice of all that was not, somehow, Judaeo-Christian. This is why dialect had to be abandoned and why Johnson himself translated his own *God's Trombones* from dialect into standard English: because dialect was a form apart, its meaning lurking beneath the surface of meaning, its meanings implicit in the forms it took in poetry—meanings ultimately derived, as we shall see below, from black mythology and black music. Not only in his language but also in the "racial" experience of Africans in the New World was to be found the Poetic Art for which Johnson so longingly searched; but because of the prescriptions he placed on Art, he would search in vain. Thus Johnson was forced to conclude that "even now [the black poet] can escape the sense of being hampered if, standing on his racial foundation, he strives to fashion something that rises above mere race and reaches out to the universal in truth and beauty."

No poet, ultimately, knows more than "race." "Mere race" was not to be risen above, but to be plunged into. While Johnson could demand the avoidance of the minstrel-vaudeville use of mispronunciation and while he could suggest that "what the colored poet in the United States needs to do is something like what Synge did for the Irish; he needs to find a form that will express the racial spirit by symbols from within rather than by symbols from without, such as the mere mutilation of English spelling and pronunciation," he did not recognize that that form, especially poetic form, had to be constructed in a language that reflected and was capable of containing the "symbols from within." That language, of course, was black speech, a coded, "danced" speech, which carried its own significations. It reflected, implicitly, a world view set apart from that contained in the languages from which it arose, be they Romantic or Bantu. Dialect contained its own hermetic, autonomous universe, to be invoked only through the spoken word. One did not believe one's eyes, were one black; one believed, said Sterling Brown, one's ears.

By the time Johnson's second Preface appeared in 1931, the abandonment of dialect was indeed complete. And with the dynamic and distinctive form of mask went the potential to express "the peculiar turn of thought" that sustains a literary movement. The black poetry of the Renaissance, without dialect, strayed further and further from black music, from the music necessary to keep verse itself the essentially untranslatable medium it is. Because the black poets saw their obligation to something called Art, they abnegated their responsibility to their language. Most were destined to remain secondary poets, because they could not master their own distinctive poetic diction. Only Jean Toomer's *Cane*, Langston Hughes's first two volumes of poetry, and Sterling Brown's *Southern Road* demonstrated the use of this "black" poetic diction, precisely because these poets were the point of consciousness of their language.

III

Ultimately, it must be to the poetry that we turn. The problem with any close reading of black poetry, particularly that in dialect, is that of translation of the "music" itself into meaningful language. This music is the poetry of the rhythmic word; the printed word cannot be fully understood as "meaning" if treated alone; there is no escape from this. Syntax itself, in these forms, becomes music. The use of dialect in poetry, for instance, must be seen in the context of the music from which it springs—black speech and black music (especially the spirituals), which is the final referent. For all its technical failings, dialect poetry at its best was an attempt to capture the movement and signification of the music that conveyed the words. It failed where it did primarily for two reasons: the poetry became a stilted literary form, devoid of the metaphorical character of the language of the spirituals, proverbs, secular songs, and folklore, from which it sought to divorce itself, and hence lost its capacity to be a verbal mirror; and out of aesthetic decision, a technical failing, or the very limitation of literary form, the poetry echoed the minstrel or plantation traditions of dialect usage rather than its vital origins.

Ray Garfield Dandridge's *Sprin Fevah* is a classic example. From the first pair of lines,

> Dar's a lazy, sortah hazy,
> Feelin' grips me, thoo and thoo;

one feels the movement of the poem bounding into triteness, a triteness of sentiment and expression. The speech sounds forced, of the sort written but never spoken or sung. It reflects not the speech patterns of the countryman whose sentiment this is intended to be but the poet's desire to entertain through novelty. It is the poem's rhyme scheme that is off; breath—the soft "a," the extended "ah's," the "oo's" in "thoo"—is constricted by a racy rhythm that any blues singer worth the weight of a steel banjo would not dare inflict upon his audience. The brisk movement, where effective in black music and good dialect, is dependent on the concrete imagery the lines can carry. Indeed, even the spirituals' detractors readily admitted the vividness and specificity of the imagery, a sort of conjure-into-being with the musical word.

> An' I feels lak doin' less dan enythin';

"Less dan enythin'," obviously, is meant here to carry the line, to convince us that the break in movement is justified by the powerful image at the end. But again, the image fails, because "less dan enythin' " can entail meanings so numerous as to border on the ridiculous in ways, say, that "less dan nuffin' " could not: Less than nothing is not very much; it is specific. This line has more problems. The poet is arbitrary in his "mere mispronunciation." If "an" and "dan" for example, are visual representations of the actual sounds produced by black speech, "doin' " must certainly fail. If one pronounced "doing" as "doin' " is intended to suggest, its spelling would be closer to "duen." "Doin' " is a poor literate translation, meant for the eye of the uninitiate, not meant to suggest a sound.

This same limitation of the visual suggestion plagues the "dough" in the first two lines of the following; but again, there are more problems:

> Dough de saw is sharp an' greasy,
> Dough de task et had' is easy,
> An' de day am fair an' breezy,
> Dar's a thief dat steals embition in de win'.

"Is" in the first two lines here is out of place. The most assaulting aspect of black dialect is the unique use of the verb "to be." No one who could have uttered this would have said "is sharp" or "is easy." He would have said "be shahp" or "be eezy." Nor would the inflection of "easy" allow it to be presented so. "Sy" would have a heavy "z" sound, and the apparent ease with which "easy" and "greasy" rhyme would have jarred. "Fair" would have been pronounced "faer." Too, one wonders strongly if "am" would be allowed to express what "be's" in this sense, since "am" seems to be used most effectively to create a musical effect to emphasis, as in "shoo am," its "a" being a diphthong.

The one line in the first stanza with some potential to be interesting is the final one:

> Dar's a thief dat steals embition in de win'.

This line is an attempt to capture the imagery of the wind so common in the spirituals, such as,

> Sometimes I feel like an eagle in de air

or, more appropriately, the common use of wind as a ful-
filler of destiny, which if it could be restrained, would re-
strain time and fate:

> Hol' de win'! Hol' de win'!
> Hol' de win', don't let it blow.

And:

> If yer wanter dream dem heavenly dreams,
> 'Way in de middle of de air;
> Lay yo' head on Jord'n's stream,
> 'Way in de middle of de air.

But once again, the imagery of *Sprin Fevah* is vague; one is
not certain if "embition" performs its stealing "in de win' "
or if our thief is out and about, preying "in de win'." The
image fails, as does the language meant to contain it.

One could find much more to criticize in the final stanza,
but the point has been made. The poem fails in its use of
the language to destroy, more visually than orally, standard
English pronunciation. And to what end, one may ask.
The heightened imagery so common to the spirituals—in
fact, the primary poetic capacity of the language—is no-
where to be found. If dialect has one overwhelming feature, it is its capacity to carry imagery compactly, its separate language not only conveying the image but focusing
it, strengthening it by contrast with its standard English
"reflection."[16]

The poem's most damning flaw by far may be its use of
the form to entertain without thought, to convey an ill-
considered humor unworthy of the form, in words vapid,
empty of imagery, and marred by the failure to conjure the
specific (such as "easy," "breezy," "greasy," "neutralize,"
"analyze," and "pursistin' "). The poem is a poor one; the
poet has mistaken simplicity for simplemindedness. (One is
reminded of Dante Gabriel Rossetti's parody of dialect
found in Stowe's *Uncle Tom's Cabin*, entitled *Uncle Ned*:
"Him tale dribble on and on widout a break, / Till you hab

no eyes for to see; / When I reach Chapter 4 I had got a headache; / So I had to let Chapter 4 be.") This poem is typical of much that was wrong with dialect poetry. Only rarely did its lines assume their full rhythmic burden, laden with allusion, rich in reference, connoting the unique turn of mind of the black; never did dialect poetry approximate the almost inexplicable modulations of the spirituals. Dialect poetry failed, too, when it tried to cram a live, spoken form into a rigid, written one, oblivious to its internal logic, unaware of its linguistic possibilities, technically inadequate to preserve the poetry as *spirit*. These errors the spirituals never made. Dialect poetry choked and wasted a spirit and produced a mediocre body of trivia.

It is right that the spirituals should be our reference point for dialect poetry, since the spirituals—"as anonymous as earth"—succeeded so well exactly where dialect was to fail: in using a new form to convey a new meaning, a meaning inseparable from belief, both of which gave rise to that form. The lines from this standard European hymn, for example,

> At this table we'll sit down,
> Christ will gird himself and serve us sweet manna all around

were translated into the lines

> Gwine to sit down at the welcome table,
> Gwine to feast off milk and honey.

This transformation is a significant one, not because it has taken a tame sentiment and made of it an assertive one but because it teaches us something about the nature of the interrelationship of sense and sound. "Gwine," for instance, is still commonly found in black speech. It, of course, is basically untranslatable; yet, with a little reflection, we must see that the full import of the word goes far beyond its referent, "I am going to," and implies far more. "Gwine" implies not only a filial devotion to a moral order but also the completion, the restoration, of harmony in what had heretofore been a universe out of step somehow. "Gwine" asserts a reordering, again this restoration rhythmic, its diphthong heightening its force on the heels of the breathily spoken "gw" sound, the "w" tempering the hard "g." "Gwine" connotes unshakeable determination, the act to come now made certain to come by the act of speech. "Gwine" leaves no room for doubt, for question, for vacillation. In part, this use of "gwine" is similar to the premise of Yoruba tragedy that through ritual a synthesis is effected to lament the primal severance of man from God. A sensitive reading of "gwine" alerts one that some essentially different thing is about to happen here, beyond the use or meaning of "I am going to." "Gwine" contains a concept, a way of looking at the world, not fully translated by "I am going to." With "Gwine," man accepts his primal place in the bosom of God; man relieves God's grief at the severance, man again interacts with God—an interaction mistakenly said to be absent from the spirituals.

When using a word we wake into resonance, as it were, its entire previous history. A text is embedded in specific historical time; it has what linguists call a diachronic structure. To read fully is to restore all that one can of the immediacies of value and intent in which speech actually occurs.

But there are other meanings here as well, lurking, if you will, somewhere between Timbuktoo and the Old City of Jerusalem. "Down," for instance, carries with it the import of its usage in the spiritual "Go Down Moses." Our poet is not "gwine to sit down," but is going to sit, down at the welcome table. The distinction, again, is crucial, for "down" in the latter sense leads from the same place appointed by God for the enactment of primal tragic action, where fate and will can meet. "Down" is the Afro-American "Fourth Stage," that place where Yahweh told Moses exactly what to say to ole Pharaoh, "way down in Egyptland," to "let my people go." Almost as strongly, "down" too implies the not-so-mythic (but mythically recalled) land from which the black man was severed, the Africa of his fathers where man was man and man was free. Here, "down" implies more than a place distinct, a place set apart, the place of fulfillment; it implies the return not only to the native land but to the native order, an inevitable order, which only God's will coupled with all the acts of

assertion contained in "gwine" can conjure. Thomas Went-
worth Higginson, in a largely overlooked passage from his
article "Negro Spirituals," in *Atlantic Monthly* (1867), off-
handedly makes a remarkably similar observation about
the spiritual "Down in the Valley."[17] The lines of the
hymn are these:

> Way down in de valley,
> Who will rise and go with me?
> You've heern talk of Jesus,
> Who set poor sinners free.

Higginson thought that

> De valley and de lonesome valley were familiar words in
> [the Negro's] religious experience. To descend into that
> region implied the same process with the "anxious-seat" of
> the camp-meeting. When a young girl was supposed to
> enter it, she bound a handkerchief by a peculiar knot over
> her head, and made it a point of honor not to change a
> single garment till the day of her baptism, so that she was
> sure of being in physical readiness for the cleansing rite,
> whatever her spiritual mood might be. More than once, in
> noticing a damsel thus mystically kerchiefed, I have asked
> some dusky attendant its meaning, and have received the
> unfailing answer,—framed with their usual indifference to
> the genders of pronouns,—'He in de lonesome valley, sa.

Higginson did not realize, of course, that the key place was
not "the valley," but "down in de valley," or more correct,
"down de valley," as the form survives today. "Table," to
return to the line "down at the welcome table," by virtue of
its position at the end of the line, is also crucial here; its
connotations of fulfillment of the Holy Word, the full rota-
tion along the circumference of Time, supplemented by the
celebration of this completion with the feast of milk and
honey, complete the strength of the signification. The line
is a noble one, its magic created through concrete images,
its associative properties both subtle and strong.

Let us examine two other examples, briefly, for the sake
of clarity. There is a particular density to black sacred language that is rooted in an almost separate mythology and

ontology melded together from African and European strains. The lines from a standard European hymn, for example, were translated from

> To hide yourself in the mountains,
> To hide yourself from God

to

> Went down to the rocks to hide my face,
> The rocks cried out no hiding place.

These lines work only because the poet found not just a different way of saying but "the" different way of saying and thus captured the especialness of that which was to be conveyed. The meaning has changed in the translation. Matters of origin, genesis, and priority, therefore, become secondary concerns in literary analysis. The spirituals make the language contain a turn of mind, subtle and sublime, poignant and compact, concrete—"the poetry of an ancient race passing through the throes of an enforced rebirth into the epoch of an alien and dominating civilization"—yet transcendent. Again the oppositions between will and fate, choice and destiny. The movement occurs through rhythm: The prodigal fleeing the wrath of God faces the unbearable sight of that wrath—the unchanging face of the rocks, daring not to utter the unspeakable name of Yahweh, answers "no hiding place" . . . "no hiding place." It is the spoken word that is holy; the prodigal must unavoidably believe his ears, not his eyes. Again, "down" is the place of confrontation, within the spirit of the soul, of the poet with the ineffable. In this instance, the *ineffable* terror of God's judgment leads to the hiding of the face; this action is related not only to the Hebrew notion of the unbearability of the countenance of Yahweh but also to the notion of the unbearability and even the unspeakableness of the name of God. It is also derived from the mode of the mask the slave used to adapt to his new world, a world he could only partially know, seen from a perspective buried in his lost world, a world he could only fragmentarily recall. The flight to the rocks, repeated to invoke the futility of the attempt to hide, suggests human attempts to flee the inexorable by seeking refuge in natural elements. Yet the rocks themselves yield to the omniscience of God: "no hiding place." To hide his face was not enough; one thinks of the Yoruba aesthetic value of character (*iwa*) and composure. The rhythm in these lines affects a presence removed from the terror of their import, and thus supports a counterpoint between that which is described and the feelings this internal movement effects. These lines suggest joy; they cannot be sung, paradoxically, without suggesting a certain joy, a resignation to the absurd. The music and intonation, therefore, are not somehow "neutral" conduits; they carry the meaning that makes the *difference* in the transformation. The context is a joyous one, tragic yet sustaining to the human dimension by the process of delineation.

A final example, given without exegesis, is the transformation of John's vision in Revelation vi.12–13:

And I beheld when he had opened the sixth seal, and lo,
there was a great earthquake; and the sun became black
as sackcloth of hair, and the moon became as blood;

And the stars of heaven fell unto the earth, even as a
fig tree casteth her untimely figs, when she is shaken
of a mighty wind.

In a remarkable translation, this awesome rendition of Judgment became:

Moon went into de poplar tree,
An' star went into blood.

Or still another, yet less resourceful:

My Lord, what a morning when de stars begin to fall,
You'll see de worl' on fire,
You'll see de moon a bleedin' an'
De moon will turn to blood.[18]

Star into blood; moon into poplar tree; the candor of the moon, dripping of blood—the full knowledge of time, when the elemental is seen to be internal, when the permanency of nature is seen to be but an extension of the essential in man, when the unity of all created things becomes manifestly fundamental—this the message of the slave, contained in a language here, as Braithwaite noted, like "wood notes wild that have scarcely yet been heard beyond the forest of their own dreams." In these images, dialect is at its most effective, and the poet not only has accepted his role as the point of consciousness of the language but has pushed that language to express that which is untranslatable.

Notes

1 The following etymological theory derives in part from *The Oxford Dictionary on Historical Principles* and in part from Theodore Thass-Thienemann, *Understanding the Symbolic Meaning of Language* and *Understanding the Unconscious Meaning of Language,* Vols. I and II of *The Interpretation of Language* (New York: Jason Aroonson, 1968, 1973).

2 "What the Twilight Says: An Overture," in *Dream on Monkey Mountain and Other Plays* (London: Jonathan Cape, 1972). All subsequent quotes are from pp. 3–40.

3 "Negro English," *Anglia,* 7 (1884), 232–79.

4 "Editorial," *Theoria to Theory,* 8:2 (1974), 202.

5 "The Fourth Stage: Through the Mysteries of Ogun to the Origin of Yoruba Tragedy," in *Myth, Literature, and the African World* (Cambridge, Eng.: Cambridge Univ. Press, 1976), pp. 140–61.

6 Pref., *The Book of American Negro Poetry* (New York: Harcourt, 1931), pp. 9–48.

7 Johnson, pp. 3–8.

8 "Some Contemporary Poets of the Negro Race," *Crisis,* 17 (April 1919), 275–80.

9 This argument, interestingly enough, would remain central to black political thought in legal attempts to strike down racist legislation.

10 For an excellent historical account, see Mary Berry and John Blassingame, "Africa, Slavery, and the Roots of Contemporary Black Culture," *Massachusetts Review,* 18 (1977), 501–16.

11 Richard Ohmann, "Prolegomena to the Analysis of Prose Style," in Philip Stevick, ed., *The Theory of the Novel* (New York: The Free Press, 1967), pp. 190–208.

12 Countée Cullen, Foreword, *Caroling Dusk* (New York: Harper, 1927), pp. vii–xii.

13 Cf. Matthew Arnold, *Culture and Anarchy* (London: Smith, Elder and Co., 1869).

14 Cf. F. R. Leavis, *New Bearings in English Poetry: A Study of the Contemporary Situation* (Ann Arbor: Univ. of Micigan Press, 1964),

p. 16: "Poetry matters because of the kind of poet who is more alive than other people, more alive in his own age. He is, as it were, at the most conscious point of the race in his time." Also, p. 42: "Losing all touch with the finer consciousness of the age it would be, not only irresponsible, but anaemic, as, indeed, Victorian poetry so commonly is." Cf. I. A. Richards, *Principles of Literary Criticism* (New York: Harcourt, 1934), p. 61: "He is the point at which the growth of the mind shows itself." Cf. W. B. Yeats, *Essays* (New York: Macmillan, 1924) p. 330: "In literature, from the lack of that spoken word which knits us to the normal man, we have lost in personality, in our delight in the whole man—blood, imagination, intellect, running together."

[15] Cf. Ernest Boyd, "The New Negro," *The Independent*, December 1925, pp. 8–11.

[16] We are forced to wonder aloud where in dialect poetry, with the notable exception of Sterling Brown, a black poet used his medium as effectively as did Eliot in *Sweeney Agonistes*, where he uses ridiculous yet sublime language and a portrayal often approaching caricature to "move" Sweeney from the role of Agamemnon to that of Orestes, from the victim to the slayer haunted by a sense of fate. The fatal knocking at the door in the final scene completes this movement. Retribution demanded of the Eumenides is "the paying of the rent," itself not only a metaphor for death, but another signification of the slang phrase itself. Eliot, in these fragments, has made the American vulgar tongue contain the rhythms and idiom common to its slang uses at the time. Yet it is expressive of more serious, almost "deadly" double entendres and puns.

[17] "Negro Spirituals," *Atlantic Monthly*, June 1867, pp. 685–94.

[18] Cf. Jean Toomer, "Blood-Burning Moon," *Cane* (New York: Boni and Liveright, 1923), pp. 51–67.

Afro-American
Literature
and Folklore

Are You a Flying Lark or a Setting Dove?

Robert Hemenway

Many Afro-American literature classes reveal a curious perversion of analytical method. Literary specialists who would never hypothesize about the social psychology of Elizabethan England feel compelled to prove that a single literary text exhibits the collective behavior of black Americans. *Invisible Man* becomes a demonstration of variance in ethnic role models; the *Narrative* of Frederick Douglass serves to advise twentieth-century undergraduates on the dynamics of race relations. The assumption is that in order to take black literature seriously one must be versed in social allegory—as if the function of the literature is to serve as an analogue to school busing. The direction of critical commentary is always outward, away from the text, toward the society at large; this might not be detrimental in itself, since no one wants to separate literature from society, but the usual understanding of social interaction arises solely from a single English teacher's rather limited experience. Uninhibited by a lack of social science training, the teacher pushes the class toward ethnic generalization. Not surprisingly, the text itself, *what* Ralph Ellison or Frederick Douglass actually wrote, the *way* he wrote it, is forgotten. One is tempted to refer to the entire phenomenon as "bad sociology," a phrase with a particularly appropriate acronym.

The sociological motif is not confined to the classroom, but appears frequently in the written commentary about Afro-American literature. Some white critics, arrogantly believing that reading black literature is synonymous with understanding it, have been transfixed by a need to make their criticism a social statement. More than happy to think of black people as social categories, not as individual human beings, these critics cannot separate Afro-American writing from their own pathological fantasies of what it must mean to be black. Thus, David Littlejohn writes, "Not all of the poems and plays and novels of the American Negro, of course are miserably bleak—only most of them; but even the few positive works still convey heavily to a white reader the sense of the 'prison,' of the debasing life sentence that being a Negro can mean in America."[1]

What Littlejohn reveals is not only a bias toward interpreting authorial artifice as racial politics but also an unexpressed belief that black literature cannot bear the weight of sophisticated literary analysis. Some black critics have unintentionally acquiesced in this conclusion by suggesting that what is important about black literature is not its literary technique but its social and political content, as if the exigencies of racism had caused manner and matter to be permanently divorced.[2]

This volume emphasizes what is literary about Afro-American literature. That does not mean black writers are to be examined in some sterile ward in a new critical hospital where the written text is formally isolated from social context, biographical origins, or political implications. It does not mean that classroom relevance is obsolete or that students should be discouraged from responding to current racial controversy. It certainly does not mean that Afro-American literature has no role in the overthrow of the system of racism permeating American institutions. It does mean that there is a concentration, as a modest corrective, on the aesthetic forms, linguistic constructions, and imaginative patterns that make Afro-American written art such a powerful and distinctive literature.

A literature assumes patterns, replicates forms, because these units communicate a shared understanding of the world. The most profound and persistent aesthetic forms of Afro-American writing arise from the traditional poetic performances of black people, those acts of creative communication called folklore. Ralph Ellison has said, "Negro folklore, evolving within a larger culture which regarded it as inferior, was an especially courageous expression. It announced the Negro's willingness to trust his own experience, his own sensibilities as to the definition of reality, rather than allow his masters to define these crucial matters for him."[3] The understanding of Afro-American aesthetics, whether in the classroom or in written discourse, must be founded on folk expression; as Zora Neale Hurston put it, folklore was what black people had before they knew there was such a thing as art.[4] Recently, Onwuchekwa Jemie stated the case succinctly: One of the most "radical energies" in Afro-American literature has been the "persistence or even predominance of elements that derive from the folk culture and oral tradition."[5] Summarizing this energy, Clyde Taylor argues:

> The folk ballad, the blues, the prayer, the sermon, the hoodoo curse, the "dozens," are basic structural and tonal reference points for Black poetry, reflective to militant. Black folk tales naturally work their way into short stories and sometimes novels. The Black folk sermon further influences Black political rhetoric. And there is an evolution in Black narratives from church testimonials to slave narratives to autobiographies and, in some cases, into novels.[6]

The evidence for these assertions seems overwhelming. In his autobiography, Frederick Douglass described the field hollers and sorrow songs of a captive people. William Wells Brown, in *Clotel*, the first Afro-American novel, paused in the action to describe the improvisatory song-making of Virginia slaves. Charles Chesnutt remembered the conjure beliefs of his childhood and created stories of fetish dolls and "goophered grape vines." In the twenties, Langston Hughes wrote blues poems, in the fifties he played the dozens with Jesse B. Semple.[7] Sterling Brown tells tall tales in verse, pays homage to the blues queens in their own idiom, and captures the rhythms of a convict's worksong on a dusty Southern Road. James Weldon Johnson adapted the metaphors of the folk preacher and commemorated the original creators of the spirituals, those "black and unknown bards." Houston Baker has argued that even Countee Cullen, the disciple of English romantic poesy, wrote testifying poems influenced by the formulaic testimonies of Afro-American Christian liturgy.[8] Among more modern writers, Cecil Brown structures his novel *The Life and Loves of Mr. Jiveass Nigger* around the cycle of John and Marster tales.[9] Al Young makes the rural tale teller into an urban hero in *Sitting Pretty*. Ernest Gaines writes of voodoo in Louisiana and graces Jane Pittman with a folk speech rich in traditional proverbs.[10] Blues formulas are everywhere in the poetry of Larry Neal, Amiri Baraka, Tom Weatherly, A. B. Spellman, Ted Joans, Bob Kaufman, Michael Harper, and Carolyn Rodgers.[11]

Why, then, are there so few studies of the interrelationship between Afro-American folklore and Afro-American literature?[12] Why does folklore analysis play such a small role in the black literature class? One answer is that conceptual models for folklore have, until recently, limited the possibilities for interpretation. So long as folklorists were concerned primarily with collecting, categorizing, and preserving the unwritten traditions of simple rural folk, there was little to do when observing references to these traditions in literature except point to their occurrence and remark upon the writer's proximity to sources. The problem was that folklore was usually conceived of as a thing, a "text," a ballad, tale, proverb, or riddle, which had been recorded in a folklore collection for the delight and information of the more literate citizenry. Literary scholars, in particular, looked at these texts with the presumptuousness of colonial missionaries arriving in a primitive land to convert the heathens. Twenty years ago, John T. Flanagan and Arthur P. Hudson, committed to the study of folklore in literature, characterized scholarly folklore collections as "raw folklore" that was "recorded or transcribed at the sources, unpolished and often rough, but authentic and untampered with." Expressing a view held widely by literary people, they noted: "Because such material lacks artistry and often subtlety it is less important as literature than as the revelation of popular mores at an untutored level. On the other hand, this very material in the hands of dramatists, musicians, painters, poets, and writers of fiction has provided a significant amount of the artistic wealth of the Western World."[13] The understanding was that folklore constituted an inferior form of literature, the inartistic folklore text becoming the end product of the folklorist's discipline.

Given this kind of condescension, it is understandable that in the last two decades folklorists have begun keeping a distance from their literary brethren and, to a certain extent, repudiating those among their tribe who have called themselves "literary folklorists." They have rightly complained about impressionistic folklore-oriented literary criticism, usually consisting of "off-hand remarks unsupported by even the tiniest shred of evidence."[14] When confronted with folklore in literature, folklorists have affirmed an emerging discipline by demanding that an author's use of folklore be carefully documented, that access to oral sources be confirmed, that the motifs, tale types, and variants of the literary usage be cited. Otherwise, how can one be sure that what the critic isolates is actually derived from folklore rather than artful invention in the folk manner? Richard Dorson, one of those most responsible for folklore's modern status as an academic discipline, has stressed that one must distinguish between folklore and fakelore— the former being documented oral traditions, the latter being popular literature such as the author-created stories about Paul Bunyan.[15] Still, even when folkloric usage has been properly corroborated, the emphasis has remained on the text. Most folk-literary analyses have consisted of either a comparison of folklore text with literary text or a search for sources that traces a literary element to its folkloric provenance.[16]

Recently, the study of folklore has undergone a paradigmatic revolution that at first glance seems to separate folklorists and literary critics even further. Most modern folklorists, many of whom refer to their discipline as folkloristics, not only reject the notion that the folklore text constitutes a literary form but also find it impossible for folklore to appear *in* literature. Such language, to their minds, is a contradiction in terms. Basing their definition of folklore on communication models that emphasize the "context" of oral tradition as much as the "text" being communicated, they argue that all one can properly refer to is a literary representation of an original folkloric phenomenon. In other words, because folklore does not exist as isolated, discrete items (texts), there is really no way for an author to appropriate a folklore item, say a riddle or a tale, and refer to this as folklore appearing *in* literature. The riddle or tale exists because it was transmitted during a folkloric "event"—a term that includes all aspects of communicative behavior—and the event manifested a network of interrelationships between tale, teller, and audience that must be observed and analyzed holistically. As Mary Ellen B. Lewis has stated, "Folklore in its totality involves a situation, a context, a collectivity of persons interacting with one another. Here a process is initiated which facilitates communication through a medium—often style and language—and results in a product, the text or item."[17] Today the "product" or "thing" arising out of the folkloric process is considered only one part of the whole. Dan Ben-Amos has explained the difference between "thing" and "process" in a 1971 essay that announced the new paradigm:

> In order to discern the uniqueness of folklore, it is first necessary to change the existing perspective we have of the subject. So far, most definitions have conceived of folklore as a collection of things. These could be either narratives, melodies, beliefs, or material objects. All of them are completed products or formulated ideas; it is possible to collect them. In fact this last characteristic has been at the base of the major portion of folklore research since its inception. The collection of things requires a methodological abstraction of objects from their actual context. No doubt this can be done; often it is essential for research purposes. Nevertheless, this abstraction is only methodological and should not be confused with, or substituted for, the true nature of the entities. Moreover, any definition of folklore on the basis of abstracted things is bound to mistake the part for the whole. To define folklore, it is necessary to examine the phenomena as they exist. In its cultural context, folklore is not an aggregate of things, but a process—a communication process, to be exact.[18]

Ben-Amos would seem to define folklore in a way that leaves little room for literary analysis. He deals with folklore as a social science, something Richard Bauman has observed: "He [Ben-Amos] is doing no more and no less than advancing the concept of a behavioral study of folklore, thereby opening the way for a behavioral science of folklore."[19]

All of this poses a considerable dilemma for the critic and teacher who acknowledges the importance of folklore to Afro-American literature. Since one cannot talk about folklore *in* literature, the best one can do is discuss folklore *and* literature, apparently two separate and quite different means of communication. One can identify an author's representation of folklore, but how can one go beyond the tired, hack-like technique of noting textual parallels? Without becoming a social scientist, how can one apply the new concepts of folkloristics?

We begin to find the answers in the fact that, although the new paradigm for folkloristics poses problems for folklore-literary study, it also promises exciting possibilities. By stressing that folklore is not a corpse-like text, fixed by the collector, the folklorist demonstrates that all folklore is dynamic, changing through time and space, as much a part of urban streets as of the cotton fields down home. Ben-Amos also provides a definition of folklore that liberates us from parochial and supremacist notions of who the folk really are. He says that folklore is not only a communication process but "artistic communication in small groups."[20] Folklore clearly is not something arcane, known only to a few "folk" living a primitive existence on an outer-bank island, isolated by poverty and circumstance from the twentieth century. Folklorists have been proving for some time that folklore is created and communicated every day, in the most contemporary and sophisticated situations.[21] The presence of folklore at all levels of society destroys that unstated superiority felt by educated people when confronted with the "lowly," "quaint" expressions of the "folk" or the "peasantry." If folklore has been observed among co-eds at Vassar, professors at Harvard, and upper-level management at General Motors, it is hard to preserve a notion of class or cultural superiority toward other small groups engaged in artistic communication.[22]

Finally, the new folkloristic paradigm offers a way out of

the universalist dilemma that has afflicted both folklore study and literary criticism. The critic has too often been obsessed with whether a literary text "transcended" all elements of race and culture to achieve a kind of ideal platonic form; in the past, the folklorist was given to constructing universal classification systems without regard to ethnographic particulars. Neither discipline was culture specific: Both the folklorist and the critic failed to recognize that cognitive, behavioral, and functional structuring of either folklore or literature is not always and everywhere the same and that both writers and tale tellers organize their performances around certain expectations of the community and culture they serve. For fólklorists, universalism resided in the motif and tale type indices (most of which were weighted toward Western European folklore); for critics, it was the familiar admonition to the black writer to write not about "Negroes" but about "human beings"—as if the two were mutually exclusive. Today, the folklorist studying speech events in Roxbury feels no compulsion to reduce his findings, paring away verbal structures special to Afro-American culture in an attempt to discover a "universal" motif.

Critics of black writing can learn a lesson from this and simply drop the universalism argument—pro or con—because it is irrelevant to culturally specific literary study. The best critics have already come to this conclusion. Sherley Williams, for example, has proposed the study of a "comparative American literature" that would recognize the uniqueness as well as the commonality of American ethnic literatures. Since whites would constitute only one such ethnic group, this would do away forever with the assumption of a white "mainstream" or an ethnocentric white standard.[23] Comparative American literature, informed by a definition of literature as a written form of culturally specific expression, would make superfluous the hackneyed debate about "protest" literature. (It would also expose the "English Department" for just what it is—another ethnic enclave.)

If folkloristics opens up new possibilities, its existence as an emerging behavioral science demands that folklore-literary study be precise in terminology and method. There may be virtue in establishing a new designation for folklore-literary analysis to distinguish it from normal literary criticism—perhaps a new name like "folklitics." Whatever the label, literary analysts will want to avoid the superficial social science of the past, to avoid becoming bad modern folklorists as well as bad sociologists.

We have to accept the fact that an author does not *use* folklore. Consciously or unconsciously, an author represents, adapts, or transforms phenomena that existed as folklore during a prior communication event. What one studies is folklore *and* literature; the location of the analysis is the interface between the two. Although literary people may want to concentrate on the "medium" of communication, the style and language that Alan Dundes has called "texture" to distinguish it from text and context, the holistic process of the folkloric event must be acknowledged.[24]

Literary critics wishing to engage in folklitics will need, as in the past, to identify the folkloric representations they discover, distinguishing between folklore and fakelore, between actual oral traditions and the mass communication mediums of popular literature and popular music. Assuming that the literary scholar is not going to do personal fieldwork, one identifies black folklore by corroborating its recording in folklore collections or, in the case of some teachers and critics, most of whom are black, by documenting its reoccurrence in personal experience. Whichever method is used, identification is a preliminary necessity and requires an acquaintance with folklore field collections and the standard aids to folklore study.

After identification, interpretation can begin, but it must be interpretation in the context of folkloristic theory. The critic must be cognizant of, and sympathetic toward, the behavioral networks that shape folklore. What performance aesthetics characterized the original folkloric event? Do these aesthetics carry over into the literary artifact?

My hypothesis is that folklore brings to literature aesthetic dynamics that the artist incorporates because they serve his or her artistic purposes. Although the folklore transformed into literature *becomes* literature, it also manifests certain vestigial communication effects, and these vestiges affect the literary audience in some of the same ways they affected the folkloric audience; if not, it is often because of the way the artist adapted the folklore. As an analytical method, then, I propose the following. The scholar (1) isolates the folkloric representation in the literary text; (2) identifies by corroborating its authenticity as a folkloric phenomenon; (3) studies the communication context of that original phenomenon to the extent that the information is available; (4) examines the literary context to determine what vestiges of oral communication seem to have been used by the artist for a literary effect; (5) considers the ways in which the author transformed and adapted the folkloric phenomena (including text, texture, and context); and (6) interprets the literary text in the light of all the information obtained. In a sense this process is circular, since the last step is also the first, the attempt to interpret the text being what first causes the critic to consider its folkloric associations. *One always begins with the literary text, and one always ends up with the literary text.* The interpretation of the literary artifact is the purpose of the entire procedure; social scientists may wish to use Afro-American literature as a source of ethnographic data, but that is not the function of folklitics. To illustrate this hypothesis and method, I offer the following analysis of Zora Hurston's first novel, *Jonah's Gourd Vine.*

II

A trained folklorist as well as a gifted novelist, Zora Neale Hurston adapts and transforms folklore for fictional purposes to a much greater extent than any other Afro-American writer. One of the most frequent complaints about Hurston's fiction is that it is *too* folkloric, that the folklore intrudes on the fictional experience. A contemporary reviewer of *Jonah's Gourd Vine* said: "She has used her characters . . . as mere pegs upon which to hang their dialect and their folkways."[25] Alain Locke called her most famous novel, *Their Eyes Were Watching God*, "folklore fiction at its best" but implied that this was a limited genre.[26]

Hurston's personal journey, from childhood in the rural

village of Eatonville, Florida (the first incorporated all black town in the state), to anthropological study at Barnard with Franz Boas, to folklore collecting expeditions in Florida, Louisiana, Alabama, Mississippi, the Bahamas, and Haiti, indicates the wealth of knowledge and extensive personal repertoire that she brought to her fiction. Her folklore collection, *Mules and Men*, although not scholarly in form, is widely acknowledged to be one of the two or three most important collections of Afro-American folklore ever recorded. Alan Lomax has called it "the most engaging, genuine, and skillfully written book in the field of folklore."[27]

Hurston easily satisfies two of the criteria that Richard Dorson has established for determining the authenticity of folkloric representations in literature.[28] It can be shown through biographical evidence that Hurston had direct contact with oral lore, and through internal evidence that she had known such things as storytelling events firsthand. Perhaps the most common scene in her fiction is a group of Eatonville storytellers, sitting on benches and nail kegs on the front porch of the Eatonville general store, swapping lies, creating what she called "crayon enlargements of life." Her autobiography reports that this was a part of her childhood that she never forgot, and she was delighted to relive it on her various collecting trips.[29]

It should not surprise that Hurston's first novel, *Jonah's Gourd Vine*, the story of a young black man's rise to respectability after Reconstruction, contains many folkloric representations. When the children play hide-and-seek around the quarters, they incorporate a traditional rhyme into their game:

> Ah got up 'bout half-past fo'
> Forty fo' robbers wuz 'round mah do'
> Ah got up and let 'em in
> Hit 'em ovah de head wid uh rollin' pin.
> All hid? All Hid?

John's "granny" tells of the folk belief that led her to bury his "nable string" under a chinaberry tree. Characters in conflict confront one another with traditional challenges such as "Youse mah race but you sho ain't mah taste." There are references to Brer Rabbit, Brer Fox, and Raw Head and Bloody Bones. The main character, John Pearson, preaches in the formal metaphors and rhythms of the folk sermon: "You are de same God, ah / Dat heard de sinner man cry / . . . Same God dat hung on Cavalry and died / Dat we might have a right tuh de tree of life." When John's wife dies, her bed is turned so that she faces the East. Almost every page of the book contains some folkloric adaptation or representation, and to a certain extent the book suffers because Hurston had not yet learned to fuse repertoire with fiction. At one point she simply transfers verbatim to the novel part of a sermon she had collected in Eau Gallie, Florida, in 1929. It was not until her two masterpieces of the late thirties, *Their Eyes Were Watching God* (1937) and *Moses Man of the Mountain* (1939), that Hurston created a fusion of folkloric idiom and fictional narrative.[30]

Having observed all of this, where does the critic go? After discovering that the same words Hurston represents as fiction are also to be found in the folklore collections, how does one go about interpreting these data? There are no real guidelines, since there are relatively few systematic and sophisticated studies of the representations of folklore in literature, and only a small number of these give any consideration to Afro-American texts.[31] It is useful, however, to ask first, what was the communication context for a given folkloric event, and, second, how did the author represent or transform that context. A good illustration is Hurston's literary representation of a special communication ritual—the verbal interchange between courting lovers.

Jonah's Gourd Vine is about the rise and fall of John Pearson, a man with great poetic talents despite his lack of education. John leaves home at the age of sixteen to escape his stepfather's cruelty, going to a plantation near Notasulga, Alabama, owned by Alf Pearson, his mother's former master (and probably his father). Tall, handsome, a new face in the neighborhood, John soon falls in love with Lucy Potts, daughter of a prosperous and proud local farmer, and their love persists despite familial opposition.

They marry and begin a family, even though John is given to periodic infidelities; eventually they leave Alabama for Florida, where they establish residence in Eatonville. With support from his wife, who is much stronger and more intelligent than he, John becomes a minister and rises in the community, becoming moderator of the South Florida Baptist Association. Although an inspired, powerful preacher, he cannot withstand the call of the flesh, and an affair with another woman contributes to his wife's death and leads to rejection of him by his congregation. Without Lucy he is bewildered and lost, uncertain how to manage his sexual freedom, confused by the misfortunes that his wife has always deflected. The novel ends with John's death, just as he is beginning to understand the nature of both his success and failure, just as he is about to begin a new life with another strong and loving woman.

The passage I wish to concentrate on occurs relatively early in this story, when John is in the process of courting Lucy. They have met surreptitiously in the woods, and they are each holding the end of a handkerchief, playfully tying knots, making what Hurston calls a "love knot." Before the knot can be tied, John pulls hard on the handkerchief, pulling Lucy toward him:

"Lucy, something been goin' on inside uh me fuh uh long time." Diffidently, "Whut, John?"

"Ah don't know, Lucy, but it boils up lak syrup in de summer time."

"Maybe you needs some sassafras root tuh thin yo' blood out."

"Naw, Lucy, Ah don't need no sassafras tea. You know whuss de matter wid me—but ack lak you dumb tuh de fact."

Lucy suddenly lost her fluency of speech. She worked furiously at the love-knot.

"Lucy, you pay much 'tention tuh birds?"

"Unhunh. De Jay bird say 'Laz'ness will kill you,' and he go to hell ev'ry Friday and totes uh grain uh sand in his mouf tuh put out de fire, and den de doves say, 'Where you *been* so long?' "

John cut her short. "Ah don't mean dat way, Lucy. Whut Ah wants tuh know is, which would you ruther be, if you

had yo' ruthers—uh lark uh flyin', uh uh dove uh settin'?"
"Ah don't know whut you talkin' 'bout, John. It mus' be
uh new riddle."
"Naw 'tain't, Lucy. Po' me, Lucy. Ahm uh one wingded
bird. Don't leave me lak dat, Lucy."
Suddenly Lucy shouted, "Look John, de knot is tied
right, ain't it pretty?"
"Yeah, Lucy iss sho pretty. We done took and tied dis
knot, Miss Lucy, less tie uh 'nother one."
"You got mo' han'kerchiefs in yo' pocket?"
"Naw. Ah ain't studyin' bout no hankerchers neither.
De knot Ah wants tuh tie wid you is de kind dat won't
come uh loose 'til us rises in judgment. You knows mah
feelings."
"How Ah know whut you got inside yo' mind?"
"Yeah yuh do too. Y'all lady people sho do make it hard
fuh us men folks. Look me in de eye Lucy. Kiss me and
loose me so Ah kin talk."
There was an awkward bumping of mouths. Lucy had
had her first kiss.
"Lucy, Ah looked up intuh Heben and Ah seen you
among de angels right 'round de throne, and when Ah
seen *you*, mah heart swole up and put wings on mah
shoulders, and Ah 'gin tuh fly 'round too, but Ah never
would uh knowed yo' name if ole Gab'ull hadn't uh whispered it tuh me."
He extended his hands appealingly.
"Miss Lucy, how bout changin' from Potts tuh Pearson?"
"Yeah, John."
"When?"
"Whenever you ready fuh me. You know mo' 'bout dat
dan Ah do."[32]

The representation of folklore that can best be documented here is the reference to birds, a context that gives
the scene a special interior drama. John's query about birds
is a ritualistic opening to a courting formula that existed
among slaves in the nineteenth century and that has a
number of twentieth-century descendants. That formula is
described below, but the significance of Hurston's representation is that Lucy, either deliberately or out of inex-
perience (she is only fourteen at the time), misunder-
stands. Her query about the jaybird refers to a widespread

belief that the jaybird goes to hell each Friday, usually as
the messenger of the devil. John, however, is not making
casual conversation about folk belief. He has entered into a
ritualistic courting procedure organized around the riddle,
"Which would you ruther be, if you had yo' ruthers—uh
lark uh flyin', uh uh dove uh settin'?" Lucy recognizes this
as a riddle, but she does not know the answer; the proper
response has been often recorded in the folklore collections: "a setting dove is a woman who has already found a
mate," while a flying lark "is a gal dat ain't made no
ttachments, but is flyin' bout lookin' fer a place ter res' her
wary [weary] haid."[33]

Courting riddles are well known to folklorists, appearing
in collections of Appalachian ballads and Sea Island narratives. The very first ballad in Francis Child's monumental
*Ballads of England and Scotland with American and Dan-
ish Variants* is entitled "Riddles Wisely Expounded," and
Child's notes refer to the several forms that riddles take, the
first of which is "a story in which one must guess riddles to
win a spouse." If one concentrated solely on text, it would
be tempting to conclude that Hurston's riddle comes directly from Afro-American folklore and indirectly from
European ballads and that it demonstrates the universal
behavior of courting lovers. Examined contextually, however, the passage suggests that Hurston was representing an
entire *style* of courting that had been preserved by black
people during slavery and may be African in origin. Examined even more closely, her representation apparently
refers to a learned social behavior between black men and
black women, a communication process that enables the
woman to negotiate her own respect, an action with important thematic implications for *Jonah's Gourd Vine*.[34]

The best account of the courting practice in slavery is by
Frank Banks in the 1894 *Southern Workman*, the journal
of Hampton Institute. Banks reports his "distinct recollection of 'Uncle Gilbert' a bald, little, dark man, who carried his spectacles on his forehead most of the time. . . .
Uncle Gilbert was very learned in the art of 'courtship' and
it was to his shop the slave lads went for instruction in
'courtship's words and ways.' " Uncle Gilbert stressed that
"courtin is a mightly ticklish bizness" and the young man

who would "git a gal wuth havin' mus' know how to talk fur her." Banks summarizes Uncle Gilbert's teachings:

> Uncle Gilbert's rule of courtship was that a "young man mus' tes' an' prove a gal befo' offerin' her his han'. Ef er gal gives a man as good anser as he gives her question, den she is all right in min'. Ef she can look him squar in de face when she talks to him, den she kin be trusted; and ef her patches is on straight, an' her close clean, den she is gwine ter keep de house straight and yer britches mended. Sich er ooman is wuth havin."[35]

Giving an answer as good as the question refers to both the specific questions asked in courtship and the verbal dueling characteristic of the slave's courtship communication. The man and woman become verbal adversaries, parrying within the cooperative security of the ritual; the fencing also takes place within a tradition of "fancy talk":

> He: My dear miss, de worl' is a howlin' wilderness full of devourin' animals, and you has got to walk through hit. Has you made up her min' to walk through hit by yersef, or wid some bol' wahyer?
>
> She: Yer 'terrigation, kin' sir, shall be answered in a lady-like manner, ef you will prove to me dat it is not for er form and er fashion dat you puts de question.
>
> He: Dear miss, I would not so impose on a lady like you as to as' her a question for a form an' a fashion. B'lieve me, kin' miss, dat I has a pertickler objick in ingagin' yer in conversation dis afternoon.
>
> She: Dear kin' sir, I has knowed many a gentleman to talk wid wise words and flatterin' looks, and at de same time he may have a deceivin' heart. May I as' yer, kin' gentle-man, ef you had de full right to address a lady in a pertick-ler manner?[36]

Kinds of questions asked in courtship conversation varied widely, and in 1895 Miss Portia Smiley contributed to *The Southern Workman* an example of courtship language in Alabama:

> Kin' lady, are yo' a standin' dove or a flyin' lark? Would you decide to trot in double harness, and will you give de

mos excrutish pleasure of rollin' de wheels of de axil, ac-
cordin' to your understandin'? If not my tracks will be col'
an' my voice will not be heard aroun' your do![37]

Corroboration for this riddle comes from Thomas Talley,
who collected a number of courtship rhymes in his *Negro
Folk Rhymes* in 1922:

> He: Is you a flyin' lark or a settin' dove?
> She: I'se a flyin' lark, my honey love.
> He: Is you a bird o' one fedder, or a bird o' two?
> She: I'se a bird o' one fedder, w'en it comes to you.
> He: Den, Mam:
>> I has desire, an' quick temptation, to jine my fence to
>> yo' plantation.[38]

What becomes obvious is that courtship's "words and
ways" in some slave communities were communication
processes that utilized verbal dueling, determined the
courtship status of the participants, served as an intellectual
test to determine their worthiness, sometimes depended on
traditional riddles, and became a formalized contest that
preserved both a duelistic style and formulaic question-
and-answer texts. Moreover, this tradition was probably
not, as Banks speculated, an imitation of white folks ways
but a courting style of African origin. Alan Dundes has included in his notes to the Banks and Smiley essays, reprinted in his *Mother Wit from the Laughing Barrel*, an
excerpt from an unpublished study of the Coniagui made
in 1941:

> I have good reason to suppose that the love life of the
> Coniagui is rather a subtle affair. One has only to observe,
> in the bustle of the market or amid the silence of the bush,
> how a young man courts the girl of his choice, to become
> convinced of this.
> Repartee is an important element in striking up an ac-
> quaintance. It might even be described as a verbal duel,
> full of proverbs and quips. The pair both want to touch
> each other, and indulge in a series of fencings and parry-
> ings in the hope of attaining their desire. Each measures the
> quickwittedness and intelligence of the other, as they try
> themselves in that "art of conference" in which Montaigne
> discovered all the elements of athletic sport.[39]

The literary analyst can hardly enter into a full-scale interpretation of the communication event that ex-slaves from Alabama apparently share with the Coniagui. In the process of interpreting *Jonah's Gourd Vine*, however, this knowledge shapes an understanding of the passage. The original scene between John and Lucy, understood contextually, becomes much more dramatic than it first appears; it assumes cultural as well as personal significance. At the time, Lucy is fourteen, considered by her mother and, to a certain extent, by her society as an age much too young for marriage. Also, she is the daughter of an upwardly mobile landholding family that has grave reservations about John, an "over the creek nigger" who works for wages and lives in the quarters. Moreover, Lucy is the smartest pupil in school, while John struggles, having come to education late in his adolescence. Lucy, in a sense, represents the new ways, John the old. When John begins his verbal courtship the reader is aware that there is a great deal that separates the two. Although they are apparently in love, the outcome of their relationship is very much in doubt.

Lucy handles herself well in the early going; she coyly matches wits in discussing John's feelings, suggesting that he needs some sassafras tea to cure his problem. The linguistic ritual is going smoothly, and John feels comfortable in advancing to the substantive question. As soon as he introduces the matter of the birds, however, Lucy apparently mistakes his meaning. She may be acting "smart," or "hard to get," but since she never gives a correct answer to the courtship riddle, even though she wants badly to accept John, it seems safe to conclude that she does not know the answer. If she did know the answer but was unaware of the need to become serious, then she would be making an even graver error. She would be revealed as out of phase with the sincerity of the situation, like a child laughing at a funeral. Her reference to the jaybird jeopardizes the relationship, for it reveals that perhaps she is too young, as well as too far removed from John's shared knowledge, to enter into marriage. The emotional demands of both are in great peril at this point, endangered by Lucy's inability to participate in the more adult ceremonies of her culture. She is vaguely aware of the folkloric context of John's riddle, but she is without access to the correct responses to participate in the performance.

John's frustration is considerable, and he impatiently emphasizes that it is not a new riddle but an old one. This is a coded message telling Lucy she should search her cultural past for an answer, while also admonishing her for being severed from traditional knowledge that is important to preserve. Lucy recognizes that John has entered the area of traditional learning—that is why she makes reference to the jay—but she is without the appropriate language to complete his actions and affirm the ritual. John attempts closure of the ceremonial act by stating that he is "a one wingded bird," probably the original of the "bird of one fedder" in the Talley version. His "Don't leave me lak dat, Lucy" is a baffled cry, referring not only to the immediate frustration of the courting situation but also to the possibility that Lucy's answers reveal an inadequate experience, perhaps rendering her unsuitable for marriage. On the one hand, she is showing herself to be uninitiated, perhaps aware of a courting style, but not yet experienced enough to know the full meaning. She is aware of form but not function; she has been a child playing an adult's game, just as children have mock weddings. On the other hand, at a subconscious level, John's plea for her not to leave him reveals a special anxiety; he does not want to be left as the isolated bearer of a tradition that can no longer be successfully communicated.

What salvages the situation is that very style of communicative behavior that frustrates John. Lucy does not know the answer to his riddle, and stymies the planned performance, but her verbal dueling, a socially learned behavior characteristic of black folkloric communication, prods John into improvising a new performance on the spot.[40] He uses the handkerchief as a physical representation of the marriage knot, and by the time he reaches the words "De knot Ah wants tuh tie wid you is de kind dat won't come uh loose 'til us rises in judgment," Lucy has begun to get the picture. It is no longer a game; she is involved in deeply significant action. By responding that she does not know John's mind, she is only asking him to spell out what she now knows is a serious proposal. If she had any doubts, John gives her a verbal signal that the sexual dueling is over, "Y'll lady people sho do make it hard fuh us men folks," and asks her to kiss him. He is indicating that, if she is to persist in her flippancy or to deny him the kiss, the situation will be lost. The kiss that follows confirms her change of attitude, and with the change John can once more salvage the traditional performance appropriate to this occasion.

He regains the rhythm of the ritual and adopts an alternative verbal strategy by invoking heaven; subconsciously, he has returned to the flying metaphor implicit in the original bird imagery. This metaphor carries a historical and a psychological significance, relating to both actual freedom in flight and the potential for flight in a sitting dove, a mental image contrasting with the constricted movement imposed on black people in America. Folk tales about black angels flying and flying Africans, Bigger Thomas' desire to be a pilot, and Ellison's "Flying Home" all come to mind.[41] The association of the lady with angelic qualities is a cliché, of course, part of many courtship situations, but from the contextual vantage point that cliché is irrelevant, since John is simply completing a courtship performance as traditional as a man dropping to his knees to propose. It is a playfully serious communication designed to climax the ritual, signifying that though Lucy may not respond to the traditional riddle, she is still capable of an appropriate response to John's seriousness. Her acceptance of the proposal follows immediately.

Even though Lucy did not know the specific answer to John's riddle and therefore endangered the performance, her culturally learned *style* enabled him to recapture the severed communication and complete the action they both desired. Although the style endangered the performance, it also *became* the performance. Lucy is skilled at verbal dueling, a cooperative communication style historically important to Afro-American culture. The courtship rhymes often depend upon this characteristic, the woman answering with wit and intelligence the queries of the man. For example:

I axed pretty Lizie to marry me,
An' what d'you reckon she said?
She said she wouldn' marry me
If ev'ybody else wus dead.

Or:

I axed Polly Ann, fer to marry me.
She say she's a-lookin' fer a Nigger dat's free.[42]

The twentieth-century analogues to these nineteenth-century situations are well reported. Claudia Mitchell-Kernan transcribes a conversation she had with a young man whom she was trying to interview in a public park:

I[Informant]: Mama, you sho is fine.
R[Researcher]: That ain't no way to talk to your mother.
                          (Laughter)
I: You married?
R: Umhm
I: Is your husband married?
                          (Laughter)
R: Very
         [After discussion of her research project]
I: Baby, you a real scholar. I can tell you want to learn.
   Now if you'll just cooperate a li'l bit, I'll show you what
   a good teacher I am. But first we got to get into my area
   of expertise.
R: I may be wrong but seems to me we already in your area
   of expertise.[43]

But what is the literary significance of these data? How does this information affect our understanding of the novel? *Jonah's Gourd Vine*, like *Their Eyes Were Watching God*, represents Hurston's attempt to work out in her own mind the position of black women in what was presumed to be a male world. John Pearson is a frequent adulterer, and his wife pays heavily for his infidelities. It is even implied that Lucy's death results from the conjuration resorted to by John's outside woman. There is a persistent tension in the novel between the institutions of society, such as marriage or the church, and the individual's need for self-expression. Since the novel is usually looked at from John's perspective, critical emphasis has been placed on the contrast between his poetic pulpit oratory, his inspired spiritual utterance, and his insistent sexual needs. But the novel can also be viewed from Lucy's perspective, especially since she is so clearly patterned after Hurston's own mother (as is John after her father), a woman who inspired her children with the ambition to "jump at de sun"; Lucy Hurston was the dominant influence in Zora's life.

Lucy Pearson strives hard to earn the respect of her community, to raise her children well, to make a good marriage despite her husband's philandering. Just as John expresses himself through the church, Lucy expresses herself through her marriage; she must be constantly on guard to keep John's behavior from threatening the respectability she has helped him earn. Hurston makes clear that John's success is largely the result of Lucy's drive: "There came the day, with Lucy's maneuvering, when John stood up in the State [Baptist] Association, and was called Moderator" (p. 189). This does not mean that Lucy is "uppity" or "dicty." Indeed, she is widely liked in Eatonville, by both men and women. She is not a prude, and she even gains respect for the way she can lead the grand march, a kind of cakewalk, at the town dance. As Joe Lindsay, one of the regulars at the Eatonville store, delights in telling Reverend Pearson: "No sinner man couldn't uh led dat march no better'n you and Lucy. Dat li'l 'oman steps it lightly, slightly, and politely" (p. 185).

Lucy is a woman who has gained respect, and Hurston understands the communicative processes whereby that respect is earned. One such process is Lucy's ability to challenge verbally her husband in distinctive, socially learned behavior that the folklorist Roger Abrahams has called "negotiating respect."[44] A good example is the following exchange between John and Lucy:

> "Lucy, is you sorry you married me instid uh some big nigger wid uh whole heap uh money and titles hung on tuh him?"
> "What make you ast me dat? If you tired uh me, jus' leave me. Another man over de fence waitin fuh yo' job."

John stood up, "Li'l Bit, Ah ain't never laid de weight uh mah hand on you in malice. Ain't never raised mah hand tuh you even when you gits mad and slaps mah jaws, but lemme tell you somethin' right now, and it ain't two, don't you never tell me no mo' whut you jus' tole me, 'cause if you do, Ahm goin' tuh kill you jes' ez sho es gun is iron. Ahm de first wid you, and Ah means tuh be de last. Ain't never no man tuh breathe in yo' face but me. You hear me? What made you say dat nohow?"

"Aw, John, you know dat's jus' uh by-word. Ah hears all de women say dat." (p. 179)

John's reply to Lucy is violent because he cannot accept the assertion of her independence as a woman. Lucy's formulaic response to his question is a form of self-expression, an opportunity for her to assert herself as an independent person. The subservient reply would be to tell John she is not sorry she married him, thus boosting his ego; that is the answer he is fishing for. But to answer in this fashion would also require a certain forfeiture of self, an offering of one's own self-image to that of the man. The success of her marriage would reside totally in John's person, and it would imply that all his transgressions are forgiven. Instead, Lucy testifies to her own sexuality and self-image, asserting her rights in a traditional style, in a ritual of interaction that provokes John into overreaction. He is out of phase with Lucy's response, just as she was to his courtship riddle. His resort to threats of violence is a male refuge, an escape from having to confront the implications of his wife's language—she may be as sexually attractive and socially free as he. Lucy's language invokes the fear of every unfaithful husband: What if his wife has the same desires as he does? Within the terms of the original metaphor, what if a sitting dove is also a flying lark?

As the critic looks back at the courtship ritual, Lucy's actions begin to make more and more sense, especially on an unconscious level. It is a scene dramatizing Lucy's assertion of self in a situation where technically she has been found wanting. Although she does not know the answer to the courtship riddle, she does know how to go about negotiating respect for herself with the man she loves. She establishes a basis for their relationship that will extend throughout marriage and will give Lucy the room to maneuver and manipulate events; despite John's physical strength, his all-too-human failings, his tendency to inflict pain, Lucy manages his career and their marriage, achieving respect in a very difficult situation. What Hurston represents in the courtship scene is not only a traditional folklore test, not only a communication style, but also a behavioral skill that enables a woman to deal with a reality in which all events manifest a moral ambiguity. Even a proposal of marriage is not an unequivocally positive event; the promise of lifetime fidelity is an ideal seldom achieved in any culture, and Lucy's response takes cognizance of that fact, even though she may not consciously think about it. Her behavior preserves her dignity and a certain autonomy in a situation that has been romantically and chauvinistically defined as the forfeiture of self, a melding of two into one. Put another way, negotiating for respect is not a static process dependent upon the institutions or instrumentalities offered to a woman by society— marriage, the home, the church—but a dynamic response to events growing out of a woman's capacity for self-expression.

The black woman affirms herself in Hurston's fiction because she has the courage and the verbal techniques to establish herself in something other than a dependent relationship with a man. It is one reason both *Jonah's Gourd Vine* and *Their Eyes Were Watching God* present such strong women; the biographical facts of Hurston's life confirm that this verbal skill was one of the dominant characteristics of her own personality. All of Hurston's heroines owe a considerable debt to her mother, a woman who conceded that her daughter "was impudent and given to talking back," but, Hurston reports, "she didn't want to 'squinch my spirit' too much for fear that I would turn out to be a mealy mouthed rag doll by the time I got grown."[45] Her heroines also owe much to "Big Sweet," the undisputed queen of a Polk County lumber camp whom Zora met in 1928; Big Sweet announces: "Lemme tell *you* something, *any* time Ah shack up wid any man Ah gives myself de privilege to go wherever he might be, night or day. Ah got de law in my mouth."[46] In *Their Eyes Were Watching*

God, the climactic moment in Janie's unhappy marriage to the domineering Joe Starks comes when she replies to his criticism:

"Nah, Ah ain't no young gal no mo' but den Ah ain't no old woman neither. Ah reckon Ah looks mah age too. But Ah'm uh woman every inch of me, and Ah knows it. Dat's uh whole lot more'n *you* kin say. You big-bellies round here and put out a lot of brag, but tain't nothin' to it but yo' big voice. Humph! Talkin' bout *me* lookin old! When you pull down yo' britches, you look lak de change uh life."[47]

I have dwelt at length on a few passages in *Jonah's Gourd Vine* to demonstrate Hurston's presentation of an Afro-American performance style. Her entire literary career, in one sense, became an attempt to represent black styles in fiction, and *Jonah's Gourd Vine* reveals her initial grappling with the problems of affirming black performance aesthetics in the midst of a predominantly white culture. But Hurston was also an early black feminist, and the fictional dynamics of the courtship scene, very interestingly, shift the emphasis of the courting ritual away from the man to the woman, thereby emphasizing the importance of Lucy's perspective to an understanding of the novel. The courting scene illustrates a common characteristic of Hurston's fiction. Her most dramatic episodes arise from men and women squaring off for a verbal duel, a situation best understood as part of the process whereby a black woman negotiates for respect, seizing the opportunity to affirm herself as a woman. In *Jonah's Gourd Vine* the most critical scene of the novel becomes Lucy's deathbed discussion with John; she tells him: "Youse livin' dirty and Ahm goin' tuh tell you 'bout it. Me and mah chillun got some rights. Big talk ain't changin' whut you doin'. You can't clean yo' self wid yo' tongue lak uh cat" (p. 204). Unable to answer in words and frustrated by his guilt, John fulfills his threat of violence and slaps his wife. From this moment his downfall begins, and after her death he dreams of the episode often, crying out for Lucy to forgive him. This is apparently the scene Hurston had in mind when she explained the title of her novel in a letter: "Oh yes, the title you didn't understand. (Jonah 4:6–10). You see the prophet of God sat up under a gourd vine that had grown up in one night. But a cut worm came along and cut it down. Great and sudden growth. One act of malice and it is withered and gone."[48]

III

The importance of folklore for interpretation of Afro-American writing is often remarked upon, but folkloric passages are seldom given detailed analysis. Hurston provides a valuable testing ground for such inquiry, since at times her novels seem direct recordings of folkloric events, as in John Pearson's funeral in *Jonah's Gourd Vine*:

> And the preacher preached a barbaric requiem poem. On the pale white horse of Death. On the cold icy hands of Death. On the golden streets of glory. Of Amen Avenue. Of Halleluyah Street. On the delight of God when such as John appeared among the singers about His throne. On the weeping sun and moon. On Death who gives a cloak to the man who walked naked in the world. And the hearers wailed with a feeling of terrible loss. They beat upon the O-go-doe, the ancient drum. O-go-doe, O-go-doe, O-go-doe! Their hearts turned to fire and their shinbones leaped unknowing to the drum. Not Kata-Kumba, the drum of triumph, that speaks of great ancestors and glorious wars. Not the little drum of kid-skin, for that is to dance with joy and to call to mind birth and creation, but O-go-doe, the voice of Death—that promises nothing, that speaks with tears only, and of the past.
>
> So at last the preacher wiped his mouth in the final way and said, "He wuz uh man, and nobody knowed 'im but God," and it was ended in rhythm. With the drumming of the feet, and the mournful dance of the heads, in rhythm, it was ended. (pp. 311–12)

The critic or teacher of Afro-American literature who interprets this last passage of the novel without extensive reference to black preaching styles and congregational responses, the traditional metaphors and images of black poetic language, African ancestralism as manifest in New World Christianity and folk belief, the tradition of atonal rhythms in Afro-American music, and the historical meaning that reverberates through the climactic trope, "he wuz uh man," will miss most of the passage's importance and a great deal of the novel's significance. Yet it is just as important to be aware of the communication context of the earlier courting scene between John and Lucy, for without it the critic will not understand that *Jonah's Gourd Vine* also says, "Here wuz a woman," here is one way a woman establishes herself in a man's world; here is one way a woman maneuvers for the space to deal with both the positive and negative effects of "manhood." The paradigm of folklore as a communication process opens up the novel to a special kind of literary analysis.

The critic who recognizes the authenticity of Hurston's representations of folkloric events acquires a special respect for her creative talent. Zora Hurston built a profound literature, brick by brick, from the rich red clay of Afro-American folklore. As a result, she could affirm both her race and her sex at a time when blacks and women were systematically denied human dignity. Her fiction celebrates black women at the very moment they were the most oppressed group in a country dedicated to institutionalizing oppression. If the teacher of Afro-American literature wishes to discuss Hurston's feminism with a class, it would be wise to understand first the folkloric context for her sexual politics and the ways her art was crafted to incorporate and celebrate a traditional communicative style.

Notes

[1] *Black on White* (New York: Viking, 1969), p. 3.
[2] I have in mind here particularly the "social realist" critics who always attack Ellison. For an interesting commentary on this phenomenon, see Larry Neal, "Ellison's Zoot Suit," *Black World*, Dec. 1970, pp. 31–52.
[3] *Shadow and Act* (New York: Signet, 1966), p. 173.
[4] See Robert Hemenway, *Zora Neale Hurston: A Literary Biography* (Urbana: Univ. of Illinois Press, 1977), p. 159.
[5] *Langston Hughes: An Introduction to the Poetry* (New York: Columbia Univ. Press, 1976), p. xiv.

6 "Black Folk Spirit and the Shape of Black Literature," *Black World* Aug. 1972, p. 35.

7 Semple does not actually "play the dozens" but he talks about it; see "Feet Live Their Own Life," in *The Best of Simple* (New York: Hill and Wang, 1961), p. 3. Jemie's *Langston Hughes* does an excellent job of discussing Hughes's dependence on folk tradition, although his distinctions between folk tradition and oral tradition are sometimes unclear.

8 *A Many-Colored Coat of Dreams: The Poetry of Countee Cullen* (Detroit: Broadside Press, 1974), p. 48.

9 William Wiggins, "The Trickster as Literary Hero: Cecil Brown's *The Life and Loves of Mr. Jiveass Nigger,*" *New York Folklore Quarterly*, 29 (1973), 269–86.

10 Helen Jaskoski, "Power Unequal to Man: The Significance of Conjure in Works by Five Afro-American Authors," *Southern Folklore Quarterly*, 38 (1974), 100.

11 See Bernard Bell, *The Folk Roots of Contemporary Afro-American Poetry* (Detroit: Broadside Press, 1974), esp. the chapter entitled "Contemporary Afro-American Poetry as Folk Art." Also, Stephen Henderson, *Understanding the New Black Poetry* (New York: Morrow, 1973).

12 I do not mean to imply that important studies have not been done. Robert O'Meally's research on Ellison, included in this volume, is one example. Sterling Brown has been a mountain of wisdom in this area for years, both in essays such as those in Langston Hughes and Arna Bontemps, eds. *The Book of Negro Folklore* (New York: Dodd, Mead, 1958), and in books such as *Negro Poetry and Drama* (Washington, D.C.: Associates in Negro Folk Education, 1937) and *The Negro in American Fiction* (Washington, D.C.: Associates in Negro Folk Education, 1937). George Kent has brilliantly dealt with folk tradition in Ellison and Hughes in chapters in his *Blackness and the Adventure of Western Culture* (Chicago: Third World Press, 1972). See also the articles by Jaskoski and Wiggins cited earlier and the following: William Wiggins, "The Structure and Dynamics of Folklore in the Novel Form: The Case of John O. Killens," *Keystone Folklore Quarterly*, 17 (1972), 92–118; Sherley Williams, *Give Birth to Brightness* (New York: Dial, 1972), pp. 218–20, and her "The Blues Roots of Contemporary Afro-American Poetry," *Massachusetts Review*, 18 (1977), 542–54 (rpt. in this volume); Robert Hemenway, "The Functions of Folklore in Chesnutt's *The Conjure Woman,*" *Journal of the Folklore Institute*, 13 (1976), 283–309.

13 *Folklore in American Literature* (Evanston, Ill.: Row, Peterson and Co., 1958), p. xiii.

14 Bernth Lindfors, "Critical Approaches to Folklore in African Literature," in *African Folklore*, ed. Richard Dorson (New York: Anchor-Doubleday, 1972), p. 227.

15 Richard Dorson, *American Folklore* (Chicago: Univ. of Chicago Press, 1959), pp. 214–16.

16 There are hundreds of such examples. See the special folklore in literature issue of the March 1973 *Southern Folklore Quarterly* as a typical example. Perhaps the best literary criticism to arise from the textual approach has been Daniel Hoffman's *Form and Fable in American Fiction* (New York: Oxford Univ. Press, 1965) and Constance Rourke's pioneering *American Humor* (New York: Harcourt, 1931).

17 Introd., *Journal of the Folklore Institute*, 13 (1976), 225. This entire number is devoted to studies of "Folklore and Literature."

18 "Toward a Definition of Folklore in Context," *Journal of American Folklore*, 84 (1971), 9. The Ben-Amos essay was first read as a paper at the 1967 meeting of the American Folklore Society and provoked commentary in the *Journal* of the society even before publication.

19 "Towards a Behavioral Theory of Folklore," *Journal of American Folklore*, 82 (1969), 167.

20 Ben-Amos, p. 13.

21 I do not mean to imply that the idea of folklore as a dynamic and contemporary phenomenon results exclusively from the Ben-Amos essay. Rather, his essay was made possible by a growing awareness among folklorists that the subject matter of their discipline was not restricted to isolated, rural groups. See Roger Abrahams, Richard Bauman, and Susan Kalčik, "American Folklore and American Studies," *American Quarterly*, 28 (1976), 373–75.

22 Richard Dorson delights in demonstrating to academic groups the extent of their own folk beliefs. The reference to co-eds comes from an anecdote told me by Robert O'Meally of a Dorson lecture begun by asking the women if they had heard in their dormitories of "the man with the hook." See also J. Barre Toelken, "The Folklore of Academe," in Jan Harold Brunvand, *The Study of American Folklore* (New York: Norton, 1968), pp. 315–37; and Alan Dundes and Carl R. Pagter, *Urban Folklore from the Paper Work Empire* (Austin: Publications of the American Folklore Society, 1975).

23 Williams, "Comparative American Literature: Notes on a Curriculum," NEH/MLA Seminar on Teaching Afro-American Literature. Yale Univ., New Haven, 10 June 1977.

24 Dundes, "Texture, Text, and Context," *Southern Folklore Quarterly*, 28 (1964), 251–65.

25 Andrew Burris, "Jonah's Gourd Vine," *Crisis*, June 1934, p. 166.

26 "Jingo, Counter-Jingo, and Us," *Opportunity*, Jan. 1938, p. 10.

27 "Zora Neale Hurston—A Life of Negro Folklore," *Sing Out!*, 10 (Oct.–Nov. 1960), 12.

28 Dorson, "The Identification of Folklore in American Literature," *Journal of American Folklore*, 70 (1957), 2–4.

29 Hurston, *Dust Tracks on a Road* (Philadelphia: Lippincott, 1942), pp. 70–77.

30 For the "door/forty-four" rhyme in a different context, see Thomas W. Talley, *Negro Folk Rhymes* (1922; rpt. Port Washington, N.Y.: Kennikat Press, 1968), p. 71. For "My race but not my taste," see Hurston's *Mules and Men* (New York: Harper 1970), p. 103. Brer Rabbit and Brer Fox are, of course, widely collected; it is perhaps relevant to remember that Joel Chandler Harris' Uncle Remus tales are literary representations of such animal tales and, although close to the original texts, are a fictionally created context. See also "Animal Tales" in *The Book of Negro Folklore*, ed. Langston Hughes and Arna Bontemps (New York: Dodd, Mead, 1958). "Raw Head and Bloody Bones" is a widely reported character; see Newbell Niles Puckett, *The Magic and Folk Beliefs of the Southern Negro* (1926; rpt. New York: Dover, 1969), p. 73. For sermons, see Hughes and Bontemps, "Amen Corner," and Bruce Rosenberg, *The Art of the American Folk Preacher* (New York: Oxford Univ. Press, 1970). For the specific reference to the

"tree of life," see Guy and Candy Carawan, *Ain't You Got a Right to the Tree of Life* (New York: Simon and Schuster, 1966), pp. 81, 188. One was turned to the East so dying would not be difficult; see Puckett, p. 81. The sermon in *Jonah's Gourd Vine* had been collected from the Rev. C. C. Lovelace at Eau Gallie, Florida, 3 May 1929, and was printed in Hurston's "Characteristics of Negro Expression," *Negro: An Anthology*, ed. Nancy Cunard (1934; rpt. New York: Ungar, 1970), pp. 35–39.

31 I am thinking here of quite technical, scholarly articles or books that could serve as models. Early studies that are useful but textually oriented are Archer Taylor, "Folklore and the Student of Literature," in *The Study of Folklore*, ed. Alan Dundes (Englewood Cliffs, N.J.: Prentice-Hall, 1965), pp. 34–42; Francis Lee Utley, "Oral Genres as a Bridge to Written Literature," *Genre*, 2 (June 1969), 91–103; and Alan Dundes, "The Study of Folklore in Literature and Culture," *Journal of American Folklore*, 78 (1965), 135–45. Newer studies that are useful are the special issue of the *Journal of the Folklore Institute*, 13 (Fall 1976); Bernth Lindfors, *Folklore in Nigerian Literature* (New York: Africana Publishing, 1973); Neil Grobman, "A Theory for the Sources and Uses of Folklore in Literature," *Folklore Preprint Series*, 4 (March 1976), no. 1; William Ferris, "Folklore and the African Novelist," *Journal of American Folklore*, 86 (Jan.–March 1973), 26–36; Mary Ellen B. Lewis, "Chinua Achebe's *Arrow of God*," *Research in African Literature*, 7 (1976), 44–52.

32 *Jonah's Gourd Vine* (1934; rpt. Philadelphia: Lippincott, 1971), pp. 124–26. All further references to this work appear in the text.

33 For references to the jaybird going to hell, see Hurston's *Mules and Men*, p. 128; Puckett, p. 549; and J. Mason Brewer, *American Negro Folklore* (Chicago: Quadrangle Books, 1968), p. 291. The answer to the riddle comes from Puckett, p. 77. It may also be worth mentioning that the "love knot" John and Lucy tie has a traditional significance; I have been unable to find love knots used in formal courting situations, but they are reported as charms to ensure a faithful mate. See Harry Middleton Hyatt, *Hoodoo, Conjuration, Witchcraft, Rootwork* (Cambridge, Md.: Western Publishing, 1973), III 2424–26. My colleague, the distinguished folklorist William Jansen, thinks that the use of the handkerchief in courting situations is also traditional in cultures other than Afro-American culture, but I have looked in vain for such a phenomenon.

34 Elsie Clews Parsons, *Folklore of the Sea Islands* (Cambridge, Mass.: Memoirs of the American Folklore Society, 1923), XVI, 162–63. Francis J. Child, *English and Scottish Popular Ballads*, ed. Helen Child Sargent and George Lyman Kittredge (Cambridge, Mass.: Riverside Press, 1904), p. 1. The standard work on riddles is Archer Taylor's *English Riddles from Oral Tradition* (Berkeley: Univ. of California Press, 1951). See also the special issue on riddling of the *Journal of American Folklore*, 89 (1976).

35 "Old Time Courtship Conversation," *Southern Workman*, 7 (1894), 147–49. I quote from the reprint in Alan Dundes, ed., *Mother Wit from the Laughing Barrel* (Englewood Cliffs, N.J.: Prentice-Hall, 1973), p. 253.

36 Dundes, *Mother Wit*, p. 254. The mode of speaking called "fancy talk" is discussed by J. L. Dillard, *Black English* (New York: Vintage, 1973), pp. 245–57.

[37] Dundes, *Mother Wit*, p. 255.

[38] Talley, p. 135.

[39] Dundes, *Mother Wit*, p. 253.

[40] This verbal dueling both within courtship situations and in other interactions is widely reported and commented upon; it takes many forms. See Roger Abrahams, "Negotiating Respect: Patterns of Presentation among Black Women," *Journal of American Folklore*, 88 (1975), 58–80; William Ferris, "Black Prose Narrative in the Mississippi Delta: An Overview," *Journal of American Folklore*, 85 (1972), 150; and Thomas Kochman, "Towards an Ethnography of American Speech Behavior," *Rappin and Stylin Out*, ed. Kochman (Urbana: Univ. of Illinois Press, 1972), pp. 241–64. Among black men in the urban situation this verbal dueling becomes "sounding" or "playing the dozens"; see Ulf Hannerz, *Soulside* (New York: Columbia Univ. Press, 1969), pp. 84, 87; William Labov, *Language in the Inner City* (Philadelphia: Univ. of Pennsylvania Press, 1972), pp. 306–08; and Claudia Mitchell-Kernan, "Signifying, Loud-talking, and Marking," in *Rappin and Stylin Out*, pp. 315–35.

[41] I have in mind the tale about a black angel who exults in his heavenly wings and flies at such breakneck speeds that he is forced to leave heaven to preserve highway safety. His closing remark is usually some variant of "Yeah, they may not let no colored folks in but while I was there I was a flying fool!" See B. A. Botkin, *A Treasury of Southern Folklore* (New York: Crown, 1949), p. 111. This tale forms the basis of Ellison's story "Flying Home," which first appeared in *Cross-Section*, ed. Edward Seaver (New York; L. B. Fischer, 1944). Tales of flying Africans are also numerous; see Hughes and Bontemps, p. 62.

[42] Talley, pp. 134, 142.

[43] Mitchell-Kernan, pp. 323–24.

[44] Abrahams is concerned with "how women assert their image and values as women." He argues that for a black woman the "essence of the negotia n involved in asserting one's role lies in a woman's being both sweet and tough depending upon her capacity to define and reasonably manipulate the situation. Ideally she has the ability to *talk sweet* with her infants and peers, but *talk smart* or *cold* with anyone who might threaten her self-image" ("Negotiating Respect," pp. 58, 62). My essay owes much to Abrahams.

[45] *Dust Tracks on a Road*, p. 29.

[46] *Mules and Men*, p. 162.

[47] *Their Eyes Were Watching God* (1937; rpt. New York: Fawcett, 1969) pp. 68–69.

[48] Zora Neale Hurston, Letter to Carl Van Vechten, 28 Feb. 1934, James Weldon Johnson Collection, Beinecke Library, Yale Univ.

Riffs and Rituals: Folklore in the Work of Ralph Ellison

Robert G. O'Meally

> Nothing great or enduring, especially in music, has ever sprung full-fledged and unprecedented from the brain of any master; the best that he gives to the world he gathers from the hearts of the people, and runs it through the alembric of his genius.
>
> —James Weldon Johnson

> Discussions of folk tradition and literature which slight the specific literary forms involved seem to me questionable.
>
> —Ralph Ellison

I

It has long been a commonplace that much of Afro-American literature has its sources in folklore, but only recently have critics begun to examine folklore as a literary tool and to analyze the ways in which folklore informs poetic or narrative structure, figurative language, characterization. This interest reflects a changing attitude toward folklore, from viewing it only as a quaint collection of stories, riddles, games—the folklore of artifact—to seeing folklore as a way of communicating, a *process* of speaking and singing under certain circumstances.[1] Folklore is not, to use Jean Toomer's phrase, "passing, soon gone." Rather it is a present and dynamic process that knows no social or racial boundaries. The effective teacher of the Afro-American literary tradition must be something of a folklorist, because some of the most skillful black writers are conscientious students of the lore, and they employ it to give shape and intensity to their work. One black writer whose fiction is steeped in folklore and whose essays place him in the vanguard of critics attempting to define the significance and use of folklore in literature is Ralph Ellison. His involvement in folklore is by no means a recent development.

Ellison has pointed out that Afro-Americans still participate vitally in an oral culture ("we are still not a reading people," he observes). For all his sophistication and insistence that writers grow up not in pool halls or picket lines but in libraries, college dropout Ellison, a kind of Rinehart in his own right, grew up in settings where folklore flourished. This is not to say that Ellison is not a sternly disciplined craftsman and student of literary traditions; he is. And a subject he has studied with great attention to language, form, and theme is black American *folklore*.

Until age nineteen Ellison lived in Oklahoma City, where a "rich babel" of folklore was alive and thriving. At Avery Chapel A.M.E. church he heard spirituals and gospel music along with the standard Methodist hymns. And for several years, as a teenager, he worked as delivery boy and clerk in J. L. Randolph's Drug Store in Oklahoma City's black section, Deep Second. Ellison recalls hearing exalted talk in the idiom as well as tales delivered in high style by older men who gathered at Randolph's on rainy and snowy days. As a youngster, Ellison also played trumpet in pick-up jazz bands in Oklahoma and in Alabama, where he attended college. Thus he heard the talk of the musicians and was immersed in jazz and the poetry of the blues.

In 1938, as a member of the Federal Writers Project in New York, Ellison worked with several other writers on a book never completed dealing with urban folklore. For this Project book, the working title of which was *Chase the White Horse*, Ellison submitted a number of game rhymes and toasts he remembered from Oklahoma City.[2] He also combed Harlem for more material, copying children's songs and sayings as well as stories told to him by the children and adults he interviewed. For *Chase the White Horse* Ellison also kept notes on the functions and the origins of the materials he collected. From 1938 to 1942 Ellison was collecting folklore during the day and writing fiction at night. By continuing to live in Harlem and by maintaining contact—sometimes in hour-long telephone conversations—with certain old friends in the South and Southwest, Ellison has remained in touch with Afro-American idiom and lore. The folkloric ingredient in Ellison's fiction is a major source of his work's enduring popularity and power.

II

In his fiction and essays, Ellison makes clear his view that the folk artist—the skilled singer or speaker in the folk idiom—is a kind of *griot* serving an ancient and vital function for Afro-Americans. During slavery, black folk songs, dances, stories, toasts, sermons, prayers, and other creations were forged from African, European, and Indian elements into distinctive Afro-American forms. Giving shape and perspective to the chaos of the slave experience, these folk art forms were, Ellison says, "what we had in the place of freedom." Through them blacks have been able to recall the past, escape and study the moment, and dream of a brighter future. There were both sacred and secular settings in which the slaves could, to use Albert L. Murray's phrase, "stomp away" the ever numerous blues.[3] These folk creations represented a triumph of the human spirit, says Ellison, through which black men and women humanized their tragic situation. Folklore provided a sense of continuity: In a simple joke was crystallized and affirmed the wisdom of the forefathers, their styles, techniques, and perspectives for survival. Blacks, says Ellison, do not need to go to Kierkegaard or Sartre or Unamuno for a "tragic sense of life" or an existential view of experience: These resound heartily in the poetry of the spirituals and the blues. By the early forties, Ellison recognized that folklore served the function classically attributed to art: It is delightful and instructive; moreover, it is vital to man's soul, for without it he cannot endure. Furthermore, blacks survived in the twentieth-century North, he says, because they transplanted their institutions and they remained conscious of the folklore in which their identity was deeply rooted.[4]

In *Shadow and Act* (1964), critic Ellison has gone so far as to say that *all* great art, from the work of the Benin masters to master works of the present, rests firmly on folk foundations.[5] Picasso, Bearden, Ailey, and Escudero are above all great manipulators of the signs and symbols of folklore. Moreover, art that is not grounded here is subject to be decadent—overly elaborate in theoretical design and false to the "note and trick of life" preserved in folk art. In Ellison's articles on black music he makes a similar point: Black music that strays too far from its folk and ritual sources—black church music, public dance music, and music of the jam session—is bound to be weak, if not in a state of decay.[6]

In 1965 Ellison asserted that folklore is generally more eclectic and complex in its vision than Afro-American fiction or poetry:

> We [blacks] have been exiled in our own land and, as for our efforts at writing, we have been little better than silent because we have not been cunning. I find this rather astounding because I feel that Negro American folklore is very powerful, wonderful, and universal. And it became so by expressing a people who were assertive, eclectic, and irreverent before all the oral and written literature that came within its grasp. It took what it needed to express its sense of life and rejected what it could not use.
>
> But what we've achieved in folklore has seldom been achieved in the novel, the short story, or poetry. In the folklore we tell what Negro experience really is. We back away from the chaos of experience and from ourselves, and we depict the humor as well as the horror of our living. We project Negro life in a metaphysical perspective and we have seen it with a complexity of vision that seldom gets into our writing. . . .[7]

Since the forties, Ellison has maintained that in order to depict the humor and the horror of our living, black writers need to reclaim some of the power locked in their folklore. In his very first published writing, a review of Waters

Turpin's *These Low Grounds* (1937), Ellison called for a greater consciousness of writing techniques and traditions among Afro-American writers.[8] He steadfastly maintained then, as he does now, that black folklore is one of the richest sources for the black writer.

In 1940, Ellison published "Stormy Weather," his longest and most searching critical review up to that time.[9] It was an important, pioneering work in establishing folklore as a criterion for evaluating black literature. Here, while reviewing one of Langston Hughes's autobiographies, *The Big Sea*, Ellison proclaims that of the New Negroes, only Hughes, much of whose poetry had been based on black speech and the blues, transcended the "bourgeois," imitative wave of black writing in the twenties and survived the shattering impact of the Great Crash. Most black writers of the twenties wrote as if they were unaware of the technical experiments by such writers as Hemingway, Stein, and Joyce; furthermore, they ignored what Ellison termed "the folk source of all Negro art." Hughes, however, emerges from the fray: "declining the ideological world of the Negro bourgeoisie, he gained his artistic soul." In Ellison's words, "Hughes's vision carried him down into the black masses to seek his literary roots. The crystallized folk experience of the blues, spirituals and folk tales became the stuff of his poetry."[10]

Obviously there is a nationalist or proletarian note struck here; there is also one that has to do with diction and rhetoric. Ellison points out that Hughes was among the first writers of the thirties to sense that the black worker spoke a "language of protest," a black urban idiom, and that "the speech pattern of this new language had long been present in Negro life, recorded in the crystallized protest of American Negro folklore." Moreover, Hughes's poetry reflected the transformation of rural folk expression into urban folk expression, which, by the thirties, was fast becoming "the basis of a new proletarian art." His radical perspective and power as a spokesman for the people derived from Hughes's having followed "the logical development of the national folklore sources of his art."[11] In other words, Hughes used the language, tone, and structure of the blues and spirituals in his work; writing from the perspective of the folk, Hughes's radicalism glowed with the energy and irony of the dozens, the toast, and the elaborate, outright lie.

Always short on praise for contemporary writers, Ellison surveys the field of forties black writers, finding most of them weak on his usual two counts: craft and use of folk materials. For example, in William Attaway's *Blood on the Forge*, the "folk" characters fail because, in Ellison's view, they are too poor of spirit. Furthermore, Ellison feels that Attaway, like other realists, is too pessimistic. His "folk" are defeated when they move North:

> Conceptually, Attaway grasped the destruction of the folk, but missed its rebirth on a higher level. The writer did not see that while the folk individual was being liquidated in the crucible of steel, he was also undergoing a fusion of new elements. Nor did Attaway see that the individual which emerged, blended of old and new, was better fitted for the problems of the industrial environment. As a result the author is so struck by the despair of his material that he fails to see any ground for hope in the material. Yet hope is there. . . .[12]

In Ellison's view, the black writer's vision is incomplete without the presence of a folk character whose consciousness is *reborn* in the modern world. The Signifying Monkey has moved North in current lore, and he "wears a box-back coat with a belt in the back."[13]

In his criticism written in the forties, Ellison champions Richard Wright as living testimony to this rebirth and vitality of black folk consciousness. For Ellison, Wright's early novellas, published as *Uncle Tom's Children*, were his best fiction; their protest and existential themes emerged not from overt Marxist or Kierkegaardian theorizing, but from the fiction itself, which was rich in folklore. It was Ellison's view, however, that while *Native Son* and *Black Boy* are monumental achievements, they are stripped of folklore and portray the "folk" in terms that are too sweepingly harsh. Despite this criticism, Ellison wrote in his important review of *Black Boy*, "Richard Wright's Blues" (1945), that *Black Boy* is filled

> with blues-tempered echoes of railroad trains, the names of Southern towns and cities, estrangements, fights and

flights, death and disappointments, charged with physical and spiritual hungers and pain. And like a blues sung by such an artist as Bessie Smith, its lyric prose evokes the paradoxical, almost surreal image of a black boy singing lustily as he probes his own grievous wound.[14]

This quality of the autobiography prompted Ellison to fashion his famous definition of the blues in written art:

The blues is an impulse to keep the painful details and episodes of a brutal existence alive in one's aching consciousness, to finger its jagged grain, and to transcend it, not by the consolation of philosophy but by squeezing from it a near-tragic, near-comic lyricism. As a form, the blues is an autobiographical chronicle of personal catastrophe expressed lyrically. . . . Their attraction lies in this, that they at once express both the agony of life and the possibility of conquering it through sheer toughness of spirit. They fall short of tragedy only in that they provide no solution, offer no scapegoat but the self.[15]

In his criticism of black literature over the last twenty-five years, Ellison has repeatedly emphasized technique and use of folklore as major criteria for evaluating black writers. Small wonder, then, that the only two contemporary black fiction writers winning Ellison's public praise—James Alan McPherson and Leon Forrest—are lauded for their uses of black folklore. McPherson's *Hue and Cry* (1971), says Ellison, "makes use of the very rich folklore which has accumulated through the experience of dining-car and Pullman porters."[16] In his Foreword to Forrest's first novel, *There Is a Tree More Ancient than Eden* (1973), Ellison is especially ecstatic: "How furiously eloquent is this man Forrest's prose, how zestful his jazz-like invention, his parody, his reference to the classics and commonplaces of literature, tall-tale and street-slum jive!"[17]

III

One familiar with Ellison's strong stand on the relationship of folklore to black literature reads Stanley Edgar

Hyman's chapter on folklore and *Invisible Man*, published in *The Promised End*, thinking it derivative of Ellison's work. Hyman identifies the "darky entertainer" as a figure from black American lore, one related to the "archetypal trickster figure, originating from Africa." This minstrel man, a professional entertainer who plays dumb, meta-morphoses, in Afro-American literature, into such characters as the wily grandfather of *Invisible Man*. This argument offends Ellison by veering toward negritude's claim that all black writing involves idiosyncratic forms traceable to an African homeland, and in "Change the Joke and Slip the Yoke," Ellison issues a sharp rejoinder to Hyman, stating that he "must disagree with him all along the way."[18] Ellison points out that when black writers *do* tap folk sources, they scrupulously avoid the "darky" figures of minstrelsy. Such characters are by no means black folk types, but *white* ones, born of the white American's peculiar psychological and ritual needs. When these white-in-blackface minstrels—like the Nigger Jim—show up in American literature, they are, at best, slightly repulsive to black readers. Furthermore, masking and "playing dumb" are *American* (and universal) games, not just black ones. Trace them to Africa and one makes a political statement, not a literary one, says Ellison. Afro-American folklore has riches indeed, Ellison says, "but for the novelist, of any cultural or racial identity, his form is his greatest freedom and his insights are where he finds them."[19] Interpret all the colors of his palette as folklore, if you change the joke, and thus limit and segregate him—you gently but firmly slip the yoke.

Having in mind Ellison's warnings, one wonders how folklore operates in Ellison's own fiction. How, extrapolating, does folklore function in Afro-American literature generally? To begin with, folklore heightens the creative tension of Ellison's prose. For example, when Mary in *Invisible Man* tells the novel's protagonist that someday he will "move on up a little higher," she quotes the title of Mahalia Jackson's gospel hit by that name.[20] Thus, she identifies herself, at least for the moment, with the values of black church folk as expressed through this song, which clearly partakes of the idiom of sacred black lore. Subtle references to blues (the Invisible Man says that he felt he had to "Open up the window and let the bad air out," quoting a line from "Buddy Bolden's Blues"); a touch of the dozens (when Jack asks, angrily, who gave the Invisible Man the authority to act alone, the Invisible Man answers, "Your ma"); sermons and sermon-like speeches; casual references to the jokes, toasts, and the signifying games of black folklore—all are elements that enrich the texture and resonance of Ellison's prose.

Folklore also influences the structure of Ellison's fiction. Several critics, following Ellison's lead, have said that *Invisible Man* is, in some sense, an extended blues. In one commentator's words,

> *Invisible Man* was *par excellence* the literary extension of the blues. It was as if Ellison had taken an everyday twelve bar blues tune (by a man from down South sitting in a manhole up North singing and signifying about how he got there) and scored it for full orchestra. . . . It had new dimensions of rhetorical resonance (based on lying and signifying). . . . It was a first rate novel, a blues odyssey, a tall tale. . . . And like the blues, and echoing the irrepressibility of America itself, it ended on a note of promise, ironic and ambiguous, but a note of promise still. The blues with no aid from existentialism have always known that there were no clear-cut solutions for the human situation.[21]

Like a blues man the Invisible Man struggles to cope with predicament after predicament (the "changes") by the magic of his words. In this sense, the young man is not so much an anti-hero (as several critics call him) as a comic hero striving for "blues heroism." In *The Hero and the Blues*, Albert Murray writes that the true "blues hero" personifies certain qualities perfected by the blues (or jazz) soloist:

> Improvisation is the ultimate human (i.e.) heroic endowment. . . . Even as flexibility or the ability to swing (or to perform with grace under pressure) is the key to . . . the charisma of the hero, and even as infinite alertness-become-dexterity is the functional source of the magic of all

master craftsmen, so may skill in the art of improvisation be that which both will enable contemporary man to be at home with his sometimes tolerable but never quite certain condition of *not* being at home in the world and will also dispose him to regard his obstacles and frustrations as well as his achievements in terms of adventures and romance.[22]

Like a blues singer, the Invisible Man recounts his story—full of the train whistles, sudden flights, and the bad men and conjure women of the blues—with style, irony, and a sense of absurdity, viewing his trials and very occasional glories in terms of adventure and bedazzled romance. Also, this soloist, playing against and with his tradition and his society, discovers his identity and his freedom, as he finds his "voice" as a solo player or singer: as he finds, if you will, his "literacy."[23]

Blues *lyrics* also float through the pages of Ellison's fiction. These blues fragments often do more than provide a picturesque setting and tone. They sometimes serve a didactic purpose, calling a young or lost black character back to a sense of his identity, which is rooted in folklore. In the factory hospital the Invisible Man is lost until his memory is jarred and he recalls the dirty-dozens and Buckeye the Rabbit. In "Out of the Hospital and under the Bar," a version of the hospital scene that Ellison published ten years after the novel appeared, the Invisible Man is jarred into self-awareness as he hears, in the recesses of his mind, a high voice calling the "How Long Blues."[24] This secular blues voice here serves a sacred function. As an Ellison hero points out in "Night-Talk" (1965), the careful listener often hears prayers and prophecies from the mouths of even quite profane speakers: God's voice "could sing through the blues and even speak through the dirty-dozens if only the players were rich-spirited and resourceful enough, comical enough, vital enough and enough aware of the disciplines of life. In the zest and richness Thou were there, yes!"[25] For Ellison, folklore is functional; it may be instructive and even *saving*.

If *Invisible Man* is in some sense an extended blues, Ellison's long-awaited second novel, published only in scattered and ill-fitting fragments (of which "Night-Talk" is one), has overtones of the blues's sacred counterpart: spirituals or gospel songs. One piece of the novel, "Juneteenth," released as a story complete in itself, consists of a sermon preached hard on Juneteenth, the anniversary of emancipation day, by two revivalists, the Reverends Hickman and Bliss.[26] Here, then, a form not always recognized as folkloric—the sermon—is used to provide a story with structure. Part of the success of "Juneteenth" derives from the responses of the congregation and of one preacher to another: It is a highly eloquent "dialogue-sermon." Interestingly, too, the story's *subject* is black identity and survival; thus the words and the form, hammered out by black folk, constitute an exuberant affirmation of Afro-American life. Rev. Hickman shouts:

> We know where we are by the way we walk. We know where we are by the way we talk. We know where we are by the way we sing. We know where we are by the way we dance. We know where we are by the way we praise the Lord on high. We know where we are because we hear a different tune in our minds and in our hearts. We know who we are because when we make the beat of our rhythm to shape our day the whole land says, Amen! It smiles, Rev. Bliss, and it moves to our time! Don't be ashamed, my brothern! Don't be cowed. Don't throw what you have away! Continue! Remember! Believe! Trust the inner beat that tells us who we are.[27]

Drawing earlier on the "Dry Bones" folk sermon mentioned by James Weldon Johnson in the Introduction to *God's Trombones*, Rev. Hickman (an ex-jazzman whose nickname is God's Trombone) taps a rich source for waking and stirring up his congregation's spirit.[28] *"Do,"* Rev. Hickman shouts, *"Do these dry bones live?!"*[29]

Like much Afro-American writing, Ellison's novel and his stories often contain entire sermons. In the Prologue to *Invisible Man*, the sermonic topic, "The Blackness of Blackness," echoes the Bible and the Black Belt sermon. Homer A. Barbee's sermon is one of the great "performances" in American literature. And it is here that Ellison consciously parodies the qualities of the hero in history and myth as outlined by Lord Raglan.[30] For instance, Raglan observes that heroes of legend and history are often born mysteriously only to encounter awesome hardship as youths. Likewise, the Founder in *Invisible Man* knew only his slave mother and suffered great trials as a baby. A note of absurdity undercuts this archetypal pattern when blind Barbee says, "I'm sure you have heard of his precarious infancy, his precious life almost destroyed by an insane cousin who splashed the babe with lye and shrivelled his seed and how, a mere babe, he lay nine days in a deathlike coma and then suddenly and miraculously recovered."[31]

Sometimes Ellison's sermons constitute the nucleus of a story. Such is the case in the first published fragment of the new novel "And Hickman Arrives" (1960).[32] In that story, "God's Trombone" preaches death and resurrection over a small coffin, which opens in mid-sermon as the small boy-preacher, Rev. Bliss, sits up in his white linen suit to inquire, innocently, "Lord, Why Hast Thou Forsaken Me?" An inspired piece of showmanship, this sermon is remembered by the delirious Rev. Bliss-become-Senator Sunraider years later, after he has been shot down on the floor of the U. S. Senate. Just as the sermons by the Prologue preacher and by Homer A. Barbee comment on the themes of *Invisible Man*, the Hickman-Bliss sermon is an integral part of "And Hickman Arrives." Indeed, the sermon—moaned, stamped, shouted, sung, and enacted —serves to raise the action of the story beyond realism to surrealism, though such "surrealistic" drama may be witnessed in certain black churches on any Sunday. In this story, a boy becomes compared with Christ; his later assassination is a kind of crucifixion. It is vitally important, too, that Bliss, who as a senator is passing for white, seems to come to himself as he recalls his black past, when under hot tents on the revival circuit, the air was tense with sermons and spirituals.

Like Charles Chesnutt, Ellison sometimes erects an entire short story around a folk tale. Such is the case in "Did You Ever Dream Lucky?" (1956) and "Flying Home" (1944). The use of folklore in these stories would satisfy even folklorists like Richard Dorson whose eye is ever vigilant for evidences of *fake*lorists in the field.[33] "Flying Home" contains allusions to the Icarus and Phoenix myths, but some of the main ore here is from the black folk mine. A young black pilot whose plane is felled, significantly, by "jim crows," meets an old black man who tells him a spirited version of "Colored Man in Heaven." This tale (recorded in Richard Dorson's *American Negro Folktales*) is presented as a parable, designed to instruct the headstrong young man in some of the paradoxes and cruelties of black life. Here again folklore soothes, delights, teaches, arms. At the end of the story the young man is able to confront his tragic predicament; he is even able to face, with less self-destructive bitterness or aggression, the vicious whites in Alabama. As in the Sterling Brown poem, "Slim in Hell," which is also based on "Colored Man in Heaven," the young man is able to deal, like Slim, with the limitations of his life in the Deep South. In Brown's version, St. Peter is surprised to learn that Slim did not know that hell was in Dixie:

> . . . Peter say, "You must
> Be crazy, I vow,
> Where'n hell dja think Hell was
> Anyhow?[34]

"Did You Ever Dream Lucky" is a contemporary Harlem story about buried treasure, a "fortune" that turns out to be worthless.[35] Several motifs from Afro-American buried treasure folk stories emerge here. Again, too, the folk story, like an Aesop fable, is a parable for delight and instruction. Complete with tale signatures, "Dream Lucky" would be fascinating to folklorists interested in transcribing folklore as performance. Here one watches folk art transmuted into literature. Here is a perplexing message contained in the simple, poetic terms of the Count Basie/ Jimmy Rushing blues that give the story its title:

> Did you ever dream lucky,
> And wake up cold in hand?
> Did you ever dream lucky, baby,
> Just to wake up cold in hand?
>
> And you didn't have a dollar,
> Somebody had your woman.[36]

IV

George W. Kent is right on target when he says that Ellison uses "folk characters" in his fiction.[37] These often heroic characters—whether from the North or South, rural or urban milieus—live in a culture that is principally oral. They speak a vernacular language infused with words from toasts and tales, the dozens and blues, spirituals and sermons. Sometimes these characters are singers or preachers —word experts; just as often they are barflies or ordinary men and women who, given the correct setting and listeners, will spin an inspired lie: that is, they will use a folklore process. The catalog of such Ellison characters includes Trueblood, "Petie Wheatstraw," Mrs. Jackson, Brother Tarp, Mary, and the Rev. Alonzo Zuber Hickman, God's Trombone. They are Ellison's strong men and women of charity and vision who have the "toughness of spirit" expressed in the blues. These characters have their feet firmly planted on the ground, and they are able and willing to help others, often through the power of their words. Most of Ellison's stories concern bright young men lost and confused in the danger-and-fun-house of American society. These "folk characters" are their guides; they are the initiators; they are mother and father.

Other "folk characters" in Ellison's prose are those around whom folk characteristics cluster. Sometimes we meet Ellison characters based on the badmen and badwomen of the blues. Also, the Invisible Man, as some critics have observed, does fall into the role of the yokel in the big city. And he acts like the stumbling Brer Bear, outmaneuvered by several Brer Rabbits: Tarp, Jack, Bledsoe. But it is usually overlooked that the Invisible Man is both the bear and the hare: If he is often duped, by the end of the book it is he who has outrun the entire field, leaving one-eyed Jack to play the role of Jack-the-Bear. Jack is also the Dirty Dog and the Marse of black folklore, keeping the "nigger boy running" until he (the Invisible Man) realizes he must stop running and assert himself. The tables are turned when the Invisible Man becomes, to some degree, *John* of the tales, outmaneuvering the Master and escaping with a modicum of freedom.

Allusions to other folk characters abound. "Petie Wheat-straw," the devil's son-in-law, is conjured. High John the Conquerer makes a brief appearance. References to the biblical Jonah, Samson, St. John, and Jesus occur, particularly in the late stories. Also, references—sometimes in blues lyrics—to such popular, if not, strictly speaking, *folk* characters as Louis Armstrong and Joe Louis are made throughout Ellison's work.

These allusions and the other uses of folklore add a dimension to Ellison's earliest fiction that propels it beyond the stark realism of the thirties. One need only compare "The Birthmark" or "Slick Gonna Learn" (realistic Ellison stories) with the Buster-and-Riley stories to see this difference. The use of folklore adds historical dimension, a sense of the past. Also, it provides a magic, a dreamlike quality missing from most social realist fiction. On the wings of folklore Ellison's characters dream of God-become-Touissant L'Ouverture breathing fire and destruction on the Napoleonic soldiers, who prove as helpless as Pharaoh's army before holy wrath. Characters fly to the moon and to heaven; they meditate on the blackness of blackness and on the rebirth of a chosen people. And for Ellison it is vital that this added dimension be grounded not only in his private fantasy world but in the lore of black folk. What some critics have called experimental or surreal in Ellison's work is often merely folk matter, dramatically rendered.

V

In sum, no longer is it enough merely to inquire about an Afro-American poem, short story, or novel:
(1) Does this work upon folkloric sources?
(2) What are those sources?
(3) How authentic are the specific folklore items?
(4) Are the items cataloged by folklorists?

Ellison's fiction and criticism suggest that we begin with a series of other, more literary questions that address directly the relationship between some texts of actual "raw" folklore—transcribed sermons, blues, spirituals, tales, toasts, dozens—and the literary work. For example:

   (1) How does each story, rhyme, or song work as an act of language? What is the structure? How are characters presented? How does the figurative language operate?
   (2) What are the ritual functions of each folkloric process? What values does each reflect? What sense of life is implied?

With a clear idea of what the black folkloric processes are, we turn to Afro-American novels, short stories, plays, and poems, asking:

   (1) What (if any) folkloric processes operate in each work?
   (2) How does each literary work's structure, figurative language, or characterization reflect that of Afro-American folklore?
   (3) Does the folklore have ritualistic meaning in the literary work?
   (4) How do the uses of folkloric processes vary from literary work to literary work?
   (5) Is the folklore skillfully integrated into the structure and meaning of a particular literary work?
   (6) Does the use of folkloric processes succeed in enriching the fabric of the literary text? Does the folklore add resonance or creative tension to the literature?

Of course, as Ralph Ellison would be the first to say, many more questions remain to be asked about a given Afro-American poem, play, short story, or novel. But these questions are vital ones. For, as Ellison has said, black literature—if not *all* great art—is erected on the firm base of folklore.

Notes

1 See Robert Hemenway's "The Function of Folklore in Charles Chesnutt's *The Conjure Woman*," *Journal of the Folklore Institute*, 13
  (1976), 283–309.
2 The manuscript of *Chase the White Horse* is on file in the Library of
  Congress, Folklore Division.
3 *Stomping the Blues* (New York: McGraw-Hill, 1976).
4 See Ellison's "Blues People," *Shadow and Act* (New York: Random,
  1964), pp. 247–58.
5 See "The Art of Fiction: An Interview," *Shadow and Act*, pp. 167–93.
6 See "Sound and the Mainstream," *Shadow and Act*, pp. 185–258.
7 "A Very Stern Discipline," *Harper's*, March 1967, p. 80.
8 "Creative and Cultural Lag," *New Challenge*, 2 (Fall 1937), 90.
9 "Stormy Weather," *New Masses*, 24 Sept. 1940, pp. 20–21.
10 "Stormy Weather," p. 20.
11 "Stormy Weather," p. 20.
12 "Transition," *Negro Quarterly*, 1 (Spring 1942), 90–91.
13 See phonograph recordings by Rudi Ray Moore; also Richard Dorson, *America in Legend* (New York: Pantheon, 1973).
14 "Richard Wright's Blues," *Shadow and Act*, p. 79.
15 "Richard Wright's Blues," pp. 78–79, 94.
16 *The Writer's Voice*, ed. George Garrett (New York: Morrow, 1973),
  p. 226.
17 Leon Forrest, *There Is a Tree More Ancient than Eden* (New York:
  Random, 1973), p. 2.
18 "Change the Joke and Slip the Yoke," *Shadow and Act*, pp. 45–59.
19 "Change the Joke," p. 59.
20 *Invisible Man* (New York: Random, 1952), p. 222.
21 Murray, *The Omni-Americans* (New York: Outerbridge, 1970), p. 167.
22 *The Hero and the Blues* (St. Louis: Univ. of Missouri Press, 1973),
  p. 107.
23 See Robert B. Stepto, "Teaching Afro-American Literature: Survey on
  Tradition; or, The Reconstruction of Instruction," in this volume.
24 "Out of the Hospital and under the Bar," *Soon, One Morning*, ed.
  Herbert Hill (New York: Knopf, 1963), pp. 242–90.
25 "Night-Talk," *Quarterly Review of Literature*, 16 (1969), 329.
26 "Juneteenth," *Quarterly Review of Literature*, 3 (1965), 262–76.
27 "Juneteenth," p. 276.
28 *God's Trombones* (New York: Viking, 1927).
29 "Juneteenth," p. 272.
30 Lord Raglan, *The Hero* (London: Watts, 1936).
31 *Invisible Man*, p. 107.
32 "And Hickman Arrives," *Noble Savage*, (1960), 5–49.
33 Dorson, *Folklore and Fakelore* (Cambridge: Harvard Univ. Press,
  1976).
34 "Slim in Hell," *Folk-Say*, 4 (1932), 249.
35 "Did You Ever Dream Lucky?" *New World Writing*, 5 (April 1954),
  134–45.
36 Count Basie and Jimmy Rushing, "Blues in the Dark," Decca Record,
  DXSB-7170, Jan. 1938.
37 Kent, *Blackness and the Adventure of American Culture* (Chicago:
  Third World, 1972), pp. 152–63, 184–201.

Theory in
Practice

I. Introduction

One of the very special qualities of the Yale seminar that prompted this volume was the interplay between the theoretical discussion of literary issues surrounding the study of Afro-American literature and the pedagogical translation of those issues into practical classroom strategies for the teaching of the literature. The second part of this book addresses the "nuts and bolts" problem of how one may "reconstruct the instruction" of Afro-American literature.

The three essays on Frederick Douglass' *Narrative* of 1845 examine different literary problems within the same text, offering a constellation of approaches to textual analysis. In their diversity, they demonstrate an underlying principle of this volume: that Afro-American literature can withstand critical scrutiny and that it only yields the wealth of its linguistic properties through close "literary" reading.

In the first essay, Robert Stepto develops a generic approach to the study of Douglass' text, identifying four "modes of narration within the slave narrative, all of which have a direct bearing on the development of subsequent Afro-American narrative forms." His discussion of such issues as "authorial control," "authenticating strategies," and "voice" raises important questions about how slave narratives may and may not be autobiographies and how the impulses of both forms reverberate in contemporary Afro-American literature.

The second piece, by Robert O'Meally, reveals another dimension in the complexity of the text—the integration of folk elements, particularly the rhetorical forms of the black sermon, into the narrative style. In concentrating on Douglass' keen ear for language and form, O'Meally affirms the importance of the oral tradition to Afro-American literature. His remarks on various characteristics of the black folk sermon provide a backdrop against which Douglass' transformations of rhetoric into personal oratory are revealed. As O'Meally asserts, the *Narrative* is "a mighty text meant, of course, to be read. But it is also a text meant to be mightily preached."

If the *Narrative* is, as Stepto and O'Meally imply, in many ways a distinctly Afro-American text, does this mean that it does not draw features from other literary traditions as well? Henry-Louis Gates, Jr., addresses this question in the last essay on Douglass, discussing the influences of the picaresque novel and sentimental fiction on the *Narrative* specifically and, more generally, on the prose style of the day. Gates suggests that the slave narrative is "a 'counter-genre,' mediating between the novel of sentiment and the picaresque, oscillating somewhere between the two in a bipolar moment, set in motion by the mode of the Confession." Through a close study of the binary oppositions in Chapter One of the *Narrative*, Gates illustrates how Douglass preorders his world through language by means of a strategy of nearly simultaneous masking and disclosure. Here, then, in the *Narrative* is an expression of the "double consciousness" that prefigures much of Afro-American literature to come.

While these three approaches offer models for critically reading an individual text, "Afro-American Literature Course Designs" suggests more general strategies for organizing entire courses in Afro-American literature. The course designs presented here grew out of a series of workshops at the Yale seminar in which participants shared their experiences in teaching black literature and attempted to redesign courses in the literature based upon the critical issues presented at the seminar and collected here in the essays of Part I. As such, the course designs represent a preliminary effort to clarify several "literary," as opposed to "socio-historical," approaches to the study and teaching of Afro-American literature. They are not meant to be road maps for courses; rather, their value lies in the new spaces they open up in our thinking about Afro-American literature.

The two course designs offered under the rubric of the survey both focus on ways other than the chronological to organize a survey course, suggesting that the internal continuity of the course resides in the literary text itself rather than on its particular "place" in literary history. For example, the linguistic approach to teaching Afro-American literature takes as its organizing principle the concept of black speech as poetic diction, an approach that allows us to "consider how language is used in particular literary forms to represent both individual preferences and the varieties of language now available to black writers to attain their individual literary voices." The thematic approach to the survey, on the other hand, proposes an organization of individual texts around such common denominators as metaphors, ritualized actions, motifs, or ongoing artistic problems.

Following the survey course designs is a brief discussion of a generic approach to black literature, and the model here is a course design for teaching black poetry. Couched in the framework of the survey, this course design suggests ways to teach black poetry through considering the points of contact between oral and folk modes, some of which derive from Africa, and the formalized written models of the Anglo-American literary tradition.

Finally, there are three models that explore interdisciplinary approaches to the teaching of Afro-American literature, each building from the principle that an intertextual study may draw its texts from many genre and art forms, including song, painting, and dance, as well as written art. Indeed, as the discussions on survey and genre indicate, Afro-American literature is inextricably bound to its oral and folk roots and as such is as full of the "sounds" and "music" of culture as of its voices. The first interdisciplinary course design proposes ways to chart the transition of oral forms into written modes; the second course design explores the significance of geography or place within the literary tradition; and the last design examines black drama in terms of its reflection of ritual, both sacred and secular, within the black community.

Henry-Louis Gates has said that "a literary text is a linguistic event," and it is this "theory" that is put into "practice" in the essays on Douglass and in the course designs.

Until we perceive Afro-American literature as an act of language, we will have missed its complexity and gleaned only a fraction of what it contributes to the larger arena of humanistic endeavors.

Dexter Fisher

II. Three Studies
of Frederick
Douglass'
Narrative (1845)

Narration, Authentication, and Authorial Control in Frederick Douglass' *Narrative* of 1845

Robert B. Stepto

The strident, moral voice of the former slave recounting, exposing, appealing, apostrophizing, and above all, *remembering* his ordeal in bondage is the single most impressive feature of a slave narrative. This voice is striking not only because of what it relates but because the slave's acquisition of that voice is quite possibly his only permanent achievement once he escapes and casts himself upon a new and larger landscape. In their most elementary form, slave narratives are, however, full of other voices that are frequently just as responsible for articulating a narrative's tale and strategy. These other voices may be those of various "characters" in the "story," but mainly they are those found in the appended documents written by slaveholders and abolitionists alike. These documents—and voices—may not always be smoothly integrated with the former slave's tale, but they are nevertheless parts of the narrative. Their primary function is, of course, to authenticate the former slave's account; in doing so, they are at least partially responsible for the narratives being accepted as historical evidence. However, in literary terms, the documents collectively create something close to a dialogue—of forms as well as of voices—which suggests that in its primal state or first phase the slave narrative is an eclectic narrative form.

When the various forms (letters, prefaces, guarantees, tales) and their accompanying voices become integrated in the slave narrative text, we are presented with another type of basic narrative which I call an integrated narrative. This type of narrative represents the second phase of narration in the slave narrative and usually yields a more sophisticated text, wherein most of the literary and rhetorical functions previously performed by several texts and voices (the appended prefaces, letters, and documents as well as the tale) are now rendered by a loosely unified single text and voice. In this second phase, the authenticating documents "come alive" in the former slave's tale as speech and even action; and the former slave—often while assuming a deferential posture toward his white friends, editors, and guarantors—carries much of the burden of introducing and authenticating his own tale. In short, a second-phase narrative is a more sophisticated narrative because the former slave's voice assumes many more responsibilities than that of recounting the tale.

Because an integrated or second-phase narrative is less a collection of texts and more a unified narrative, we may say that, in terms of narration, the integrated narrative is in the process of becoming—irrespective of authorial intent—a generic narrative, by which I mean a narrative of discernible genre such as history, fiction, essay, or autobiography. This process is no simple "gourd vine" activity: An integrated narrative does not become a generic narrative "overnight," and, indeed, there are no assurances that in becoming a new type of narrative it is transformed automatically into a distinctive generic text. What we discover, then, is a third phase to slave narrative narration wherein two developments may occur: The integrated narrative (Phase II) is dominated either by its tale or by its authenticating strategies. In the first instance, the narrative and moral energies of the former slave's voice and tale so resolutely dominate those of the narrative's authenticating machinery (voices, documents, rhetorical strategies) that the narrative becomes in thrust and purpose far more metaphorical than rhetorical. When the integrated narrative becomes in this way a figurative account of action, landscape, and heroic self-transformation, it is so close generically to history, fiction, and autobiography that I term it a generic narrative.

In the second instance, the authenticating machinery either remains as important as the tale or actually becomes, usually for some purpose residing outside the text, the dominant and motivating feature of the narrative. Since this is also a sophisticated narrative phase, figurative presentations of action, landscape, and self may also occur, but such developments are rare and always ancillary to the central thrust of the text. When the authenticating machinery is dominant in this fashion, the integrated narrative becomes an authenticating narrative.

As these remarks suggest, one reason for investigating the phases of slave narrative narration is to gain a clearer view of how some slave narrative types become generic narratives and how, in turn, generic narratives—once formed, shaped, and set in motion by certain distinctly Afro-American cultural imperatives—have roots in the slave narratives. This bears as well on our ability to distinguish between narrative modes and forms and to describe what we see. When, for example, a historian or literary critic calls a slave narrative an autobiography, what he *sees* is, most likely, a narrative told in the first person that possesses literary features distinguishing it from the ordinary documents providing historical and sociological data. But a slave narrative is not necessarily an autobiography. We need to know the finer shades between the more easily discernible categories of narration, and we must discover whether these stops arrange themselves in progressive, contrapuntal, or dialectic fashion—or whether they possess any arrangement at all. As the scheme described above and diagrammed below suggests, I believe there are at least four identifiable modes of narration within the slave narrative, all of which have a direct bearing on the development of subsequent Afro-American narrative forms.

Phase I: basic narrative (a): "eclectic narrative"—authenticating documents and strategies (sometimes including one by the author of the tale) *appended* to the tale

Phase II: basic narrative (b): "integrated narrative"—authenticating documents and strategies integrated into the tale
and formally becoming voices and/or characters in the
tale

Phase III:

(a) "generic narrative"—authenticating documents and
strategies are totally subsumed by the tale; the slave
narrative becomes an identifiable generic text, e.g., autobiography, etc.

(b) "authenticating narrative"
—the tale is subsumed by the
authenticating strategy; the
slave narrative becomes an
authenticating document for
other, usually generic, texts,
e.g., novel, history

II

What we observe in the first two phases of slave narrative narration is the former slave's ultimate lack of control
over his own narrative occasioned primarily by the demands of audience and authentication. This dilemma is not
unique to the authors of these narratives; indeed, many
modern black writers still do not control their personal history once it assumes literary form. For this reason, Frederick Douglass' *Narrative of the Life of Frederick Douglass
an American Slave Written by Himself* (1845) seems all
the more a remarkable literary achievement. Because it
contains several segregated narrative texts—a preface, a
prefatory letter, the tale, an appendix—it appears to be, in
terms of the narrative phases, a rather primitive slave narrative. But each of the ancillary texts seems to be drawn to
the tale by some sort of extraordinary gravitational pull or
magnetic attraction. There is, in short, a dynamic energy
between the tale and each supporting text; the Douglass
narrative is an integrated narrative of a very special order.
While the integrating process does, in a small way, pursue

the conventional path of creating characters out of authenticating texts (Wm. Lloyd Garrison silently enters Douglass' tale at the very end), its new and major thrust is the creation of that aforementioned energy that binds the supporting texts to the tale while at the same time removing them from participation in the narrative's rhetorical and authenticating strategies. In short, Douglass' tale dominates the narrative and does so because it alone authenticates the narrative.

The introductory texts to the tale are two in number: a Preface by Wm. Lloyd Garrison, the famous abolitionist and editor of *The Liberator*; and a "Letter from Wendell Phillips, Esq.," who was equally renowned as an abolitionist, a crusading lawyer, and a judge. In theory, each of these introductory documents should be a classic guarantee written almost exclusively to a white reading public, concerned primarily and ritualistically with the white validation of a newfound black voice, and removed from the tale in such ways that the guarantee and tale vie silently and surreptitiously for control of the narrative as a whole. But these entries simply are not fashioned that way. To be sure, Garrison offers a conventional guarantee when he writes:

> Mr. DOUGLASS has very properly chosen to write his own Narrative, in his own style, and according to the best of his ability, rather than to employ some one else. It is, therefore, entirely his own production; and . . . it is, in my judgment, highly creditable to his head and heart.

And Phillips, while addressing Douglass, most certainly offers a guarantee to "another" audience as well:

> Every one who has heard you speak has felt, and, I am confident, every one who reads your book will feel, persuaded that you give them a fair specimen of the whole truth. No one-sided portrait,—no wholesale complaints,—but strict justice done, whenever individual kindliness has neutralized, for a moment, the deadly system with which it was strangely allied.

But these passages dominate neither the tone nor the substance of their respective texts.

Garrison is far more interested in writing history (specifically that of the 1841 Nantucket Anti-Slavery Convention and the launching of Douglass' career as a lecture agent for various antislavery societies) and recording his own place in it. His declaration, "I shall never forget his [Douglass'] first speech at the convention," is followed shortly thereafter by "*I rose*, and declared that Patrick Henry of revolutionary fame, never made a speech more eloquent in the cause of liberty. . . . *I reminded* the audience of the peril which surrounded this self-emancipated young man. . . . *I appealed* to them, whether they would ever allow him to be carried back into slavery,—law or no law, constitution or no constitution" (italics added). His Preface ends, not with a reference to Douglass or to his tale, but with an apostrophe very much like one he would use to exhort and arouse an antislavery assembly. In short, with the following cry, Garrison hardly guarantees Douglass' tale but reenacts his own abolitionist career instead:

> Reader! are you with the man-stealers in sympathy and purpose, or on the side of their down-trodden victims? If with the former, then are you the foe of God and man. If with the latter, what are you prepared to do and dare in their behalf? Be faithful, be vigilant, be untiring in your efforts to break every yoke, and let the oppressed go free. Come what may—cost what may—inscribe on the banner which you unfurl to the breeze, as your religious and political motto—NO COMPROMISE WITH SLAVERY! NO UNION WITH SLAVEHOLDERS!"

In the light of this closure and (no matter how hard we try to ignore it) the friction that developed between Garrison and Douglass in later years, we might be tempted to see Garrison's Preface at war with Douglass' tale for authorial control of the narrative as a whole. Certainly, there is a tension, but that tension is stunted by Garrison's enthusiasm for Douglass' tale:

> This *Narrative* contains many affecting incidents, many *passages* of great eloquence and power; but I think the most thrilling one of them all is the *description* DOUGLASS

> gives of his feelings, as he stood soliloquizing respecting
> his fate, and the chances of his one day being a free man.
> . . . Who can read that *passage*, and be insensible to its
> pathos and sublimity? (italics added)

What Garrison does, probably subconsciously, is an un-
usual and extraordinary thing—he becomes the first guarantor we have seen who not only directs the reader to the
tale but also acknowledges the tale's singular rhetorical
power. Thus, Garrison enters the tale by being at the
Nantucket Convention with Douglass in 1841 and by
authenticating the impact of the tale, not its facts. He fashions his own apostrophe, but finally he remains a member
of Douglass' audience far more than he assumes the posture of a competing or superior voice. In this way, Garrison's Preface stands outside Douglass' tale but is steadfastly
bound to it.

This is even more so the case for Wendell Phillips' "Letter." It contains passages that seem to be addressed to
credulous readers in need of a "visible" authority's guarantee, but by and large the "Letter" is directed to Frederick
Douglass alone. It opens with "My Dear Friend," and there
are many extraliterary reasons for wondering initially if the
friend is actually Frederick. Shortly thereafter, however,
Phillips declares, "I am glad the time has come when the
'lions write history,' " and it becomes clear that he not only
addresses Douglass but also writes in response to the tale.
These features, plus Phillips' specific references to how
Douglass acquired his "ABC" and learned of "where the
'white sails' of the Chesapeake were bound," serve to in-
tegrate Phillips' "Letter" into Douglass' tale. Above all, we
must see in what terms the "Letter" is a cultural and linguistic event: Like the Garrison document, it presents its
author as a member of Douglass' audience, but the act of
letterwriting, of correspondence, implies a moral and linguistic parity between a white guarantor and black author
that we have not seen before and that we do not always see
in American literary history *after* 1845. In short, the tone
and posture initiated in Garrison's Preface are completed
and confirmed in Phillips' "Letter," and while these documents are integrated into Douglass' tale, they remain
segregated outside the tale in the all-important sense that

they yield Douglass sufficient narrative and rhetorical space in which to render personal history in—and as—a literary form.

What marks Douglass' narration and control of his tale is his extraordinary ability to pursue several types of writing with ease and with a degree of simultaneity. The principal types of writing we discover in the tale are syncretic phrasing, introspective analysis, internalized documentation, and participant-observation. Of course, each of these types has its accompanying authorial posture, the result being that even the telling of the tale (as distinct from the content of the tale) yields a portrait of a complex individual marvelously facile in the tones, shapes, and dimensions of his voice.

Douglass' syncretic phrasing is often discussed, and the passage most widely quoted is probably "My feet have been so cracked with the frost, that the pen with which I am writing might be laid in the gashes." The remarkable clarity of this language needs no commentary, but what one admires as well is Douglass' ability to startlingly conjoin past and present and to do so with images that not only stand for different periods in his personal history but also, in their fusion, speak of his evolution from slavery to freedom. The pen, symbolizing the quest for literacy fulfilled, actually takes measure of the wounds of the past, and this measuring process becomes a metaphor in and of itself for the artful composition of travail transcended. While I admire this passage, the syncretic phrases I find even more intriguing are those that pursue a kind of acrid punning upon the names of Douglass' oppressors. A minor example appears early in the tale, when Douglass deftly sums up an overseer's character by writing, "Mr. Severe was rightly named: he was a cruel man." Here, Douglass is content with "glossing" the name; but late in the tale, just before attempting to escape in 1835, Douglass takes another oppressor's name and does not so much gloss it or play with it as *work upon* it to such an extent that, riddled with irony, it is devoid of its original meaning:

> At the close of the year 1834, Mr. Freeland again hired me of my master, for the year 1835. But, by this time, I began to want to live *upon free land* as well as *with Freeland*; and

> I was no longer content, therefore, to live with him or any other slaveholder.

Of course, this is effective writing—far more effective than what is found in the average slave narrative—but the point I wish to make is that Douglass seems to fashion these passages for both his readership and himself. Each example of his wit and increasing facility with language charts his ever-shortening path to literacy; thus, in their way, Douglass' syncretic phrases reveal his emerging comprehension of freedom and literacy and are another introspective tool by which he may benchmark his personal history.

But the celebrated passages of introspective analysis are even more pithy and direct. In these, Douglass fashions language as finely honed and balanced as an aphorism or Popean couplet, and thereby orders his personal history with neat, distinct, and credible moments of transition. When Mr. Auld forbids Mrs. Auld to instruct Douglass in the ABC, for example, Douglass relates:

> From that moment, I understood the pathway from slavery to freedom. . . . Whilst I was saddened by the thought of losing the aid of my kind mistress, I was gladdened by the invaluable instruction which, by the merest accident, I gained from my master.

The clarity of Douglass' revelation is as unmistakable as it is remarkable. As rhetoric, the passage is successful because its nearly extravagant beginning is finally rendered quite acceptable by the masterly balance and internal rhyming of "saddened" and "gladdened," which is persuasive because it is pleasant and because it offers the illusion of a reasoned conclusion.

Balance is an important feature of two other equally celebrated passages that quite significantly open and close Douglass' telling of his relations with Mr. Covey, an odd (because he worked in the fields alongside the slaves) but vicious overseer. At the beginning of the episode, in which Douglass finally fights back and draws Covey's blood, he writes:

You have seen how a man was made a slave; you shall see how a slave was made a man.

And at the end of the episode, to bring matters linguistically and narratively full circle, Douglass declares:

> I now resolved that, however long I might remain a slave in form, the day has passed forever when I could be a slave in fact. I did not hesitate to let it be known of me, that the white man who expected to succeed in whipping, must also succeed in killing me.

The sheer poetry of these statements is not lost on us, nor is the fact of why the poetry was created in the first place. One might suppose that in another age Douglass' determination and rage might take a more effusive expression, but I cannot imagine that to be the case. In the first place, his linguistic model is obviously scriptural; and in the second, his goal is the presentation of a historical self, not the record of temporary hysteria. This latter point persuades me that Douglass is about the business of discovering how personal history may be transformed into autobiography. Douglass' passages of introspective analysis almost single-handedly create fresh space for themselves in the American literary canon.

Instead of reproducing letters and other documents written by white guarantors within the tale or transforming guarantors into characters, Douglass internalizes documents that, like the syncretic and introspective passages, order his personal history. For example, Douglass' discussion of slave songs begins with phrases such as "wild songs" and "unmeaning jargon" but concludes, quite typically for him, with a study of how he grew to "hear" the songs and how the hearing affords yet another illumination of his path from slavery to freedom:

> I did not, when a slave, understand the deep meaning of those rude and apparently incoherent songs. I was myself within the circle; so that I neither saw nor heard as those without might see and hear. They told a tale of woe which was then altogether beyond my feeble comprehension. . . . Every tone was a testimony against slavery, and a prayer to

God for deliverance from chains. The hearing of those wild
notes always depressed my spirit, and filled me with ineffable sadness. I have frequently found myself in tears while
hearing them. The mere recurrence to those songs, even
now, afflicts me; and while I am writing these lines, an expression of feeling has already found its way down my
cheek.

The tears of the past and present interflow, and Douglass
not only documents his saga of enslavement but also, with
typical recourse to syncretic phrasing and introspective
analysis, advances his presentation of self.

Douglass' other internalized documents are employed
with comparable efficiency as we see in the episode where
he attempts an escape in 1835. In this episode, the document reproduced is the pass or "protection" Douglass
wrote for himself and his compatriots in the escape plan:

"This is to certify that I, the undersigned, have given the
bearer, my servant, full liberty to go to Baltimore, and
spend the Easter holidays. Written with mine own hand,
&c., 1835.
                                    "WILLIAM HAMILTON,
"Near St. Michael's, in Talbot county, Maryland."

The protection exhibits Douglass' increasingly refined sense
of how to manipulate language—he has indeed come a
long way from that day Mr. Auld halted his ABC lessons—
but even more impressive, I believe, is the act of reproducing the document itself. We know from the tale that when
their scheme was thwarted, each slave managed to destroy
his pass, so Douglass reproduces his language from memory, and there is no reason to doubt a single jot of his
recollection. My point here is simply that Douglass can
draw so easily from the wellsprings of memory because the
protection is not a mere scrap of memorabilia but rather a
veritable road sign on his path to freedom and literacy. In
this sense, his protection assumes a place in Afro-American
letters as a key antecedent to such documents as the fast-
yellowing notes of James Weldon Johnson's *Ex-Coloured
Man* and "The Voodoo of Hell's Half Acre" in Richard
Wright's *Black Boy*.

All of the types of narrative discourse discussed thus far

reveal features of Douglass' particular posture as a participant-observer narrator. But the syncretic phrases, introspective studies, and internalized documents only exhibit Douglass as a teller and doer, and part of the great effect of his tale depends upon what Douglass does not tell, what he refuses to reenact in print. Late in the tale, at the beginning of Chapter xi, Douglass writes:

> I now come to that part of my life during which I planned, and finally succeeded in making, my escape from slavery. But before narrating any of the peculiar circumstances, I deem it proper to make known my intention not to state all the facts connected with the transaction. . . . I deeply regret the necessity that impels me to suppress any thing of importance connected with my experience in slavery. It would afford me great pleasure indeed, as well as materially add to the interest of my narrative, were I at liberty to gratify a curiosity, which I know exists. . . . But I must deprive myself of this pleasure, and the curious gratification which such a statement would afford. I would allow myself to suffer under the greatest imputations which evil-minded men might suggest, rather than exculpate myself, and thereby run the hazard of closing the slightest avenue by which a brother slave might clear himself of the chains and fetters of slavery.

It has been argued that one way to test a slave narrative's authenticity is by gauging how much space the narrator gives to relating his escape as opposed to describing the conditions of his captivity. If the adventure, excitement, and perils of the escape seem to be the raison d'être for the narrative's composition, then the narrative is quite possibly an exceedingly adulterated slave's tale or a bald fiction. The theory does not always work perfectly: Henry "Box" Brown's narrative and that of William and Ellen Craft are predominantly recollections of extraordinary escapes, and yet, as far as we can tell, these are authentic tales. But the theory nevertheless has great merit, and I have often wondered to what extent it derives from the example of Douglass' tale and emotionally, if not absolutely rationally, from his fulminations against those authors who unwittingly excavate the underground railroad and expose it to the morally thin mid-nineteenth-century American air. Doug-

lass' tale is spectacularly free of suspicion, because he never
tells a detail of his escape to New York, and it is this
marvelously rhetorical omission or silence that both sophis-
ticates and authenticates his posture as a participant-observer narrator. When a narrator wrests this kind of
preeminent authorial control from the ancillary voices "circling" his narrative, we may say that he controls the
presentation of his personal history and that his tale is becoming autobiographical. In this light the last few sentences of Douglass' tale take on special meaning:

> But, while attending an anti-slavery convention at Nan-
> tucket, on the 11th of August, 1841, I felt strongly moved
> to speak. . . . It was a severe cross, and I took it up re-
> luctantly. The truth was, I felt myself a slave, and the idea
> of speaking to white people weighed me down. I spoke
> but a few moments, when I felt a degree of freedom, and
> said what I desired with considerable ease. From that time
> until now, I have been engaged in pleading the case of my
> brethren—with what success, and what devotion, I leave
> those acquainted with my labors to decide.

With these words, the narrative, as many have remarked,
comes full circle, taking us back, not to the beginning of
the *tale*, but rather to Garrison's prefatory remarks on the
Convention and Douglass' first public address. This return
may be pleasing in terms of the sense of symmetry it affords, but it is also a remarkable feat of rhetorical strategy: Having traveled with Douglass through his account of
his life, we arrive in Nantucket in 1841 to hear him speak
and, in effect, to become, along with Mr. Garrison, his
audience. The final effect is that Douglass reinforces his
posture as an articulate hero while supplanting Garrison as
the definitive historian of his past.

Even more important, I think, is the final image Douglass bestows of a slave shedding his last fetter and becoming a man by first finding his voice and then, as sure as light
follows dawn, speaking "with considerable ease." In one
brilliant stroke, the quest for freedom and literacy implied
from the start even by the narrative's title is resolutely
consummated.

The final text of the narrative, the Appendix, is a discourse by Douglass on his view of Christianity and Chris-

tian practice as opposed to what he exposed in his tale to be the bankrupt, immoral faith of slaveholders. As rhetorical strategy, the discourse is effective generally because it lends weight and substance to what passes for a conventional complaint of slave narrative narrators and because Douglass' exhibition of faith can only enhance his already considerable posture as an articulate hero. But more specifically, the discourse is most efficacious because at its heart lies a vitriolic poem written by a Northern Methodist minister, which Douglass introduces by writing

> I conclude these remarks by copying the following portrait of the religion of the south, (which is, by communion and fellowship, the religion of the north,) which I soberly affirm is "true to life," and without caricature or the slightest exaggeration.

The poem is strong and imbued with considerable irony, but what we must appreciate here is the effect of the white Northerner's poem conjoined with Douglass' authentication of the poem. The tables are clearly reversed. Douglass has controlled his personal history and at the same time fulfilled the prophecy suggested in his implicit authentication of Garrison's Preface: He has explicitly authenticated what is conventionally a white Northerner's validating text. Douglass' narrative thus offers what is unquestionably our best portrait in Afro-American letters of the requisite act of assuming authorial control. An author can go no further than Douglass did without writing all the texts constituting the narrative himself.

References

Blassingame, John W. *The Slave Community*. New York: Oxford Univ. Press, 1971.

Cox, James. "Autobiography and America." *Virginia Quarterly Review*, 47 (1971), 252–77.

Douglass, Frederick. *Narrative of the Life of Frederick Douglass an American Slave Written by Himself*. 1845; rpt. Cambridge: Belknap-Harvard Univ. Press, 1960.

Reed, Ishmael. *Mumbo Jumbo*. New York: Doubleday, 1972.

Stone, Albert E. "Identity and Art in Frederick Douglass' 'Narrative.' " *CLA Journal*, 17 (1973), 192–213.

Frederick Douglass' 1845 *Narrative*
The Text Was Meant to Be Preached

Robert G. O'Meally

Typically, scholars and teachers dealing with Frederick Douglass' *Narrative of the Life of an American Slave* (1845) are concerned with the crucial issue of religion, because the tensions and ironies generated by the sustained contrast between white and black religions constitute a vital "unity" in the work. Slavery sends Old Master to the devil, while the slave's forthright struggle for freedom is a noble, saving quest. Douglass' search for identity—paralleling the search of many and varied American autobiographers before him—is tightly bound with his quest for freedom and for truth. The *Narrative* presents scholars and teachers with a variety of religious questions. How does Douglass reconcile his professed Christianity with his evidently pagan faith in Sandy Jenkins' root? Why does Christian Douglass condone (even applaud!) the slaves' constant "sinning" against (lying to, stealing from, even the threatened killing of) the upholders of slavery? What is suggested by the fact that the most fervently religious whites treat their slaves more barbarously than do even the "unsaved" whites? While such topics are integral to a discussion of Douglass' *Narrative* and its relation to religion, they leave untouched a vital dimension of this broad subject.

The *Narrative* does more than touch upon questions often pondered by black preachers. Its very form and substance are directly influenced by the Afro-American preacher and his vehicle for ritual expression, the sermon. In this sense, Douglass' *Narrative* of 1845 *is* a sermon, and, specifically, it is a black sermon. This is a text meant to be read and pondered; it is also a Clarion call to spiritual affirmation and action: This is a text meant to be preached.

II

The Afro-American sermon is a folkloric process. More than a body of picturesque items for the catalog, the black sermon is a set of oratorical conventions and techniques used by black preachers in the context of the Sunday morning (or weeknight revival) worship service. The black sermon—especially as delivered in churches of independent denominations, which developed in relative isolation from white control—is distinctive in structure, in diction, and in the values it reflects.[1]

Certain aspects of the black sermon's structure vary greatly from preacher to preacher; indeed, the black congregation expects its preacher to have idiosyncrasies in his manner and form of presentation.[2] In keeping with the thinking of the seemingly remote American Puritans, black church men and women view their preacher's personal style and "voice" as bespeaking his discovery of a personal Christian identity and a home in Christiandom; each telling of The Story is as different in detail as each individual teller. In shaping his sermon, a black preacher may follow the American Puritan formula: doctrine, reasons, uses.[3] Or he may use a historical, an analytical, or a narrative scheme for organizing his presentation of the Word. In any case, most Afro-American preachers pace themselves with care, beginning slowly, perhaps with citations from the Bible, or with a prayer, or with a deliberate statement and restatement of the topic for the day.

Most black preachers also build toward at least one ringing crescendo in their sermons, a point when their words are rhythmically sung or chanted in a modified, "ritual" voice. Here the call-response pattern is most marked; the preacher's words are answered by the congregation's phrases, "All right!" "Yes, brother!" "Say *that!*" Sometimes the preacher will rock in rhythm and chant visions of golden heaven and warnings of white-hot hell to his listeners. Sometimes he becomes "laughing-happy" as he walks the pulpit, declaring in words half-sung, half-spoken, how glad he is to be saved by the grace of the Lord.[4] In this crescendo section of the sermon, the highly rhythmical language is closer to poetry than it is to prose. Such chanting may occur only at the conclusion of the sermon, or there may be several such poetical sections. In them the preacher seems possessed; the words are not his own, but the Spirit's.

Classic rhetorical and narrative techniques also abound in the Afro-American sermon. One notes the rich use of metaphors and figures of speech, such as repetitions, apostrophes, puns, rhymes, and hyperboles. A good preacher will not just report as a third-person narrator what the Bible says, but he will address the congregation as a first-person observer: "I can see John," the preacher might say, "walking in Jerusalem *early* one Sunday morning."[5] He is a master of rhetorical and narrative devices.

Characteristically, too, Afro-American sermons are replete with stories from the Bible, folklore, current events, and virtually any source whatsoever.[6] Whether or not this storytelling aspect of the black preacher is an African "survival," as some researchers claim, the consistent use of stories determines the black sermon's characteristic structure. Some stories may provide the text for a sermon, while others occur repeatedly as background material.

James Weldon Johnson notes that certain narrative "folk sermons" are repeated in pulpits Sunday after Sunday.[7] Or, a section of one well-known sermon may be affixed to another sermon. Some of these "folk sermons" include "The Valley of Dry Bones," based on Ezekiel's vision; the "Train Sermon," in which God and Satan are portrayed as train conductors transporting saints and sinners to heaven and to hell; and the "Heavenly March," featuring man on his lengthy trek from a fallen world to a heavenly home. Johnson's own famous poem, "The Creation," is based on another "folk sermon" in which the preacher narrates the story of the world from its birth to the day of final Judgment.[8]

Black sermons are framed in highly figurative language. Using tropes, particularly from the Bible, spirituals, and other sermons, the black preacher's language—especially in chanted sections of his sermon—is often dramatic and full of imagery. In one transcription of a black sermon, a preacher speaks in exalted language of the Creator's mightiness:

> I vision God wringing
> A storm from the heavens
> Rocking the world
> Like an earthquake;
> Blazing the sea
> Wid a trail er fire.
> His eye the lightening's flash,
> His voice the thunder's roll.
> Wid one hand He snatched
> The sun from its socket,
> And the other He clapped across the moon.
> I vision God standing
> On a mountain
> Of burnished gold,
> Blowing his breath
> Of silver clouds
> Over the world,
> His eye the lightening's flash,
> His voice the thunder's roll.[9]

Like other American preachers, the black preacher speaks to his listeners' hearts as well as to their minds. He persuades his congregation not only through linear, logical argumentation but also through the skillful painting of word pictures and the dramatic telling of stories. His tone is exhortative: He implores his listeners to save themselves from the flaming jaws of hell and to win a resting place in heaven. The black preacher may speak in mild, soothing prose, or he may, filled with the spirit, speak in the fiery, poetical tongue of the Holy Spirit. The black preacher's strongest weapon against the devil has been his inspired use of the highly conventionalized craft of sacred black oratory—a folkloric process.

III

The influences of the black sermon on black literature have been direct and constant. The Afro-American playwright, poet, fiction writer, and essayist have all drawn from the Afro-American sermon. Scenes in black literature occur in church; characters recollect particularly inspiring or oppressive sermons; a character is called upon to speak and falls into the cadences of the black sermon, using the familiar Old Testament black sermonic stories and images. In his essays, James Baldwin, who preached when he was in his teens, employs the techniques of the sermon as he speaks to his readers' hearts and souls about their sins and their hope for salvation.[10] Just as one finds continuity in tone and purpose from the sermons of the Puritans to the essays of such writers as Emerson and Thoreau, one discovers continuity in the Afro-American literary tradition from the black sermon—still very much alive in the black community—to the Afro-American narrative, essay, novel, story, and poem.

What, then, is *sermonic* about Douglass' *Narrative*? First of all, the introductory notes by William Lloyd Garrison and Wendell Phillips, both fiery orators and spearheads of the abolition movement, prepare the reader for a spiritual message. In his Preface, Garrison recalls Douglass' first speech at an antislavery convention. Thunderous applause follows the ex-slave's words, and Garrison says, "I never hated slavery so intensely as at that moment; certainly my perception of the enormous outrage which is inflicted by it, on the godlike nature of its victims was rendered far more clear." And then, in stormy, revivalist style, Garrison rises and appeals to the convention, "whether they would ever allow him [Douglass] to be carried back into slavery,—law or no law, constitution or no constitution. The response was unanimous and in thunder—tones—'No!' 'Will you succor and protect him as a brother-man—a resident of the old Bay State?' 'Yes!' shouted the whole mass."[11]

As if introducing the preacher of the hour, Garrison says that Douglass "excels in pathos, wit, comparison, imitation, strength of reasoning, and fluency of language" (p. 7).

Moreover, in Douglass one finds "that union of head and heart, which is indispensable to an enlightenment of the heads and winning the hearts of others. . . . May he continue to 'grow in grace, and in the knowledge of God' that he may be increasingly serviceable in the cause of bleeding humanity, whether at home or abroad" (p. 7). As for Douglass' present narrative, says Garrison, it grips its readers' hearts:

> He who can peruse it without a tearful eye, a heaving breast, an afflicted spirit,—without being filled with an unutterable abhorrence of slavery and all its abettors, and animated with a determination to seek the immediate overthrow of that execrable system,—without trembling for the fate of this country in the hands of a righteous God, who is ever on the side of the oppressed, and whose arm is not shortened that it cannot save,—must have a flinty heart, and be qualified to act the part of a trafficker "in slaves and the souls of men." (p. 9)

The choices, Garrison states, are but two: enrollment in the righteous war against slavery or participation in the infernal traffic in "the souls of men."

In his turn, Wendell Phillips prepares the way for Douglass' "sermon." In his laudatory letter to the author, Phillips speaks of Southern white slave masters as infrequent "converts." Most often, the true freedom fighter detests slavery in his heart even "before he is ready to lay the first stone of his anti-slavery life" (p. 18). Phillips thanks Douglass especially for his testimony about slavery in parts of the country where slaves are supposedly treated most humanely. If things are so abominable in Maryland, says Phillips, think of slave life in "that Valley of the Shadow of Death, where the Mississippi sweeps along" (p. 18).

Douglass' account of his life serves the ritual purpose announced in the prefatory notes: The ex-slave comes before his readers to try to save their souls. His purpose is conversion. In incident upon incident, he shows the slaveholder's vile corruption, his lust and cruelty, his appetite for unchecked power, his vulgarity and drunkenness, his cowardice, and his damning hypocrisy. Slavery, says Douglass, brings sin and death to the slaveholder. Come to the abolition movement, then, and be redeemed. Take, as Douglass has done, the abolitionist paper as a Bible and freedom for all men as your heaven. Addressed to whites, the *Narrative* is a sermon pitting the dismal hell of slavery against the bright heaven of freedom.

Douglass' portrayal of himself and of his fellow slaves is in keeping with the text's ritual function. Like a preacher, he has been touched by God, *called* for a special, holy purpose. Providence protects Douglass from ignorance and despair. Providence selects him to extend his vision of freedom and, concretely, to move to Baltimore. The unexplained selection of Douglass to go to Baltimore he sees as "the first plain manifestation of that kind providence which has ever attended me, and marked my life with so many favors" (p. 56). Of this "providential" removal to Baltimore Douglass further writes:

> I may be deemed superstitious, and even egotistical, in regarding this event as a special interposition of divine Providence in my favor. But I should be false to the earliest sentiments of my soul, if I suppressed the opinion. . . . From my earliest recollection, I date the entertainment of a deep conviction that slavery would not always be able to hold me within its foul embrace; and in the darkest hours of my career in slavery, this living word of faith and spirit of hope departed not from me, but remained like ministering angels to cheer me through the gloom. This good spirit was from God, and to him I offer thanksgiving and praise. (p. 56)

In his effort to convert white slaveholders and to reassure white abolitionists, Douglass attempts to refute certain racist conceptions about blacks. He presents blacks as a heroic people suffering under the lash of slavery but struggling to stay alive to obtain freedom. To convince whites to aid slaves in their quest for freedom Douglass tackles the crude, prejudiced assumptions—which slavers say are upheld by Scripture—that blacks somehow *deserve* slavery, that they enjoy and feel protected under slavery. Of the notion that blacks are the cursed descendants of Ham, Douglass writes, "if the lineal descendants of Ham are alone to be scripturally enslaved, it is certain that slavery at the south must soon become unscriptural; for thousands are ushered into the world, annually, who, like myself, owe their existence to white fathers, and those fathers most frequently their own masters" (p. 27). Furthermore, if cursed, what of the unshakable conviction of the learned and eloquent Douglass that he is, in fact, chosen by God to help set black people free?

What, then, of the assumption of the plantation novel and the minstrel show that blacks are contented with "their place" as slaves at the crushing bottom of the American social order? Douglass explains that a slave answers affirmatively to a stranger's question, "Do you have a kind master?" because the questioner may be a spy hired by the master. Or the slave on a very large plantation who complains about his master to a white stranger may later learn that the white stranger was, in fact, his master. One slave makes this error with Colonel Lloyd, and, in a few weeks, the complainer is told by his overseer that, for finding fault with his master, he is now being sold into Georgia. Thus, if a slave says his master is kind, it is because he has learned the maxim among his brethren "A still tongue makes a wise head." By suppressing the truth rather than taking the consequences of telling it foolishly, slaves "prove themselves a part of the human family" (p. 43).

At times, slaves from different plantations may argue or even fight over who has the best, the kindest, or the manliest master. "Slaves are like other people and imbibe prejudices quite common to others," explains Douglass. "They think their own better than that of others." Simultaneously, however, slaves who publicly uphold their masters' fairness and goodness, "execrate their masters" privately (p. 43).

Do not the slaves' songs prove their contentedness and joy in bondage? "It is impossible," says Douglass, "to conceive of a greater mistake." Indeed, he says,

> The songs of the slave represent the sorrows of his heart; and he is relieved by them, only as an aching heart is relieved by its tears. At least, such is my experience. I have often sung to drown my sorrow, but seldom to express my happiness. Crying for joy, and singing for joy, were alike uncommon to me while in the jaws of slavery. (p. 38)

Instead of expressing mirth, these songs Douglass heard as a slave "told a tale of woe which was then altogether beyond my feeble comprehension; they were tones loud, long, and deep; they breathed the prayer and complaint of souls boiling over with the bitterest anguish. Every tone was a testimony against slavery, and a prayer to God for deliverance from chains." These songs, Douglass recalls, gave him his "first glimmering conception of the dehumanizing character of slavery" (p. 37). In other words, these songs "prove" the black man's deep, complex humanity. Therefore, whites, come forth, implies Douglass, and join the fight to free these God's children!

The tone of Douglass' *Narrative* is unrelentingly exhortative. Slaveholders are warned that they tread the road toward hell, for even as their crimes subject the slave to misery, they doom the master to destruction. Douglass describes his aged grandmother's abandonment in an isolated cabin in the woods. Then in dramatic, rhythmical language, he warns that,

> My poor old grandmother, the devoted mother of twelve children, is left all alone, in yonder hut, before a few dim embers. She stands—she sits—she staggers—she falls—she groans—she dies—and there are none of her children or grandchildren present, to wipe from her wrinkled brow the cold sweat of death, or to place beneath the sod her fallen remains. Will not a righteous God visit for these things? (p. 78)

Later in the text, Douglass exhorts white readers to sympathize with the escaping slave's plight. To comprehend the escapee's situation, the white sympathizer "must needs experience it, or imagine himself in similar circumstances" (p. 144). In a voice one imagines to be as strong and varied in pitch as a trombone, Douglass reaches a crescendo, in black sermon style, when speaking in highly imagistic language of the white man who would comprehend the escaped slave's feelings:

> Let him be a fugitive slave in a strange land—a land given up to be the hunting ground for slaveholders—whose inhabitants are legalized kidnappers—where he is every

moment subjected to the terrible liability of being seized upon by his fellowmen, as the hideous crocodile seizes upon his prey!—I say, let him place himself in my situation—without home or friends—without money or credit—wanting shelter, and no money to buy it,—and at the same time let him feel that he is pursued by merciless men-hunters, and in total darkness as to what to do, where to go, or where to stay,—perfectly helpless both as to the means of defence and means of escape,—in the midst of plenty, yet suffering the terrible gnawings of hunger,—in the midst of houses, yet having no home,—among fellow-men, yet feeling as if in the midst of wild beasts, whose greediness to swallow up the trembling and half-famished fugitive is only equalled by that with which the monsters of the deep swallow up the helpless fish upon which they subsist,—I say, let him be placed in that most trying situation,—the situation in which I was placed,—then, and not till then, will he fully appreciate the hardships of, and know how to sympathize with, the toil-worn and whip-scarred fugitive slave. (p. 144)

In this passage Douglass, like a black preacher, uses a variety of oratorical techniques: alliteration, repetition, parallelism. Also, using conjunctions, commas, and dashes, Douglass indicates the dramatic pauses between phrases and the surging rhythms in the sermon-like prose.

Like a sermon, too, Douglass' *Narrative* argues not only by stern reason but also with tales that may be termed *parables*. One of the most forceful of these parables, one threaded quite successfully into the *Narrative*, is the parable of poor Mrs. Auld. Residing in the border state of Maryland, in the relatively large city of Baltimore, Mrs. Auld, who has never owned a slave before she owns Frederick Douglass, is truly a good woman. Before her marriage, Mrs. Auld worked as a weaver, "dependent upon her own industry for a living." When eight-year-old Douglass is brought into the Auld household, Mrs. Auld is disposed to treat him with human respect and kindness. Indeed, "her face was made of heavenly smiles, and her voice was tranquil music." Douglass obviously presents this woman as a glowing model of Christian charity: "When I went there," he writes, "she was a pious, warm, and tender-hearted woman. There was no sorrow or suffering for which she had not a tear. She had bread for the hungry, clothes for the naked, and comfort for every mourner within her reach" (p. 64). Soon after Douglass arrives in her home, Mrs. Auld begins to do as she has done for her own son; she commences teaching Douglass the alphabet.

Before long, of course, this "kind heart" is blasted by the "fatal poison of irresponsible power" (p. 57). In Douglass' words, Mrs. Auld's "cheerful eye, under the influence of slavery, soon became red with rage; that voice, made all of sweet accord, changed to one of harsh and horrid discord; and that angelic face gave place to that of a demon" (p. 58). In response to her husband's warning that education "would *spoil* the best nigger in the world," she forbids Douglass' further instruction. In fact, she becomes at last "even more violent than her husband himself" in the application of this precept that slave education is a danger (p. 58). Thus, even the mildest forms of slavery—in providential Baltimore—turn the most angelic face to that of a "harsh and horrid" devil.

The central paradox of the story of Mrs. Auld is that Mr. Auld's vitriolic warning against learning actually serves to make Douglass double his efforts to gain literacy. Mr. Auld's words to his wife prove prophetic:

> "Now," said he, "if you teach that nigger . . . how to read, there would be no keeping him. It would forever unfit him to be a slave. He would at once become unmanageable, and of no value to his master. As to himself, it could do him no good, but a great deal of harm. It would make him discontented and unhappy. (p. 58)

Douglass overhears this warning and feels that at last he comprehends the source of the white man's power to enslave blacks. "From that moment," writes Douglass, "I understood the pathway from slavery to freedom." Also, from that moment on, Douglass' holy search for identity and freedom is knotted to his determined quest for literacy and knowledge. For the skill of literacy, "I owe almost as much to the bitter opposition of my master," writes Douglass, "as to the kindly aid of my mistress. I acknowledge the benefit of both" (p. 59). It is as if the providentially guided Douglass receives truth from the mouths of family and friends, and even from the mouths of his most indefatigable enemies. And like a preacher he reports his successes (the Good Word) in exalted prose and in parables.

A second major parable in the *Narrative* concerns the slave-breaker Edward Covey and the wise old slave Sandy Jenkins. Like Mrs. Auld, Covey is a hard worker whose diligence fails to shield him from the blight of slavery. Sent to Covey's plantation to be "broken," Douglass, in a sense, breaks Covey. Douglass leaves the slave-breaker's plantation stronger than ever in his personal resolution to break free. At first, the deceptive Covey, with his killing work schedule and "tiger-like" ferocity, seems to have succeeded in "taming" Douglass. "I was broken," says Douglass, "in body, soul, and spirit. My natural elasticity was crushed, my intellect languished, the disposition to read departed, the cheerful spark that lingered about my eye died; the dark night of slavery closed in upon me; and behold a man transformed into a brute!" (p. 95). On Sundays, his only free day, Douglass would lounge in a "beast-like stupor" under a tree. His thoughts of killing himself and Covey are checked only by fear and dim hope.

Somehow, though, Douglass' spirits are rekindled. First, he observes the white sails of the ships piloting the Chesapeake Bay—through identification with their bold freedom, and through soliloquies to them and to God, Douglass finds his hopes revived. He too will try to sail to freedom. Quoting a line from a spiritual, he says, "There is a better day coming" (p. 97).

Second, he faces down Covey. "You have seen how a man was made a slave," writes Douglass. "You shall see how a slave was made a man" (p. 97). One day he faints and is unable to do his work. Covey orders him to arise and return to his labor, but Douglass says, "I made no effort to comply, having now made up my mind to let him do his worst." Then Douglass runs off to his master, Mr. Thomas Auld, to express fear that Covey will kill him. But Auld merely sends Douglass back to the slave-breaker. Back at Covey's, Douglass is chased into the woods by the slave-breaker, who wields a cowskin. Ordinarily, running away

could only make things worse for Douglass: "My behavior," he says, "was altogether unaccountable" (p. 101).
Providence seems to be with him though. In the woods,
Douglass meets his old acquaintance Sandy Jenkins, who
advises him to return to Covey. But Jenkins does not send
Douglass back to Covey unarmed. Jenkins directs Douglass
to a part of the woods where he can find a certain root,
which, Douglass says, "if I would take some of it with me,
carrying it *always on my right side*, would render it impossible for Mr. Covey, or any other white man, to whip me"
(p. 102). In the years that he has carried his root, Jenkins
says, he had never been beaten, and he never expects to be
again. Douglass seeks relief from Covey by petition to
Auld, then by attempted escape, and then by the spiritual
guidance—dependent upon personal fortitude and faith—
symbolized by the old slave's root.

Upon his return to Covey's, Douglass is spared an initial
attack, presumably because Covey, a leader in his church,
does not want to work or whip slaves on Sunday. Monday
morning, however, Covey comes forth with a rope and—
"from whence came the spirit I don't know," says Douglass
—the slave resolves to fight. They fight for nearly two
hours, Douglass emerging unscarred and Covey bloodied.
This fight marks an important rite of passage for Douglass:

> This battle with Mr. Covey was the turning-point in my
> career as a slave. It rekindled the few expiring embers of
> freedom, and revived within me a sense of my own man-
> hood. It recalled the departed self-confidence, and inspired
> me again with a determination to be free. . . . I now re-
> solved that, however long I might remain a slave in form,
> the day had passed forever when I could be a slave in fact.
> I did not hesitate to let it be known of me, that the white
> man who expected to succeed in whipping, must also
> succeed in killing me.
>
> From this time I was never again what might be called
> fairly whipped, though I remained a slave four years after-
> wards. I had several fights, but was never whipped. (p. 105)

Thus we see Douglass, Providence's hero, maneuvering
through deadly dangers. His straightforwardness and courage defeat the serpentine and Pharisee-like Covey. Doug-

lass' hope returns through identification with the white sails on the Bay. He is also given heart by the root, a symbol of spiritual and natural power as well as of the supreme power of hope and faith.

As in a successful black sermon, these parables are well woven into the whole cloth of the *Narrative*. They illustrate the corrupting power of slavery upon whites; they illustrate the power of the slave to overcome the slaveowner and to return, mysteriously—and by the power of Providence—to the winding road to freedom. Douglass' *Narrative* is alive with allusions to the Bible. Inevitably, the war waged is between the devil of slavery and the righteous, angry God of freedom. Chapter iii commences with a description of Colonel Lloyd's garden. In its beauty and power to tempt, this "large and finely cultivated garden" recalls the Garden of Eden:

> This garden was probably the greatest attraction of the place. During the summer months, people came from far and near—from Baltimore, Easton, and Annapolis—to see it. It abounded in fruits of almost every description, from the hardy apple of the north to the delicate orange of the south. This garden was not the least source of trouble on the plantation. Its excellent fruit was quite a temptation to the hungry swarms of boys, as well as the older slaves, belonging to the colonel, few of whom had the virtue or the vice to resist it. (p. 39)

This Eden, though carefully tended as God commanded, is vile and corrupt. Colonel Lloyd, merciless owner of the garden and gardeners, forbids the slaves to eat any of its excellent fruits. To enforce his rule he has tarred the garden fence; any slave with tar on his person was deemed guilty of fruit theft and was "severely whipped." This is an Eden controlled not by God but by greedy, selfish, slaveholding man.

Or is this garden under the charge of the devil? As noted, slavery turns the heart of "heavenly" Mrs. Auld to flinty stone. And Mr. Plummer, Douglass' first overseer, is "a miserable drunkard, a profane swearer" known to "cut and slash women's heads so horribly" that even the master becomes enraged. This enraged master, Captain Anthony, *himself* seems "to take great pleasure in whipping a slave." In a grueling scene, he whips Douglass' aunt Hester, a favorite of Anthony's, until only the master's fatigue stops the gory spectacle. "The louder she screamed, the harder he whipped; and where the blood ran fastest, there he whipped longest" (p. 28). Mr. Severe would curse and groan as he whipped the slave women, seeming "to take pleasure in manifesting this fiendish barbarity." Colonel Lloyd renders especially vicious beatings to slaves assigned to the care of his horses. When a horse "did not move fast enough or hold high enough," the slaves were punished. "I have seen Colonel Lloyd make old Barney, a man between fifty and sixty years of age, uncover his bald head, kneel down upon the cold, damp ground, and receive upon his naked and toil-worn shoulders more than thirty lashes at the time" (p. 41). Other slaveowners and overseers, both men and women, kill their slaves in cold blood.

One of the men termed "a good overseer" by the slaves is Mr. Hopkins, who, at least is not quite so profane, noisy, or cruel as his colleagues. "He whipped, but seemed to take no pleasure in it." His tenure as overseer is a short one, conjectures Douglass, because he lacks the brutality and severity demanded by the master.

Covey is the most devil-like slaveholder in the *Narrative*. Hypocritical, masterful at deception, clever, untiring, seemingly omnipresent, Covey is called "The Snake" by the slaves. In one of the *Narrative*'s most unforgettable portraits, Douglass tells us that through a cornfield where Covey's slaves work, The Snake would:

> . . . sometimes crawl on his hands and knees to avoid detection, and all at once he would rise nearly in our midst, and scream out, "Ha, ha! Come, come! Dash on, dash on!" This being his mode of attack, it was never safe to stop a single minute. His comings were like a thief in the night. He appeared to us as being ever at hand. He was under every tree, behind every stump, in every bush, and at every window, on the plantation. He would sometimes mount his horse, as if bound to St. Michael's, a distance of seven miles, and in half an hour afterwards you would see him coiled up in the corner of the woodfence, watching every motion of the slaves. (p. 92)

The Snake has built his reputation on being able to reduce spirited men like Douglass to the level of docile, manageable slaves. Under Covey's dominion—before Douglass
gains a kind of dominion over Covey—Douglass feels himself "transformed into a brute. " In the symbolic geography
of this text the Garden is ruled—at least for the moment—
by none other than his majesty, the infernal Snake, Satan.

   Douglass makes clear that slavery, not the slaveowner, is
the supreme Devil in this text: slavery, with its "robes
crimsoned with the blood of millions." Mrs. Auld falls from
"heavenliness" to the hell of slavery. As a boy Douglass
learns from Sheridan's speeches in behalf of Catholic
emancipation that "the power of truth [holds sway] over
the conscience of even a slaveholder" (p. 66). These white
slaveholders, if devil-like, are nonetheless capable of redemption.

   Colonel Lloyd, in fact, is described as possessing wealth
equal almost to that of Job—the Old Testament's model of
supreme faithfulness. Finally, however, the effect of the
comparison is ironical, for Lloyd is a man of increasing
cruelty; his very wealth seems to provide his temptation to
do evil, and Lloyd yields to temptation with relish.

   There are several places in the *Narrative* where American slavery is compared with the holding of the Old Testament Jews in captivity. Douglass points out that, the more
he read, the more he viewed his enslavers as "successful
robbers, who had left their homes, and gone to Africa, and
stolen us from our homes, and *in a strange land* reduced us
to slavery" (italics mine). Later in the *Narrative* Douglass
describes the fugitive slave in the North as a dweller "in a
strange land." The language here and the parallel situations recall the biblical psalm that reads

> By the rivers of Babylon, there we
> sat down, yea, we wept, when
> we remembered Zion
>   we hanged our harps upon the
> willows in the midst thereof.
>   For there they that carried us away
> captive required of us a song; and
> they that wasted us required of us
> mirth, saying, Sing us one of the
> songs of Zion

How shall we sing the Lord's
Song in a strange land?[12]

This allusion is even more suggestive when one considers
Douglass' careful explanation of the slaves' songs, demanded, in a sense, and misunderstood by the captors,
who, thinking the songs joyous, feel the more justified in
their ownership of the black singers.

In the *Narrative*, Douglass calls on the Old Testament
God to free His black children. "For what does he hold the
thunders in his right hand, if not to smite the oppressor,
and deliver the spoiled out of the hand of the spoiler?" (p.
96). Douglass also manifests certain characteristics of an
Old Testament hero. He becomes Daniel, blessed with
supernatural powers of perception and protected by God's
special favor. Like Daniel, thrown into a den of lions for
refusing to refrain from praying, Douglass never loses faith
while he lives in the very "jaws of slavery." Upon being
returned from the Lloyd Plantation to Baltimore, Douglass
felt he had "escaped a worse than lion's jaws" (p. 100).
Captain Auld in St. Michael's was a vicious, ineffectual
master who, Douglass tells us, "Might have passed for a
lion, but for his ears" (p. 83). Escaping for a brief time
from Covey, Douglass, sick and scarred, returns to Auld.
The runaway slave supposes himself to have "looked like a
man who had escaped a den of wild beasts, and barely
escaped them" (p. 100). Unlike Daniel, Douglass actually
has to battle with the lions, tigers, and "the Snake" in the
den of slavery. Like Daniel, though, he is protected, and
once he has Sandy's root on his right side he can never be
beaten. Providentially, too, Douglass is eventually rescued
from the crushing jaws of slavery.

Douglass' account of his life follows the pattern of the
life of a mythic or historic hero—or a hero of Scripture.
His birth, if not virginal, as is so often the case with the
archetypal hero, is cloaked in mystery. He is never sure
who his father is or even when, exactly, he himself was
born. Nor does he feel very close to his natural family;
slavery kept mother from son, and brother from sister, so
that natural familial bonds were felt only remotely. Like
Joseph (the biblical son sold into slavery by his brothers)

and like Moses, Douglass feels sure he has been selected by heaven for special favor. And like Jesus, he prays for redemption and resurrection from "the coffin of slavery to the heaven of freedom" (p. 105). Christ-like, too, is Douglass' faltering faith at the torturous nadir of his enslavement. Under Covey's lash, Douglass nearly surrenders to the bestial slave system, and to murder and suicide. But Douglass turns from the false religion of such "Pharisees" as Covey; like Jesus, Douglass criticizes white institutionalized worship but clings to his faith in a personal Father.

Douglass' personal sense of ethics contradicts the codes of such men as Covey. For instance, Douglass hails the slave's trickery of the master as wit, if not wisdom. Douglass also approves the attempted assassination of a black informer on runaway slaves; such is justice. Moreover, although Douglass disclaims "ignorant" and "superstitious" belief in the power of the root, his true feeling about root power emerges from the *Narrative*. Clearly, the root, be it pagan or nonpagan, gives Douglass the strength to master Covey. This "superstition" seems no contradiction in Douglass, for he is presented as a hero who transcends strict adherence to existing law. He is the possessor of pure religion; God speaks directly to him. Like a Christ or a Moses, he not only follows God's law, he *gives* the law. Clearly, this pure, felt religion of real experience with Providence is not the religion of the white slaveholding churchmen who merely use Christianity to justify their crimes.

Douglass' rejection of the slaveholder's false religion parallels the rejection of popular conceptions of God by such diverse American writers as Benjamin Franklin, Thomas Paine, and—writing a full century after the *Narrative*'s publication—James Baldwin.[13] Like these writers, Douglass replaces the hollow religion of form for a deep, personal religion—in his case, the religion of abolition, which he practices and preaches with fervent passions.

Furthermore, like many black preachers, Douglass' true religion is a practical one that seeks a "heaven" on earth as well as on high. Salvation is not only a personal matter; Douglass labors for the freedom of a *people*. Once free (or at least freer) in Massachusetts, he joins the abolition movement: "It was a severe cross," he writes, "and I took it

up reluctantly." His *Narrative* is, then, not only the spiritual journey of one soul but also a testimony and a warning, written with the earnest hope that it "may do something toward throwing light on the American slave system,
and hastening the glad day of deliverance to the millions of
my brethren" (p. 162). Like a black sermon, it is the story
of a people under the guidance of Providence.

Douglass' message is the message of the progressive
black preacher: Be hopeful and faithful, but do not fail to
fight for the freedom of your brother men. Douglass recognizes that the God of freedom respects the slave who may
lie, cheat, steal, or even kill to stay alive and to struggle for
freedom. This freedom ethic, "preached" by Douglass, was
in the tradition of many militant black preachers, including
the black preacher and pamphleteer, Rev. Henry Highland
Garnet.[14]

Douglass' *Narrative* is, in its way, a holy book—one full
of marvels, demonstrating God's active participation in a
vile and fallen world. The *Narrative* is a warning of the
terror of God's fury. It is also an account of a black Moses'
flight "from slavery to freedom." It is an invitation to join
"the church" of abolition, a church that offers freedom not
only to the slave and the sympathetic white Northerner
but also to the most murderous and bloodthirsty Southern
dealers in human flesh. Sinners, Douglass seems to chant,
black sermon-style, you are in the hands of an angry God!

Clearly, this is an autobiography, a slave narrative, a
fiction-like work shaped by oratory as well as the sentimental romance. But Douglass, who grew up hearing sermons
on the plantation and who heard and delivered them
throughout his life, produced, in this greatest account of his
life, a text shaped by the form and the processes of speaking characteristic of the black sermon. This is a mighty text
meant, of course, to be read. But it is also a text meant to
be mightily preached.

Notes

[1] See Henry Mitchell, *Black Preaching* (Philadelphia: Lippincott, 1970).
[2] Mitchell, pp. 162–63.
[3] Perry Miller, ed. *The American Puritans* (Garden City, N.Y.: Double-
      day, 1956), p. 165.

4 Ralph Ellison, "Hidden Name and Complex Fate," *Shadow and Act* (New York: Random, 1964), p. 158.

5 Mitchell, p. 172.

6 Mitchell, p. 98.

7 Johnson, *God's Trombones* (New York: Viking, 1927), p. 1.

8 Johnson, pp. 1–7.

9 Arna Bontemps and Langston Hughes, ed., *Book of Negro Folklore* (New York: Dodd, Mead, 1958), p. 250.

10 For a discussion of this, see David Levin, "Baldwin's Autobiographical Essays: The Problem of Identity," *Massachusetts Review*, 5 (1964), 239–47.

11 Frederick Douglass, *Narrative of the Life of Frederick Douglass an American Slave* (1845; rpt. Cambridge: Harvard Univ. Press), 1848), pp. 4–6. All subsequent references are to this edition.

12 Ps. cxxxvii, King James Version.

13 Levin, p. 242.

14 See Henry Highland Garnet, "An Address to the Slaves of America," *Appeal*, ed. Garnet (1848), 89–96; rpt. in *Negro Caravan*, ed. Sterling A. Brown, Arthur P. Davis, Ullyses Lee (New York: Dryden Press, 1941), pp. 600–06.

Binary Oppositions in Chapter One of *Narrative of the Life of Frederick Douglass an American Slave Written by Himself*

Henry-Louis Gates, Jr.

I was not hunting for my liberty, but also hunting for my name.
—William Wells Brown, 1849

Whatever may be the ill or favored condition of the slave in the matter of mere personal treatment, it is the chattel relation that robs him of his manhood.
—James Pennington, 1849

When at last in a race a new principle appears, an idea,—that conserves it; ideas only save races. If the black man is feeble and not important to the existing races, not on a parity with the best race, the black man must serve, and be exterminated. But if the black man carries in his bosom an indispensable element of a new and coming civilization; for the sake of that element, no wrong nor strength nor circumstance can hurt him: he will survive and play his part. . . . I esteem the occasion of this jubilee to be the proud discovery that the black race can contend with the white: that in the great anthem which we call history, a piece of many parts and vast compass, after playing a long time a very low and subdued accom-

paniment, they perceive the time arrived when they can strike in with effect and take a master's part in the music.
—Emerson, 1844

The white race will only respect those who oppose their usurpation, and acknowledge as equals those who will not submit to their rule. . . . We must make an issue, create an event and establish for ourselves a position. This is essentially necessary for our effective elevation as a people, directing our destiny and redeeming ourselves as a race.
—Martin R. Delany, 1854

Autobiographical forms in English and in French assumed narrative priority toward the end of the eighteenth century; they shaped themselves principally around military exploits, court intrigues, and spiritual quests. As Stephen Butterfield has outlined, "Elizabethan sea dogs and generals of the War of the Spanish Succession wrote of strenuous campaigns, grand strategy, and gory battles. The memoirs of Louis XIV's great commander, the Prince of Condé, for example, thrilled thousands in Europe and America, as did the 'inside stories' of the nefarious, clandestine doings of the great European courts. The memoirs of the Cardinal De Retz, which told the Machiavellian intrigues of French government during Louis XIV's minority and of the cabal behind the election of a Pope, captivated a large audience. Even more titillating were personal accounts of the boudoir escapades of noblemen and their mistresses. Nell Gwyn, Madame Pompadour, and even the fictitious Fanny Hill were legends if not idols in their day. More edifying but no less marvelous were the autobiographies of spiritual pilgrimage—such as the graphic accounts of Loyola, John Bunyan, and the Quaker George Fox. Their mystical experiences and miraculous deliverances filled readers with awe and wonder." It is no surprise, then, that the narratives of the escaped slave became, during the three decades before the Civil War, the most popular form of written discourse in the country. Its audience was built to order. And the expectations created by this peculiar autobiographical convention, as well as by two other literary traditions, had a profound effect on the shape of discourse in the slave narrative. I am thinking here of the marked (but generally unheralded) tradition of the sentimental novel and, more especially, of the particularly American transmutation of the European picaresque. The slave narrative, I suggest, is a "countergenre," a mediation between the novel of sentiment and the picaresque, oscillating somewhere between the two in a bipolar moment, set in motion by the mode of the Confession. (Indeed, as we shall see, the slave narrative spawned its formal negation, the plantation novel.)

Claudio Guillén's seminal typology of the picaresque,[1] outlined as seven "characteristics" of that form and derived from numerous examples in Spanish and French literature, provides a curious counterpoint to the morphology of the slave narratives and aids remarkably in delineating what has proved to be an elusive, but recurring, narrative structure.

The picaro, who is after all a type of character, only becomes one at a certain point in his career, just as a man or woman "becomes" a slave only at a certain (and structurally crucial) point of perception in his or her "career." Both the picaro and the slave narrators are orphans; both, in fact, are outsiders. The picaresque is a pseudo-autobiography, whereas the slave narratives often tend toward quasi-autobiography. Yet in both, "life is at the same time revived and judged, presented and remembered." In both forms, the narrator's point of view is partial and prejudiced, although the total view "of both is reflective, philosophical, and critical on moral or religious grounds."[2] In both, there is a general stress on the material level of existence or indeed of *subsistence*, such as sordid facts, hunger, and money. There is in the narration of both a profusion of objects and detail. Both the picaro and the slave, as outsiders, comment on if not parody collective social institutions. Moreover, both, in their odysseys, move horizontally through space and vertically through society.

If we combine these resemblances with certain characteristics of the sentimental novel, such as florid asides, stilted rhetoric, severe piety, melodramatic conversation, destruction of the family unit, violation of womanhood, abuse of innocence, punishment of assertion, and the rags-to-riches success story, we can see that the slave narrative grafted together the conventions of two separate literary traditions and became its own form, utilizing popular conventions to affect its reader in much the same way as did cheap, popular fiction. Lydia Child, we recall, was not only the amanuensis for the escaped slave, Harriet Jacobs, but also a successful author in the sentimental tradition. (That the plantation novel was the antithesis or negation of the slave narrative becomes apparent when we consider its conventions. From 1824, when George Tucker published *The Valley of the Shenandoah*, the plantation novel concerned itself with aristocratic, virtuous masters; beast-like, docile slaves; great manor houses; squalid field quarters; and idealized, alabaster womanhood—all obvious negations of themes common to the slave narratives. Indeed, within two years of the publication in 1852 of Harriet Beecher Stowe's *Uncle Tom's Cabin*, at least fourteen plantation novels appeared.)

It should not surprise us, then, that the narratives were popular, since the use of well-established and well-received narrative conventions was meant to ensure commercial and hence political success. By at least one account, the sale of the slave narratives reached such profound proportions that a critic was moved to complain that the "shelves of booksellers groan under the weight of Sambo's woes, done up in covers! . . . We hate this niggerism, and hope it may be done away with. . . . If we are threatened with any more negro stories—here goes." These "literary nigritudes" [sic], as he calls them, were "stories" whose "editions run to hundreds of thousands."[3] Marion Wilson Starling recalls Gladstone's belief that not more than about five percent of the books published in England had a sale of more than five hundred copies; between 1835 and 1863, no fewer than ten of these were slave narratives.[4] So popular were they in England that a considerable number were published at London or Manchester before they were published in America, if at all. Nor should it surprise us that of these, the more popular were those that defined the genre structurally. It was Frederick Douglass' *Narrative* of 1845 that exploited the potential of and came to determine the shape of language in the slave narrative.

Douglass' *Narrative*, in its initial edition of five thousand copies, was sold out in four months. Within a year, four more editions of two thousand copies each were published. In the British Isles, five editions appeared, two in Ireland in 1846 and three in England in 1846 and 1847. Within the five years after its appearance, a total of some thirty thousand copies of the *Narrative* had been published in the English-speaking world. By 1848, a French edition, a paperback, was being sold in the stalls. *Littells Living Age*, an American periodical, gave an estimate of its sweep in the British Isles after one year's circulation: "Taking all together, not less than one million persons in Great Britain and Ireland have been excited by the book and its commentators."[5]

Of the scores of reviews of the *Narrative*, two, especially, discuss the work in terms of its literary merits. One review, published initially in the *New York Tribune* and reprinted in *The Liberator*, attempts to place the work in the larger tradition of the narrative tale as a literary form.

> Considered merely as a narrative, we have never read one more simple, true, coherent, and warm with genuine feeling. It is an excellent piece of writing, and on that score to be prized as a specimen of the powers of the black race, which prejudice persists in disputing. We prize highly all evidence of this kind, and it is becoming more abundant.[6]

Even more telling is the review from the *Lynn Pioneer* reprinted in the same issue of *The Liberator*; this review was perhaps the first to attempt to attach a priority to the *Narrative*'s form and thereby place Douglass directly in a major literary tradition.

> It is evidently drawn with a nice eye, and the coloring is chaste and subdued, rather than extravagant or overwrought. Thrilling as it is, and full of the most burning eloquence, it is yet simple and unimpassioned.

Although its "eloquence is the eloquence of truth," and so "is as simple and touching as the impulses of childhood," yet its "message" transcends even its superior moral content: "There are passages in it which would brighten the reputation of any author,—while the book, as a whole, judged as a mere work of art, would widen the fame of Bunyan or De Foe."[7] Leaving the matter of "truth" to the historians,[8] these reviews argue correctly that despite the intention of the author for his autobiography to be a major document in the abolitionist struggle and regardless of Douglass' meticulous attempt at documentation, the *Narrative* falls into the larger class of the heroic fugitive with some important modifications that are related to the confession and the picaresque forms (hence, Bunyan and Defoe), a peculiar blend that would mark Afro-American fiction at least from the publication of James Weldon Johnson's *Autobiography of an Ex-Coloured Man.*

These resemblances between confession and picaresque informed the narrative shape of Afro-American fiction in much the same way as they did in the English and American novel. As Robert Scholes and Robert Kellogg maintain

> The similarity in narrative stance between picaresque and confession enables the two to blend easily, making possible an entirely fictional narrative which is more in the spirit of the confession than the picaresque, such as *Moll Flanders* and *Great Expectations.*

But this same blend makes possible a different sort of sublime narrative, "one that is *picaresque* in spirit but which employs actual materials from the author's life, such as [Wells's] *Tono-Bungay.*" Into this class fall slave narratives, the polemical Afro-American first-person form the influence of which would shape the development of point of view in black fiction for the next one hundred years, precisely because

> By turning the direction of the narrative inward the author almost inevitably presents a central character who is an example of something. By turning the direction of the nar-

rative outward the author almost inevitably exposes weaknesses in society. First-person narrative is thus a ready vehicle for ideas.[9]

It is this first-person narration, utilized precisely in this manner, that is the first great shaping characteristic of the slave narratives. But there is another formal influence on the slave narratives the effect of which is telling: this is the American romance.

Like Herman Melville's marvelous romance, *Pierre*, the slave narratives utilize as a structural principle the irony of seeming innocence. Here in American society, both say, is to be found as much that is contrary to moral order as could be found in pre-revolutionary Europe. The novelty of American innocence is, however, the refusal or failure to recognize evil while participating in that evil. As with other American romantic modes of narration, the language of the slave narratives remains primarily an expression of the self, a conduit for particularly personal emotion. In this sort of narrative, language was meant to be a necessary but unfortunate instrument merely. In the slave narratives, this structuring of the self couples with the minute explication of gross evil and human depravity, and does so with such sheer intent as to make for a tyranny of point. If the matter of the shaping of the self can come only after the slave is free, in the context of an autobiographical narrative where he first posits that full self, then slavery indeed dehumanizes and must in no uncertain terms be abolished, by violence if necessary, since it is by nature a violent institution. The irony here is tyranically romantic: Illusion and substance are patterned antitheses.

As with other examples of romance, the narratives turn on an unconsummated love: The slave and the ex-slave are the dark ladies of the new country destined to expire for unrequited love. Yet the leitmotif of the journey north and the concomitant evolution of consciousness within the slave —from an identity as property and object to a sublime identity as a human being and subject—display in the first person the selfsame spirit of the New World's personal experience with Titanic nature that Franklin's *Autobiography* has come to symbolize. The author of the slave narrative, in his flight through the wilderness (re-created in vivid detailed descriptions of the relation between man and land on the plantation and off), seems to be arguing strongly that man can "study nature" to know himself. The two great precepts—the former Emersonian and the latter Cartesian—in the American adventure become one. Further, as with the American symbolists, the odyssey is a process of *becoming*: Whitman, for instance, is less concerned with explorations of emotion than with exploration as a mode of consciousness. Slave narratives not only describe the voyage but also enact the voyage so that their content is primarily a reflection of their literary method. Theirs is a structure in which the writer and his subject merge into the stream of language. Language indeed is primarily a perception of reality. Yet, unlike the American symbolists, these writers of slave narratives want not so much to adopt a novel stance from which the world assumes new shapes as to impose a new form onto the world. There can be no qualification as to the nature of slavery; there can be no equivocation.

Stephen Butterfield explicates[10] this idea rather well by contrasting the levels of diction in the slave narrative *The Life of John Thompson*[11] with a remarkably similar passage from Herman Melville's *Moby-Dick*.

The first is from Thompson:

The harpoon is sharp, and barbed at one end, so that when it has once entered the animal, it is difficult to draw it out again, and has attached to its other end a pole, two inches thick and five feet long. Attached to this is a line 75 to 100 fathoms in length, which is coiled into the bow of the boat.

Melville follows:

Thus the whale-line folds the whole boat in its complicated coils, twisting and writhing about it in almost every direction. All the oarsmen are involved in its perilous contortions; so that to the timid eye of the landsman they seem as festooning their limbs.

There is a difference here of rhetorical strategies that distinguishes the two. Melville's language is symbolic and weighted with ambiguous moral meanings: The serpentine rope allows for no innocence; "all the oarsmen" are involved, even those who have nothing to do with coiling it in the tub; the crew lives with the serpent and by the serpent, necessarily for their livelihood, unaware of the nature of the coil yet contaminated and imperiled by its inherent danger. Melville thus depicts the metaphysical necessity of evil.

John Thompson's language is distinguished formally from the concrete and symbolistic devices in Melville. Thompson allows the imagery of a whaling voyage to carry moral and allegorical meanings, yet he means his narration to be descriptive and realistic; his concern is with verisimilitude. There can be nothing morally ambiguous about the need to abolish slavery, and there can be little ambiguity about the reason for the suffering of the slave. "The slave narrative," Butterfield concludes, "does not see oppression in terms of a symbol-structure that transforms evil into a metaphysical necessity. For to do so would have been to locate the source of evil outside the master-slave relationship, and thus would have cut the ideological ground from under the entire thrust of the abolitionist movement."[12] Thompson means not so much to narrate as to convey a message, a value system; as with the black sermon, the slave's narrative functions as a single sign. And the nature of Frederick Douglass' rhetorical strategy directly reflects this sentiment through the use of what rhetoricians have called antitheses and of what the structuralists have come to call the binary opposition.

In the act of interpretation, we establish a sign relationship between the description and a meaning. The relations most crucial to structural analysis are functional binary oppositions. Roman Jakobson and Morris Halle argue in *Fundamentals of Language* that binary oppositions are inherent in all languages, that they are, indeed, a fundamental principle of language formation itself.[13] Many structuralists, seizing on Jakobson's formulation, hold the binary opposition to be a fundamental operation of the human mind, basic to the production of meaning. Levi-

Strauss, who turned topsy-turvy the way we examine mythological discourse, describes the binary opposition as "this elementary logic which is the smallest common denominator of all thought."[14] Levi-Strauss' model of opposition and mediation, which sees the binary opposition as an underlying structural pattern as well as a method for revealing that pattern, has in its many variants become a most satisfying mechanism for retrieving almost primal social contradictions, long ago "resolved" in the mediated structure itself.[15] Perhaps it is not irresponsible or premature to call Levi-Strauss' contribution to human understanding a classic one.

Frederic Jameson, in *The Prison-House of Language,* maintains that

> the binary opposition is . . . at the outset a heuristic principle, that instrument of analysis on which the mythological hermeneutic is founded. We would ourselves be tempted to describe it as a technique for stimulating perception, when faced with a mass of apparently homogeneous data to which the mind and the eyes are numb: a way of forcing ourselves to perceive difference and identity in a wholly new language the very sounds of which we cannot yet distinguish from each other. It is a decoding or deciphering device, or alternately a technique of language learning.

How does this "decoding device" work as a tool to practical criticism? When any two terms are set in opposition to each other the reader is forced to explore qualitative similarities and differences, to make some connection, and, therefore, to derive some meaning from points of disjunction. If one opposes A to B, for instance, and X to Y, the two cases become similar as long as each involves the presence and absence of a given feature. In short, two terms are brought together by some quality that they share and are then opposed and made to signify the absence and presence of that quality. The relation between presence and absence, positive and negative signs, is the simplest form of the binary opposition. These relations, Jameson concludes, "embody a tension 'in which one of the two terms of the binary opposition is apprehended as positively having a certain feature while the other is apprehended as deprived of the feature in question.' "[16]

Frederick Douglass' *Narrative* attempts with painstaking verisimilitude to reproduce a system of signs that we have come to call plantation culture, from the initial paragraph of Chapter i:

> I was born in Tuckahoe, near Hillsborough, and about twelve miles from Easton, in Talbot County, Maryland. I have no accurate knowledge of my age, never having seen any authentic record containing it. By far the larger part of the slaves know as little of their ages as horses know of theirs, and it is the wish of most masters within my knowledge to keep their slaves thus ignorant. I do not remember to have ever met a slave who could tell of his birthday, they seldom come nearer to it than planting-time, harvest-time, cherry-time, spring-time, or fall-time. A want of information concerning my own was a source of unhappiness to me even during childhood. The white children could tell their ages. I could not tell why I ought to be deprived of the same privilege. I was not allowed to make any inquiries of my master concerning it. He deemed such inquiries on the part of a slave improper and impertinent, and evidence of a restless spirit. The nearest estimate I can give makes me now between twenty-seven and twenty-eight years of age. I come to this, from hearing my master say, some time during 1835, I was about seventeen years old.[17]

We see an ordering of the world based on a profoundly relational type of thinking, in which a strict barrier of difference or opposition forms the basis of a class rather than, as in other classification schemes, an ordering based on resemblances or the identify of two or more elements. In the text, we can say that these binary oppositions produce through separation the most inflexible of barriers: that of meaning. We, the readers, must exploit the oppositions and give them a place in a larger symbolic structure. Douglass' narrative strategy seems to be this: He brings together two terms in special relationships suggested by some quality that they share; then, by opposing two seemingly unrelated elements, such as the sheep, cattle, or horses on the plantation and the specimen of life known as slave, Douglass' language is made to signify the presence and absence of some quality—in this case, humanity.[18] Douglass uses this device to explicate the slave's understanding of himself and of his relation to the world through the system of the perceptions that defined the world the planters made. Not only does his *Narrative* come to concern itself with two diametrically opposed notions of genesis, origins, and meaning itself, but its structure actually turns on an opposition between nature and culture as well. Finally and, for our purposes, crucially, Douglass' method of complex mediation—and the ironic reversals so peculiar to his text—suggests overwhelmingly the completely arbitrary relation between description and meaning, between signifier and signified, between sign and referent.

Douglass uses these oppositions to create a unity on a symbolic level, not only through physical opposition but also through an opposition of space and time. The *Narrative* begins "I was born in Tuckahoe, near Hillsborough, and about twelve miles from Easton, in Talbot County, Maryland." Douglass knows the physical circumstances of his birth: Tuckahoe, we know, is near Hillsborough and is twelve miles from Easton. Though his place of birth is fairly definite, his date of birth is not for him to know: "I have no accurate knowledge of my age," he admits, because "any authentic record containing it" would be in the possession of others. Indeed, this opposition, or counterpoint, between that which is *knowable* in the world of the slave and that which is *not*, abounds throughout this chapter. Already we know that the world of the master and the world of the slave are separated by an inflexible barrier of meaning. The knowledge the slave has of his circumstances he must deduce from the *earth*; a quantity such as time, our understanding of which is *cultural* and not *natural*, derives from a nonmaterial source, let us say the *heavens*: "The white children could tell their ages. I could not."

The deprivation of the means to tell the time is the very structural center of this initial paragraph: "A want of information concerning my own [birthday] was a source of unhappiness to me even during childhood." This state of disequilibrium motivates the slave's search for his humanity as well as Douglass' search for his text. This deprivation has created that gap in the slave's imagination between self and other, between black and white. What is more, it has apparently created a relation of likeness between the slave and the animals. "By far," Douglass confesses, "the large part of slaves know as little of their ages as horses know of theirs." This deprivation is not accidental; it is systematic: "it is the wish of most masters within my knowledge to keep their slaves thus ignorant." Douglass, in his subtle juxtaposition here of "masters" and "knowledge" and of "slaves" and "ignorance," again introduces homologous terms. "I do not remember to have ever met a slave," Douglass emphasizes, "who could tell of his birthday." Slaves, he seems to conclude, are they who cannot plot their course by the linear progression of the calendar. Here, Douglass summarizes the symbolic code of this world, which makes the slave's closest blood relations the horses and which makes his very notion of time a cyclical one, diametrically opposed to the master's linear conception: "They [the slaves] seldom come nearer to [the notion of time] than planting-time, harvest-time, cherry-time, spring-time, or fall-time." The slave had arrived, but not *in time* to partake at the welcome table of human culture.

For Douglass, the bonds of blood kinship are the primary metaphors of human culture.[19] As an animal would know its mother, so Douglass knows his. "My mother was named Harriet Bailey. She was the daughter of Isaac and Betsey Bailey." Both of whom were "colored," Douglass notes, "and quite dark." His mother "was of a darker complexion" even than either grandparent. His father, on the other hand, is some indefinite "white man," suggested through innuendo to be his master: "The opinion was also whispered," he says, "that my master was my father." His master was his father; his father his master: "of the correctness of this opinion," Douglass concludes, "I know nothing," only and precisely because "the means of knowing was withheld from me." Two paragraphs below, having reflected on the death of his mother, Douglass repeats this peculiar unity twice again. "Called thus suddenly away," he commences, "she left me without the slightest intimation of who my father was." Yet Douglass repeats "the whisper that my father was my master" as he launches into a description of the rank odiousness of a system "that slaveholders have ordained, and by law established," in which the patrilinear succession of the planter has been forcibly replaced by a matrilinear succession for the slave: "the children of slave women shall in all cases follow the condition of their mothers." The planters therefore make of the "gratification of their wicked desires," spits Douglass, a thing "profitable as well as pleasurable." Further, the end result of "this cunning arrangement" is that "the slaveholder, in cases not a few, sustains to his slaves the double relation of master and father." "I know of such cases," he opens his sixth paragraph, using a declaration of verisimilitude as a transition to introduce another opposition, this one between the fertile slave-lover-mother and the planter's barren wife.

The profound ambiguity of this relationship between father and son and master and slave persists, if only because the two terms "father" and "master" are here embodied in one, with no mediation between them. It is a rather grotesque bond that links Douglass to his parent, a bond that embodies "the distorted and unnatural relationship endemic to slavery."[20] It is as if the usually implied primal tension between father and son is rendered apparent in the daily contact between father-master-human and son-slave-animal, a contact that occurs, significantly, only during the light of day.

Douglass' contact with his mother ("to know her as such," he qualifies) never occurred "more than four or five times in my life." Each of these visits, he recalls, "was of short duration," and each, he repeats over and over, took place "at night." Douglass continues: "[My mother] made her journey to see me in the night, travelling the whole distance," he mentions as if an afterthought, "on foot." "I do not recollect of ever seeing my mother," he repeats one sentence later, "by the light of day. She was with me in the *night*" (emphasis added). Always she returned to a Mr. Stewart's plantation, some twelve miles away, "long before I waked" so as to be at the plantation before dawn, since she "was a field hand, and a whipping is the penalty of not being in the field at sunrise." The slaves, metaphorically, "owned" the night, while the master owned the day. By the fourth paragraph of the narrative, the terms of our homology—the symbolic code of this world—are developed further to include relations of the animal, the mother, the slave, the night, the earth, matrilinear succession, and nature opposed to relations of the human being, the father, the master, the daylight, the heavens, patrilinear succession, and culture. Douglass, in short, opposes the absolute and the eternal to the mortal and the finite. Our list, certainly, could be expanded to include oppositions between spiritual/material, aristocratic/base, civilized/barbaric, sterile/fertile, enterprise/sloth, force/principle, fact/imagination, linear/cyclical, thinking/feeling, rational/irrational, chivalry/cowardice, grace/brutishness, pure/cursed, and human/beastly.

Yet the code, Douglass proceeds to show, stands in defiance of the natural *and* moral order. Here Douglass commences as mediator and as trickster to reverse the relations of the opposition. That the relation between the slave-son and his master-father was an unnatural one and even grotesque, as are the results of any defilement of Order, is reflected in the nature of the relation between the plantation mistress and the planter's illegitimate offspring. "She is ever disposed to find fault with them," laments Douglass; "she is never better pleased than when she sees them under the lash." Indeed, it is the white mistress who often compels her husband, the master, to sell "this class of his slaves, out of deference to the feelings of his white wife." But it is the priority of the economic relation over the kinship tie that is the true perversion of nature in this world: "It is often the dictate of humanity for a man to sell his own children to human flesh-mongers," Douglass observes tellingly. Here we see the ultimate reversal: For it is now the mistress, the proverbial carrier of culture, who demands that the master's son be delivered up to the "human flesh-mongers" and traded for consumption. Douglass has here defined American cannibalism, a consumption of human flesh dictated by a system that could only be demonic.

Douglass' narrative demonstrates not only how the deprivation of the hallmarks of identity can affect the slave but also how the slaveowner's world negates and even perverts those very values on which it is built. Deprivation of a birth date, a name, a family structure, and legal rights makes of the deprived a brute, a subhuman, says Douglass, until he comes to a consciousness of these relations; yet, it is the human depriver who is the actual barbarian, structuring his existence on the consumption of human flesh. Just as the mulatto son is a mediation between two opposed terms, man and animal, so too has Douglass' text become the complex mediator between the world as the master would have it and the world as the slave knows it really is. Douglass has subverted the terms of the code he was meant to mediate: He has been a trickster. As with all mediations the trickster is a mediator and his mediation is a trick—only a trick; for there can be no mediation in this world. Douglass' narrative has aimed to destroy that symbolic code that created the false oppositions themselves. The oppositions, all along, were only arbitrary, not fixed.

Douglass first suggests that the symbolic code created in this text is arbitrary and not fixed, human-imposed not divinely ordained in an ironic aside on the myth of the curse of Ham, which comes in the very center of the seventh paragraph of the narrative and which is meant to be an elaboration on the ramifications of "this class of slaves" who are the fruit of the unnatural liaison between animal and man. If the justification of this order is the curse on Ham and his tribe, if Ham's tribe signifies the black African, and if this prescription for enslavement is scriptural, then, Douglass argues, "it is certain that slavery at the south must soon become unscriptural; for thousands are ushered into the world, annually, who, like myself, owe their existence to white fathers, and those fathers," he repeats for the fourth time, are "most frequently their own masters."

As if to underscore the falsity of this notion of an imposed, inflexibly divine order, Douglass inverts a standard Christian symbol, that of the straight and narrow gate to Paradise. The severe beating of his Aunt Hester, who "happened," Douglass advises us parenthetically, "to be absent when my master desired her presence," is the occasion of this inversion. "It struck me with awful force," he remembers. "It was the blood-stained gate," he writes, "the entrance to the hell of slavery, through which I was about to pass. It was," he concludes, "a most terrible spectacle." This startling image suggests that of the archetypal necromancer, Faustus, in whose final vision the usual serene presence of the Cross is stained with warm and dripping blood.

Douglass has posited the completely arbitrary nature of the sign. The master's actions belie the metaphysical suppositions on which is based the order of his world: It is an order ostensibly imposed by the Father of Adam, yet one in fact exposed by the sons of Ham. It is a world the oppositions of which have generated their own mediator, Douglass himself. This mulatto son, half-animal, half-man, writes a text (which is itself another mediation) in which he can expose the arbitrary nature of the signs found in this world, the very process necessary to the destruction of this world. "You have seen how a man was made a slave," Douglass writes at the structural center of his *Narrative*, "you shall see how a slave was made a man."[21] As with all mediation, Douglass has constructed a system of perception that becomes the plot development in the text but that results in an inversion of the initial state of the oppositions through the operations of the mediator himself, as indicated in this diagram:

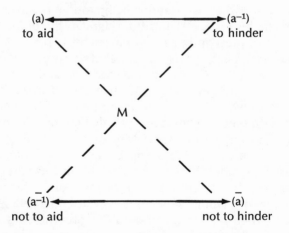

With this narrative gesture alone, slave has become master, creature has become man, object has become subject. What more telling embodiment of Emersonian idealism and its "capacity" to transubstantiate a material reality! Not only has an *idea* made subject of object, but creature has assumed self and the assumption of self has created a race. For, as with all myths of origins, the relation of self to race is a relation of synecdoche. As Michael Cooke maintains concerning the characteristics of black autobiography:

> The self is the source of the system of which it is a part, creates what it discovers, and although (as Coleridge realized) it is nothing unto itself, it is the possibility of everything for itself. Autobiography is the coordination of the self as content—everything available in memory, perception, understanding, imagination, desire—and the self as shaped, formed in terms of a perspective and pattern of interpretation.[22]

If we step outside the self-imposed confines of Chapter i to seek textual evidence, the case becomes even stronger. The opposition between culture and nature is clearly contained in a description of a slave meal, found in Chapter v.[23] "We were not regularly allowanced. Our food was coarse corn meal boiled. This was called *mush*. It was put into a large wooden tray or trough, and set down upon the ground. The children were then called, like so many pigs, and like so many pigs they would come and devour the mush; some with oyster-shells, others with pieces of shingle, some with naked hands, and none with spoons. He that ate fastest got most; he that was strongest secured the best place; and few left the trough satisfied." The slave, we read, did not eat food; he ate mush. He did not eat with a spoon; he ate with pieces of shingle, or on oyster shells, or with his naked hands. Again we see the obvious culture-nature opposition at play. When the slave, in another place, accepts the comparison with and identity of a "bad sheep," he again has inverted the terms, supplied as always by the master, so that the unfavorable meaning that this has for the master is supplanted by the favorable meaning it has for the slave. There is in this world the planter has made, Douglass maintains, an ironic relation between appearance and reality. "Slaves sing most," he writes at the end of Chapter ii, "when they are most unhappy. . . . The singing of a man cast away upon a desolate island might be as appropriately considered as evidence of contentment and happiness, as the singing of a slave; the songs of the one and of the other are prompted by the same emotion."

Finally, Douglass concludes his second chapter with a discourse on the nature of interpretation, which we could perhaps call the first charting of the black hermeneutical circle and which we could take again as a declaration of the arbitrary relation between a sign and its referent, between the signifier and the signified. The slaves, he writes, "would compose and sing as they went along, consulting neither time nor tune. The thought that came up, came out—if not in the word, [then] in the sound;—and as frequently in the one as in the other."[24] Douglass describes here a certain convergence of perception peculiar only to members of a very specific culture: The thought could very well be embodied nonverbally, in the sound if not in the word. What is more, sound and sense could very well operate at odds to create through tension a dialectical relation. Douglass remarks: "They would sometimes sing the most pathetic sentiment in the most rapturous tone, and the most rapturous sentiment in the most pathetic tone. . . . They would thus sing as a chorus to words which to many would seem unmeaning jargon, but which, nevertheless, were full of meaning to themselves." Yet the decoding of these cryptic messages did not, as some of us have postulated, depend on some sort of mystical union with their texts. "I did not, when a slave," Douglass admits, "understand the deep meaning of those rude and apparently incoherent songs." "Meaning," on the contrary, came only with a certain aesthetic distance and an acceptance of the critical imperative. "I was myself within the circle," he concludes, "so that I neither saw nor heard as those without might see and hear." There exists always the danger, Douglass seems to say, that the meanings of nonlinguistic signs will seem "natural"; one must view them with a certain detachment to see that their meanings are in fact merely the "products" of a certain culture, the result of shared assumptions and conventions. Not only is meaning culture-bound and the referents of all signs an assigned relation, Douglass tells us, but *how* we read determines *what* we read, in the truest sense of the hermeneutical circle.

Notes

1 *Literature as System: Essays toward the Theory of Literary History* (Princeton Univ. Press, 1971), pp. 71–106 and esp. pp. 135–58.

2 Guillén, p. 81.

3 George R. Graham, "Black Letters; or Uncle Tom-Foolery in Literature," *Graham's Illustrated Magazine of Literature, Romance, Art, and Fashion*, 42 Feb. 1853, p. 209.

4 Starling, *The Slave Narrative: Its Place in American Literary History,* Diss. New York Univ. 1946, pp. 47–48.

5 "Narrative of Frederick Douglass," *Littell's Living Age*, 1 April 1846, p. 47.

6 *New York Tribune*, 10 June 1845, p. 1, col. 1; rpt. in *Liberator*, 30 May 1845, p. 97.

7 *Lynn Pioneer*; rpt. in *Liberator*, 30 May 1845, p. 86.

8 See esp. John Blassingame, "Black Autobiography as History and Literature," *Black Scholar*, 5:4 (Dec. 1973–Jan. 1974), 2–9; and his *Slave Testimony: Two Centuries of Letters, Speeches, Interviews, and Autobiographies* (Baton Rouge: Louisiana State Univ. Press, 1977).

9 Scholes and Kellogg, *The Nature of Narrative* (New York: Oxford Univ. Press, 1966), p. 76.

10 *Black Autobiography in America* (Amherst: Univ. of Massachusetts Press, 1974), p. 36.

11 Thompson, *The Life of John Thompson, a Fugitive Slave, Containing His History of Twenty-Five Years in Bondage and His Providential Escape* (Worcester: n.p., 1856), p. 113.

12 Butterfield, p. 37.

13 *Fundamentals of Language* (The Hague: Mouton, 1971), pp. 4, 47–49.

14 *Totemism* (New York: Penguin, 1969), p. 130.

15 What has this rather "obvious" model of human thought to do with the study of mundane literature generally and with the study of Afro-American literature specifically? It has forced us to alter irrevocably certain long-held assumptions about the relation between sign and referent, between signifier and signified. It has forced us to remember that we must not always mean what we say; or to remember what queries we intended to resolve when we first organized a discourse in a particular way. What's more, this rather simple formulation has taught us to recognize texts where we find them and to read these texts as they demand to be read. Yet, we keepers of the black critical activity have yet to graft fifty years of systematic thinking about literature onto the consideration of our own. The study of Afro-American folklore, for instance, remains preoccupied with unresolvable matters of genesis or with limitless catalogs and motif indices. Afraid that Brer Rabbit is "merely" a trickster or that Anansi spiders merely spin webs, we reduce these myths to their simplest thematic terms— the perennial relation between the wily, persecuted black and the not-too-clever, persecuting white. This reduction belies our own belief in the philosophical value of these mental constructs. We admit, albeit inadvertently, a nagging suspicion that these are

the primitive artifacts of childish minds, grappling with a complex Western world and its languages, three thousand years and a world removed. These myths, as the slave narratives would, did not so much "narrate" as they did convey a value system; they functioned, much like a black sermon, as a single sign. The use of binary opposition, for instance, allows us to perceive much deeper "meanings" than a simplistic racial symbolism allows. Refusal to use sophisticated analysis on our own literature smacks of a symbolic inferiority complex as blatant as were treatments of skin lightener and hair straightener.

[16] *The Prison-House of Language: A Critical Account of Structuralism and Russian Formalism* (Princeton: Princeton Univ. Press, 1972), pp. 113; 35, citing Troubetskoy's *Principes de phonologie*. See also Jonathan Culler, *Structuralist Poetics: Structuralism, Linguistics, and the Study of Literature* (Ithaca: Cornell Univ. Press, 1975), pp. 93, 225–27; Roland Barthes, *S/Z, An Essay*, trans. Richard Miller (New York: Hill and Wang, 1975), p. 24.

[17] *Narrative* (Boston: Anti-Slavery Office, 1845), p. 1. All subsequent quotes, unless indicated, are from pp. 1–7.

[18] There is overwhelming textual evidence that Douglass was a consummate stylist who, contrary to popular myth, learned the craft of the essayist self-consciously. The importance of Caleb Bingham's *The Columbian Orator* (Boston: Manning and Loring, 1797) to Douglass' art is well established. John Blassingame is convinced of Douglass' use of Bingham's rhetorical advice in his writing, especially of antitheses. (Personal interview with John Blassingame, 7 May 1976.) For an estimation of the role of language in the political struggle of antebellum blacks see Alexander Crummell, "The English Language in Liberia," in his *The Future of Africa* (New York: Scribners, 1862), pp. 9–57.

[19] See also Nancy T. Clasby, "Frederick Douglass's *Narrative*: A Content Analysis," *CLA Journal*, 14 (1971), 244.

[20] Clasby, p. 245.

[21] Douglass, p. 77.

[22] "Modern Black Autobiography in the Tradition," in *Romanticism, Vistas, Instances, and Continuities*, ed. David Thorburn and Geoffrey Hartman (Ithaca: Cornell Univ. Press, 1973), p. 258.

[23] Douglass, pp. 13–15.

[24] Douglass, p. 30.

Afro-American
Literature
Course Designs

Rethinking the Afro-American
Literature Survey Course

> In the closed circle I have fashioned. In the alien
> language of another tribe. I make these documents for
> some heart who will recognize me truthfully. Who
> will know what I am and what I wanted beneath the
> maze of meanings and attitudes that shape the reality
> of everything.
>
> —Amiri Baraka

Afro-American literature is, above all, an act of language.
This is not to deny that Afro-American literature has been
informed by its authors' experiences as members of a group
faced historically with exile, enslavement, and political
oppression. However, to read Afro-American literature
simply as a document of Afro-American history is to deny
the importance of its formal and linguistic properties.
Richard Palmer points out that a full understanding of any
literary work is "linguistic, historical and ontological."[1] To
achieve such an understanding of an Afro-American literary
work, it is necessary to recognize that the dual origin of
Afro-American literature (i.e., African and Euro-American)
produces unique *forms* and *usages* that not only are present
in many works representing many literary periods but also
are collectively a primary reason certain texts within the
canon of Afro-American literature speak to or illuminate
one another. It is this concept of "resonance" among texts
that helps us distinguish between the "canon" and the
"history" of Afro-American literature. According to North-

rop Frye, "literature develops historically within a limited orbit of language, reference, allusion, beliefs, transmitted and shared tradition."[2] While historical circumstances may influence that orbit, history cannot determine the precise nature of the linguistic events enacted within the orbit. In short, no historical circumstance or event can "explain" a literary work.

The previous sentence might seem to belabor a truism of modern criticism, but when we look at the typical structure of Afro-American literature survey courses as they are taught in many American colleges and universities, we see a truism often contradicted by practice. Extraliterary criteria are allowed to dictate the organization of many survey courses. These criteria are most typically historical (e.g., grouping literary works under historical designations like "The Slave Period" or "The Negro Nadir"), but they also can be social (e.g., using the literature to chart the effect on the black community of the civil rights movement) or economic (e.g., reading the works as expressions of an oppressed social class). What these approaches neglect is an adequate treatment of the text in literary terms. And what is needed as a full corrective to them is a series of approaches to survey courses that work within a framework of Afro-American *literary* history. Such approaches should clarify and apply those concepts of literary criticism that will best ensure an analysis of Afro-American literature as literature and create a valid internal chronology for the works studied. The approaches detailed below do not, certainly, exhaust the possibilities, nor are they necessarily mutually exclusive, but they do fulfill in some measure the demands made by the literature itself.

Descriptions and Methodologies

An essential principle to keep in mind when designing an Afro-American literature survey course is that the black literary tradition has evolved out of the cultural traditions, intellectual influences, and folkways of several civilizations and continents. To teach selected works by black authors out of the context of the Afro-American literary tradition does a disservice to the tradition, to the text, and to those elements of form, style, and content that distinguish the works of black authors, especially (1) the use of black speech as literary diction, (2) the dramatic impact of folk material on all genres, and (3) the pervasive presence, throughout the literary history, of the black narrator's "dual consciousness." Any valid critical approach can be used to examine Afro-American literature, because useful criticism cuts across racial and cultural lines and assures analysis of the literature as literature vis-à-vis literary history and that history's cultural context. In short, Octavio Paz or Northrop Frye may illuminate Afro-American literature as much as Stephen Henderson or Darwin Turner does.

To design an effective survey course, a teacher must necessarily grapple with the problem of determining what central approach or organizing principle will provide the means for demonstrating the nature of the tradition and the relationships (or "resonances") among the works the tradition comprises: In short, what does the teacher want students to take away from the course? In the past, many of us (taking our cue from the best anthologies) have organized our courses chronologically and have progressed temporally from work to work. However, though some temporal relationships must necessarily exist, a strictly chronological approach to literary history is unsatisfactory, because it does not take into account the essential dynamic that exists not only between the history of culture and the history of its art forms but also among the literary texts themselves. An effective course, for example, will focus on the way certain literary texts relate linguistically to one another rather than on how they fit into a chronological scheme. This "intertextual" approach to survey courses, based as it is upon the linguistic dimensions of literary history, encourages the "close" reading of individual texts, because the emphasis has been placed on charting the movement—that is, the transitions—between texts within a literary tradition. It also allows for greater flexibility in the selection of texts to be studied. For example, since the goal is now to teach a literary tradition and not a literary chronology, almost any single work can be omitted from an overview of Afro-American literature without actually dismantling the tradition.

Unquestionably, the Afro-American survey is an important course, whether it is taught as a gateway to a fully developed Afro-American major or as the sole course students can take in the field. We suggest that there are many possibilities for variation, imagination, and interpretation in the central design of the course. What follows are two ways in which a survey course in Afro-American literature can be planned to focus on a literary rather than a socio-historical principle.

Design A. Linguistic Approaches to Teaching Afro-American Literature

The idea of viewing the history of Afro-American literature as a search for a language capable of rendering the complexity of Afro-American life is a potent means of organizing the varied and constantly growing body of material we call Afro-American literature. We have long recognized the important influence of the interaction of a black oral culture with the literate traditions of Europe and America in the shaping of Afro-American literature. Both traditions are the black writer's heritage. But the black oral tradition is not a formless sea in which myths, archetypes, narrative structures, and salient themes float. Nor is it an eddy in the mainstream of American language in which oddments of quaint expressions and colorful terms peculiar to the black speech community whirl about. That oral tradition is also a language with a grammar, a syntax, and standards of eloquence of its own, a fact well substantiated by an imposing array of recent linguistic scholarship. The Afro-American artist is just as bicultural, just as much an heir to legitimate linguistic traditions, in the area of language as he is in the area of literary forms: Black speech is to formal English as the oral tradition is to the literate tradition.

The addition of the idea that black speech exists in a creatively tense relationship with formal English to the more familiar notion of oral versus literate traditions yields

a system for mapping the Afro-American literary landscape:

Formal English

Oral Tradition   Literate Tradition

Black Speech

We will turn to the practical advantage of this mapping
device momentarily, but first let us consider the benefits
that accrue from discussing Afro-American literature in
reference to its linguistic or vertical axis. The opposition of
black speech to formal English requires the analysis of a
work in terms of its language: Literature will be analyzed
as literature. But the limitations of pure formalism can be
avoided just as well. Black speech did not become acceptable as poetic diction, or even recognized as speech, without a fight. The history of this struggle is clearly a part of
the larger quest for freedom. Furthermore, black speech is
the result of Africans coming to terms with Europeans in
America: The linguistic phenomenon is summoned into
being by a specific historical context. Clearly, we have a
means of mediating the claims of pure formalism and reductionist historicism. Finally, the idea of black speech as
poetic diction can be applied to other literatures of the
African diaspora and of Africa itself. What Afro-Americans have done with English can be compared with what
black Cubans have done with Spanish and with what the
Senegalese have done with French.

Practically speaking, the idea of black speech as poetic
diction cannot stand alone as a principle of organization in
a survey course. The horizontal axis of oral versus written
forms inevitably comes into play because poetic diction
exists in poems. We hasten to add that even our map has its
shortcomings. It might allow us to note that a sermon in
God's Trombones and a Langston Hughes blues have the
same "value" on our horizontal axis (both forms are in the
oral tradition) but quite different values on our vertical
axis (James Weldon Johnson's language is closer to formal
English than is the language of Hughes). Yet this says nothing about whether one poem is more successful than the

other. The function of the map is to rationalize the landscape in objective terms, not arbitrarily to designate one corner of it as more sacred than another; a work hallows a particular place, a particular place does not sanctify whatever work chances to fall on it.

A survey course would do well to begin, however, by tracing the development of black speech in historical terms and proceeding to analyze the intricate developments that attended its exploitation as a poetic resource. In essence, the task of the black poet has been not to purify the language of the tribe but to establish a place for the tribe's language in poetry. The first task of the teacher of the survey is to establish a clear sense of what black speech is, putting particular stress on the characteristics of black figurative language. J. L. Dillard's account of the creation of black speech in *Black English* and Robbins Burling's *English in Black and White* are useful and fascinating reading. From here one might take up Dunbar and the tradition of dialect verse, noting the significant ways in which the works of Dunbar and other dialect poets depart from black speech. James Weldon Johnson's attempt to find a literary analogue for the folk sermon in *God's Trombones* and his reflections on the difficulties—literary and political—confronting the black poet seeking to adopt the voice of his people are indispensable. The efforts of Hughes and Sterling Brown to explore the possibilities of black speech as poetic diction would seem to follow quite naturally. One might conclude this section of the survey, a section that could be adequately treated in about five weeks, with any of a number of recent works that are virtuoso demonstrations of the resources of black speech. The fiction of Toni Cade Bambara and June Jordan and the poetry of Sherley Williams come immediately to mind.

Once we have established black speech as a poetic diction mediating between the vertical and horizontal axes, we can consider how language is used in particular literary forms to represent both individual preferences and the varieties of language now available to black writers to attain their individual literary voices. We can also begin to analyze selected works within the canon of a single author or to compare the works of several authors. For example, Richard Wright uses formal language in *Native Son* and black speech patterns in *Uncle Tom's Children*. And Ralph Ellison uses language close to oral traditions in *Invisible Man*, while William Demby employs a more modernist language in *The Catacombs*. Thus, within the body of Afro-American literature there is a variety of black linguistic postures that might be studied. In terms of methodology, a teacher might begin by suggesting works that clearly relate to one of the four areas (*Native Son* as formal English; *His Own Where* as black speech, etc.) and then suggest other works that, in comparison, might further illuminate those uses of language or might, in fact, supersede those very same categories, such as *Invisible Man* and *Cane*.

Design B. Thematic Approaches to Teaching Afro-American Literature

An Afro-American survey course can be managed around a limited number of major course themes. These can be metaphors (e.g., the wearing of the mask), ritualized actions (e.g., the varied manifestations of the "call and response" pattern), motifs (e.g., the heroic black), ongoing artistic problems (e.g., audience), or any of a number of other possibilities. The basic idea for selecting a limited number of themes (three or four) is that (1) they will provide a manageable number of internal (as opposed to extraliterary) transitions; and (2) they will create a valid intertextual basis on which to establish the course. The themes chosen should present something of a homogeneous group and should permit a treatment of a number of the major works in the Afro-American literary canon. One or two of the themes chosen should focus attention on the formal and structural patterns of the works studied.

The themes can be postulated at the beginning of the course, but they should be developed and expanded as each successive work is studied. The following list suggests how one of the themes mentioned above, the metaphor of masking, might be traced through ten works:

(1) The masking of the freedom quest in the spirituals
(2) The masking of literacy in Douglass' *Narrative*

  (3) The employment of the nostalgic antebellum mask by Uncle Julius in Chesnutt's *The Conjure Woman*

  (4) Dunbar's dialect mask

  (5) The capitulation to the mask in Johnson's *Autobiography of an Ex-Colored Man*

  (6) The ultimate uselessness of the mask in Hughes' "Father and Son" (the humble, subservient brother, as well as the rebellious brother, is destroyed by the white mob)

  (7) The inability to manipulate the mask in Wright's *Native Son*

  (8) The movements away from male societal mask in Hurston's *Their Eyes Were Watching God*

  (9) The ironic adoption of the revolutionary mask in Nikki Giovanni's poetry

  (10) The irreducible reality of the mask in *Invisible Man*

This theme can be easily related to African roots, for the mask (always "in motion") is one of the central artifacts of African civilization. Establishing such a relation further focuses the course on form and its transformations within the Afro-American literary tradition.

This "major themes" methodology has the further advantage of providing the students with an immediate basis for the interpretation of each assigned work—that is, the three or four themes can be turned into a basic set of "questions" to ask about each work.

Sample Course Design

Linking themes: (1) "Call and Response" as recurrent ritualized pattern

               (2) The motif of the heroic black

               (3) The black authors' problem of identifying their audience

Week 1: Oral literature: spirituals, work songs, gospel songs, blues, etc.

Week 2: Oral literature: sermons, folktales, jokes, etc.

Week 3: Douglass' *Narrative* (perhaps supplemented by short selections from other slave narratives—e.g., Gustavus Vassa's work)

Week 4:   Chesnutt's *The Wife of His Youth and Other Stories*
Week 5:   Washington's *Up from Slavery*
Week 6:   Du Bois' *The Souls of Black Folk*
Week 7:   Toomer's *Cane*
Week 8:   Hurston's *Their Eyes Were Watching God*
Week 9:   Wright's *Native Son*
Week 10: Baraka's *Dutchman*
Week 11: Ellison's *Invisible Man*
Week 12: The poetry of Gwendolyn Brooks
Week 13: Neo-black poetry
Week 14: Neo-black poetry

Three brief comments on this design by way of explanation:

(1) The course begins with an analysis of "call and response" as an African pattern carried over and reshaped as a major organizing principle for Afro-American oral and musical arts. *Up from Slavery*, on the other hand, employs "call and response" in a symbolic way: Washington, as August Meier shows us, manipulated the myths and symbols of the white American success syndrome (the call) to achieve a virtually unfailing response (power, prestige, respect, position, wealth, and influence). At the course end, in neo-black poetry, we see again that there is often a pervasive reliance on "call and response" as an informing pattern.

(2) The "heroic black" metamorphoses from the Moses figure of the spirituals and the Stackolee figure of the folktales into, for instance, the "blue-veined" Mr. Ryder in "The Wife of His Youth" (who breaks an advantageous engagement to acknowledge his long-lost slave wife), the antihero Kabnis in *Cane*, the increasingly free heroine of *Their Eyes Were Watching God*, the struggling character in Brooks's "Anniad," and the rebellious cultural nationalist persona of some neoblack poetry.

(3) Unlike oral Afro-American literature, which was (and is) meant to be consumed directly by the Afro-American community, early written works, like Douglass' *Narrative* of 1845, move beyond their oral literature basis to address a mixed racial audience, probably, of necessity,

more white than black. *Invisible Man*'s closing sentence—
"Who knows but that, on the lower frequencies, I speak for
you?"—evidences a continued authorial concern with the
dual audience created by the pressures of racism. The very
multiplicity of contemporary views on the proper themes
and legitimate formats for black poetry (and other genres)
suggests that the problem of audience still helps condition
Afro-American literature.

Notes

1 "Toward Reopening the Question: What Is Interpretation," in *Her-meneutics* (Evanston, Illinois: Northwestern Univ. Press, 1969),
p. 228.
2 "The Critical Path: An Essay on the Social Context of Literary Criti-cism," *Daedalus*, 99 (Spring 1970), p. 276.

Rethinking the Afro-American Genre Course

The generic approach is one means of clarifying literary traditions in terms of specific literary forms: narrative, lyric, and dramatic. Observing the behavior and function of the shaping elements that define specific forms and studying these elements intertextually inform a literary history. More often than not, Afro-American writers transform, or improvise upon, traditional genres by employing motifs, forms, and techniques found in Afro-American oral traditions. What follows is one example of a generic approach to teaching Afro-American literature.

A Course Design for Teaching Black Poetry

Afro-American poetry emerges from a convergence of Anglo-American and African literary traditions. The poetry yields observable, significant evidence of the influence not only of written Western literary forms but also of verbal forms informed by mostly African folk sources (e.g., oral literature, sermons, tales, proverbs, and black speech). The resulting poetic tradition and characteristics of texts (e.g., elements of form, theme, and subject) within the tradition possess great scope, significance, and variety and, indeed, encourage our study of Afro-American poetry in courses of at least a semester's length. Because Afro-American poetry comprises a large body of literature, evolves from a definable tradition, and shares common characteristics, it deserves study in its own right.

One critical approach to the teaching of the poetry seeks to define an Afro-American literary poetic tradition and to place poets and poetry alike in that tradition. The organizing framework is the survey, which is chosen for the following reasons:

(1) It establishes the parameters of the tradition.
(2) It includes a wide scope of materials focusing on poetry and poets that illuminate, embellish, and transform the tradition.
(3) It examines a poet's literary career in time.
(4) It studies the concept of a literary tradition (literary history), a concept students often lack.
(5) It develops a critical vocabulary with which to describe, define, and evaluate Afro-American poetry.
(6) It is the most feasible format for most colleges to implement.

Content and Methodology

This Black Poetry Survey is structured to give the student an overview of the poetry through focus on those writers and works that illuminate both the Afro-American poetic tradition and those pivotal moments or transitions within the development of the tradition. Subjects for study include the sources of the black poetic tradition and the characteristic elements of the literature. The texts are studied on the basis of the following:

(1) The development of a black poetic diction
(2) The evolution of poetic voices speaking/singing in certain modes of articulation and performance, including the sermonic, the blues, and tale-telling
(3) "Black uses" of traditional poetic genres such as the lyric and narrative poems
(4) The development of specifically black poetic genres, such as the sermonic or the blues poem
(5) Identification of central images, metaphors, and symbols that recur in the literature

A methodology of comparative textual analysis emerges from the identification of a black poetic tradition as a convergence of African and Anglo-American literatures, oral and written.

Within the schema outlined above, it becomes clear that the African's acquisition of spoken English and the subsequent transformation of that language into something Afro-American were pivotal to the development of a black poetic tradition. In the Americas, Africans imposed their own systems of thought, literature, and aesthetic sensibility on the new language and in the process created something new. This "something new" became a distinctive mode of language filled with irony, ambiguity, and indirection alongside of concrete, vivid metaphor. Distinctive forms such as spirituals, work songs, blues, gospel, sermons, testimonies, and narrative poems became in their own right literary genres.

The next pivotal moment in the development of a black poetic tradition was the beginning of a written poetic tradition. In its earliest stages, a conscious imitation of British and American literary forms and conventions can be observed. Lucy Terry imitates the popular broadside ballad; Jupiter Hammon imitates the lyrics and forms of the Methodist hymnal; and Phillis Wheatley imitates the neoclassical poetry of the elite. Correctness and fidelity to the models are the major concerns of the "mockingbirds." As the literature develops, black poets master, adapt, and subsequently transform the traditional forms (as evidenced in the development of the sonnet from Dunbar through Cullen, McKay, Walker, Hayden, and Brooks).

An element of the black poetic tradition that should be introduced early in the course is the development of a black poetic aesthetic; that is, what makes a poem a good poem? From African traditions comes the Afro-American concept of the functionality of art: Good art embellishes the communal activities through which it is created. Furthermore, a concept of art as a source of moral uplift manifests itself not only in the abolitionist, temperance, and feminist poems of Frances Harper and other nineteenth-century poets but also in the social protest poetry of the 1920s, 1930s, and early 1940s. The two concepts merge in the definitions of poetic function posited by the Black Arts poets of the late 1960s.

Another aspect of the tradition to be examined is the importance of the performance mode in the black poetic tradition. The dramatic character of the poetry, the voices in the poetry, and the relationship of poem to reader all enter into this aspect of study. Equally important, perhaps, is the long tradition of oral readings by poets from Frances Harper through Paul Laurence Dunbar, Langston Hughes, Sterling Brown, LeRoi Jones, and Ted Joans to Nikki Giovanni, Madhubuti, and others. Poetry in the black poetic tradition is an act of communication.

What becomes evident is that, while it is important to teach the development of a black poetic tradition in time (i.e., with some attention to chronology), it is equally important to relate works from differing times and contexts to one another and to key elements of the tradition. Within this framework, the instructor is free to examine as many or as few texts by a single author as are necessary to illuminate particular elements of form, structure, or tradition. In addition, the instructor is free to return to a given poet and reintroduce new works or new aspects of that poet's work as another element of or development in the tradition. The ultimate goal of our methodology is to enable the student to read poems critically within a definable literary tradition.

A general outline for a black poetry survey course might read:

Unit One: The beginnings of a black poetic tradition emerging from oral (mostly African) and written (Anglo-American) poetic traditions. Acquisition and transformation of language within the demands of particular and cultural contexts. Imitation of Anglo-American literary forms.

Unit Two: The beginnings of an original poetic voice as cultural imperatives impinge on the imitated literary forms. Use of folklore and folk speech. Placement of dialect poetry within tradition. Mastering of Anglo-American literary forms.

Unit Three: Toward a black poetic diction. Conscious use of folk speech and forms. Adaptation of Anglo-American literary forms to culturally specific subjects and themes. Expression of lyric impulse in both Afro-American (e.g., blues) and Anglo-American (e.g., sonnet) literary forms.

Unit Four: Perfection of use of Anglo-American literary forms. Relationship between Afro-American and Anglo-American poetic traditions in modern era.

Unit Five: Black beat poetry as transition, reintroducing black musical forms into the tradition. Use of oral performances of poetry (often with musical accompaniment). Widening of possible subjects and language of poetry.

Unit Six: The Black Arts Movement as a conscious attempt to return written poetry to the folk through transformation of black speech into black poetic diction. Transformation of popular music forms (jazz and soul) into literary forms. Conscious linking of poetry to African tradition.

Unit Seven: Infusion into contemporary "literary" poetry oral elements such as colloquial speech, oral poetic genres.

Pedagogical concerns include the following suggestions on course and class preparation:

(1) Poets should be selected on the basis of their relationship to the tradition being defined and studied.

(2) An instructor should be familiar with as many as possible of an author's published works beyond what has been anthologized.

(3) Since this may be the student's first or only poetry course, it will probably be necessary to introduce several approaches to discussing poetry.

(4) Poets whose careers span several pivotal moments or periods in literary history should be studied at each point that their work is important in that history.

(5) Possible texts might include a comprehensive anthology and complete volume(s) by one or more poets with supplementary duplicated materials.

(6) The instructor should have an adequate background in the forms of the oral tradition.

(7) The instructor should have an adequate knowledge of the Anglo-American poetic tradition.

(8) The instructor should have an adequate knowledge

of American popular culture as it influences the Afro-American poetic tradition.

(9) The discussion of texts should be supplemented with records, tapes, assignments to attend poetry readings, and filmed interviews.

Rethinking the Interdisciplinary Course Embracing Afro-American Literature

In Afro-American culture, language, music, dance, and the rituals of community—both secular and religious—are inextricably interrelated. The relationships go far beyond the thematic resonance or recurrence of religious rituals or musical performances in works of art. Rather, Afro-American culture produces forms of expression that are developed from the rituals of community and are transformed by individual artists in music, dance, and literature.

It is therefore useful to bring to bear on the artistic products of this culture a range of bright lights provided by the various human sciences. The analysis of cultural texts —poems, paintings, novels, spirituals, sculpture, folktales, jazz, plays, films, gospels, autobiographies, sermons, blues —by appropriate methods will reveal the interrelated structures, origins, and functions of the culture's expressive forms.

Each of the following three course designs is conceived as interdisciplinary rather than multidisciplinary; that is, parallel courses in the individual disciplines that are brought to bear upon Afro-American creativity—art history, music, theater, intellectual history, folklore, and religion—will not yield comparable instruction.

While each of these courses can be taught by a team, none of them requires this instructional approach. A teacher of literature trained in formal analysis and willing to read in other areas of the human sciences should be able to transform any one of these designs into an effective course.

Description and Methodology

Sample Course Design #1—Black Literature and the Arts:
Shape That Thing

An interdisciplinary course in Afro-American literature might begin with materials from the African oral tradition and the European written tradition. One possibility might be to trace the transformation of a story from the Bible (e.g., the story of Moses, Abraham's children, or Joseph) into sermons, spirituals, and folktales, and then to study the transformation of an Anansi, the spider story, into tale, song, and written tale in order to illustrate some of the origins of, and changes within, Afro-American art forms. A second activity might be to examine aspects of myth, ritual, diction, iconography, rhetoric, and rhythm in early work songs, blues, sacred music, and sermons.

A third unit might examine how a slave narrative, such as Solomon Northup's *Twelve Years a Slave*, retells the archetypal story of the harrowing of hell, while offering a self-portrait of the author-as-artist and astute observations on slave life and culture.

Further study of nineteenth-century materials will suggest an interdisciplinary examination of the minstrel show. (A text is available in Dailey Paskman's *Gentlemen, Be Seated*; criticism—for the teacher, not the class—is available in Robert Toll's *Blacking Up*.) The dehumanizing mask placed on blacks by the minstrel tradition informs the plantation school of post–Civil War writing and draws forth a range of response from black artists. Texts that might be examined include poems by Frances E. W. Harper and Paul Laurence Dunbar, Henry O. Tanner's painting "The Banjo Lesson," James Weldon Johnson's *God's Trombones*, and some early black films.

A fifth unit might compare the blues textually with plantation poems, contrasting the shallow and dehumanized artificiality of the latter with the richly emotional, heroic, stoic, and ironic humanity of the former. Items to be examined might include classic blues singing, heroic portraiture by artists like William Scott, poems by Sterling Brown and Langston Hughes, and paintings by Horace Pippin.

Moving well into the twentieth century, we might next study Richard Wright's writings from the late 1930s and early 1940s in relation to folk materials, painting (Jacob Lawrence), and music (Paul Robeson). The sense of the heroic, stoic, and ironic in naturalist, socialist, and "protest" thought is a theme that might unify the whole.

Finally, a discussion of how fictional narrative may be reinvented in alignment with folk speech, blues, history, and Western literary history as evidenced by Ralph Ellison's essays (especially "Richard Wright's Blues") and novel, *Invisible Man*, might be a way to conclude. Here, useful additional texts are provided by Edward K. ("Duke") Ellington and Romare Bearden.

Sample Course Design #2—Symbolic Geography in Afro-American Literature: The Myth of Escape

This course examines the persistence of certain fundamental impulses in Afro-American culture by tracing the evolution of expressive forms (oral and written, visual, verbal and musical) within the boundaries of a symbolic geography special to Afro-American life.

One way to examine these developments is to look at some examples of transformations of given forms (the Babylonian captivity story in the Bible; trickster figures in African folktales) into Afro-American tales, spirituals, and sermons. These texts reveal a desire for freedom and self-realization—literacy, power, art-making—within the specific context of the North as a symbol of freedom. The "North" is, at times, the city, the Promised Land, Africa, and non-Western religion.

The *Narrative of the Life of Frederick Douglass* embodies the myth of the escape North. Douglass is delivered by Providence first to the city, then to the North to literacy and leadership. Du Bois' *The Souls of Black Folk* introduces the invisible history of the black South by defining the "journey" of the black spirit within the symbolic boundary of the Black Belt. He invokes the songs, the Bible, the traditions of hope and self-transformation, but he also shows the dissolution of that hope as he takes us through the spiritual journey.

Both Dunbar's *The Sport of the Gods* and Toomer's *Cane* challenge the myth of geographical freedom and add resonance and complexity to the values attached to the "North." Despite this challenge, the desire for movement from the hell and home of the South remains a theme and a metaphor: The sound of the train is in blues music, again with biblical resonances of the journey through tribulation; there are the rhythms of the train in Ellington's "A Train," Baraka's subway train in *Dutchman*, the blues poems of train porters, Wright's stories of the escape North—train, song, poems, blues, journey, freedom, escape.

The city—the Heavenly City, the Promised Land—becomes an iron nightmare. Wright's *Native Son*, Petry's *The Street*, Baldwin's *Another Country* and Hughes's *Simple Stories* present variously distorted images of the northern Canaan. Gwendolyn Brooks, Sterling Brown, and Langston Hughes all explore the continuing vitality of the road, the city, and the North as symbols of literal and imaginative freedom.

Autobiographies develop further the search for freedom in the process of growing up, testing the myth of northerly freedom, depicting the spiritual journey within the geographical one, as Malcolm travels east and then East to find his ultimate spiritual place. The recognition of the insubstantiality of the literal North and of the ambiguity of constant movement as a mode of existence leads, ironically, to the vitalizing power of "prison" as metaphor in the work of Etheridge Knight and Eldridge Cleaver. Although it is the antithesis of the Promised Land, "prison," like "slavery," gives birth to brightness.

Sample Course Design #3—Blackface/Black Form:
The Invisible History of Afro-American Drama

Drama is a collaborative and communal art relying not only on a printed text but also on visual and oral elements of performance. Because of its immediacy, drama must use a system of signs—gesture, language, character types, setting—to communicate clearly and effectively with an audience responsive to those signs. An interdisciplinary approach to Afro-American drama might discuss the origins of the dramatic impulse in Afro-American culture and the distinctive expressive forms of that culture as the materials from which the playwright builds his work:

(1) Analyze the performance aspects and ritual function of Afro-American church services and secular music. Discuss gesture (dance and physical movement), singing, lyrics, sermon rhetoric and imagery, the relationships between minister and congregation and soloist and congregation.

(2) Analyze irony, images, tone, function, and performance aspects of blues and blues-based secular music. Discuss the dramatic situation and impulse in lyric forms.

(3) In some or all of the following plays, discuss how each playwright mines the religious and musical expressions of Afro-American culture to create effective dramatic language, characters, dramatic space or setting, and a ritual situation: Langston Hughes's *Tambourines to Glory*, James Baldwin's *The Amen Corner*, Philip Hayes Dean's *The Sty of the Blind Pig*, and Amiri Baraka's *The Baptism*.

(4) The minstrel show, a white dramatic form imposed on aspiring Afro-American performers and dramatists, inhibited the development of authentic dramatic forms by severely restricting the range of characters and themes. Analyze the minstrel show's songs, dialogue, situations, costumes, and characterization (text: Paskman's *Gentlemen, Be Seated*). The achievement of black playwrights in the face of these restrictions is considerable. Sissle and Balek's *Shuffle Along*, the plays of Langston Hughes, Willis Richardson, and Lorraine Hansberry all struggle toward excellence and authenticity under this burden.

(5) Other writers seized the dramatic possibilities of the minstrel show and exploited them. Discuss the conflict between face and mask, the ambiguity of racial identity and role, and all the attendant ironies that are manipulated to great effect in Ossie Davis' *Purlie*

Victorious, Baraka's *Great Goodness of Life (A Coon Show)* and *Dutchman*, Charles Gordone's *No Place to Be Somebody*, and Douglas Turner Ward's *Day of Absence*.

(6) Other plays connect formally to the rituals of the Afro-American community. In these works the authors attempt to imitate the function of Afro-American religious services—celebrating, purifying, and perpetuating the community. Discuss the ritual form of plays like Adrienne Kennedy's *Funnyhouse of a Negro* and *A Rat's Mass*, or Baraka's *The Slave*, *Madheart (A Morality Play)*, and *Slave Ship*.

Appendix

References

Note: The following works were required reading for the Yale seminar and have been included here for those readers who would like to pursue some of the ideas that lie behind the essays in this volume.

—Editors

Ben-Amos, Dan. "Toward a Definition of Folklore in Context." *Journal of American Folklore*, 84 (Jan.–March 1971), 3–15.

Ellison, Ralph. "Change the Joke and Slip the Yoke." In *Shadow and Act*. New York: Random, 1964, pp. 45–59.

Hartman, Geoffrey. "Toward Literary History." In *Beyond Formalism*. New Haven: Yale Univ. Press, 1970, pp. 356–86.

Henderson, Stephen. Preface. *Understanding the New Black Poetry*. New York: Morrow, 1973.

Hurston, Zora Neale. "Characteristics of Negro Expression." In *Negro Anthology*. Ed. Nancy Cunard. London: Wishart and Co., 1934, pp. 24–31.

Johnson, James Weldon. Preface. *God's Trombones: Seven Negro Sermons in Verse*. New York: Viking, 1927.

Lévi-Strauss, Claude. "The Structural Study of Myth." In *Structural Anthropology*. 1963; New York: Basic Books, 1976, pp. 206–31.

Murray, Gilbert. "The Mólpe." In *The Classical Tradition in Poetry*. New York: Russell, 1927, pp. 28–51.

Palmer, Richard. "Toward Reopening the Question: What Is Interpretation?" In *Hermeneutics*. Evanston, Ill.: Northwestern Univ. Press, 1969, p. 223–41.

Paz, Octavio. "Critique of the Pyramid." In *The Other Mexico*. New York: Grove, 1972, pp. 69–112.

Soyinka, Wole. "Appendix: The Fourth Stage." In *Myth, Literature, and the African World*. Cambridge, Eng.: Cambridge Univ. Press, 1976, pp. 140–61.

Walcott, Derek. Introd. "What the Twilight Says: An Overture." In *Dream on Monkey Mountain*. New York: Farrar, Straus, 1970.

Wellek, René, and Austin Warren. "The Mode of Existence of a Literary Work of Art." In *Theory of Literature*. New York: Harcourt, 1968, pp. 142–57.

Wimsatt, William. "What to Say about a Poem." In *Hateful Contraries*. Lexington: Univ. of Kentucky Press, 1965, pp. 215–45.

Wimsatt, William, and Cleanth Brooks. Epilogue. In *Literary Criticism: A Short History*. New York: Knopf, 1966.